PRINCIPLES OF COACHING FOOTBALL

PRINCIPLES OF COACHING FOOTBALL

Mike Bobo
Spike Dykes

TEXAS TECH UNIVERSITY

Allyn and Bacon
Boston • London • Toronto • Sydney • Tokyo • Singapore

Series Editor: Suzy Spivey
Series Editorial Assistant: Amy Braddock
Manufacturing Buyer: Suzanne Lareau
Advertising Manager: Anne Morrison
Editorial Production Services: Omegatype Typography, Inc.

Internet: www.abacon.com
America Online: keyword: College Online

Portions of this book first appeared in *Principles of Coaching Football*
by Mike Bobo, © 1987 by Wm. C. Brown, Co.

Library of Congress Cataloging-in-Publication Data

Bobo, Mike.
    Principles of coaching football / Mike Bobo, Spike Dykes.
        p.   cm.
    Includes bibliographical references and index.
    ISBN 0-205-26253-8
    1. Football—Coaching—United States.   2. School sports—Coaching—
United States.   I. Dykes, Spike.   II. Title.
GV956.6.B623   1998
796.322'07'7—dc21   97-29510
                                                                CIP

Printed in the United States of America

10   9   8   7   6   5   4   3   2   1   02   01   00   99   98

This book is dedicated to the people in my life who have been the source of my strength, support, encouragement, joy, and love—no matter what the won–lost column showed: to Mackie, my lovely wife; to Bo, our son, and Tracie, his wife; and to Shell, our daughter.

Mike Bobo

This book is dedicated to all the great assistant coaches that have worked for me and with me through the years. Certainly any degree of success achieved goes to these folks and the great players I have had the privilege of coaching.

Spike Dykes

CONTENTS

PREFACE

This text was written primarily for those individuals who aspire to become football coaches. Several texts are on the market which thoroughly discuss the college game from the head coach's point of view and/or the nature of the coaching profession and the successful coach. Although most undergraduate students who wish to coach imagine themselves as the encyclopedia of knowledge and master of strategy directing "their" team to victory before a throng of 75,000 screaming fans, the vast majority of coaches begin their careers in the junior high school, teaching elementary football fundamentals to eager, and often immature, youngsters. It is these fundamentals which this text addresses.

Among those coaching younger athletes we find true teachers: coaches with an opportunity to introduce football fundamentals and greatly influence the lives of young people. With these thoughts in mind, this text gives the reader a basis from which to build a general knowledge of the game of football. This material is not new and no claim is made by the authors as to the originality of many of the ideas and concepts contained herein. The authors wish to make it clear, however, that the interpretation, application, and organization of these concepts are of our own design, and drawn from our own experiences. The systems of play used in this text are "sample" systems that we feel illustrate coaching concepts. Our intent is to illustrate techniques; any formation play calling, defensive titles, and so forth, do not refer to any specific system used by any school to our knowledge.

Although this book is primarily concerned with the mechanical aspects of the game, our general coaching philosophy is also expressed throughout the text. In the first two chapters the reader will find an overview of the "why" of coaching and information on how research can impact on the game of football. These will be followed by a scouting chapter. The scouting information is followed by five chapters on the offensive game. These chapters are continued with the all-important kicking game to round out the offensive considerations of the text. The defensive game is addressed in the next three chapters. Throughout these sections "typical" defensive and offensive patterns have been used. The feeling is that if young coaches can master one or two basic formations, both offensively and defensively, they can broaden their knowledge base to encompass other systems easily. In addition, drills are illustrated to give the beginning coach a start at teaching the fundamentals. It should always be borne in mind that there is no single best system for all football teams. Truly, the more you learn about this game, the less you'll feel you know.

The above chapters complete the mechanical aspects of the text, which up to this point is intended to serve as a well-rounded instructional text. Basics have been stressed throughout, and it is hoped that this text will provide the practical introduction to a profession that can be as rewarding as any that we know. Final chapters on public relations, player–coach relationships, psychology, and attitude end the text with what we hope will give aspiring football coaches a few tools to add to their repertoire when beginning their coaching careers.

ACKNOWLEDGMENTS

We would like to thank the following reviewers for their comments on the manuscript: Robert Denton, Baylor University; M. Gene Lee, Metropolitan State College of Denver; Peter Mazzaferro, Bridgewater State College; Ron Puhl, Bloomsburg University; and Ron Randleman, Sam Houston State University.

M. B.
S. D.

PRINCIPLES OF COACHING FOOTBALL

1

THE NATURE AND BENEFITS
OF THE GAME OF FOOTBALL

Chapter Objectives

After completing this chapter, the reader should be able to:

- Write or state their own philosophy concerning the value of football in the educational process.
- List the possible problems associated with coaching football as a profession.
- List the possible advantages, both extrinsic and intrinsic, of the coaching profession.
- Discuss the possible problems that will be encountered by a first-year coach, with parents, teachers, and students.

PHILOSOPHY OF FOOTBALL COACHING

The importance of the relationship between a football coach and a young football player cannot be overemphasized. The coach has great influence on developing youth. Many years after players have stopped playing football they will still remember "Coach Smith." They might not be able to remember the name of their

English or mathematics teacher, but chances are they *will* be able to remember their football coaches.

It would be difficult to find a life's work more rewarding than coaching football. It is, without question, a multifaceted profession. The skilled coach is a teacher, a technician, a strategist, a disciplinarian, a motivator, an organizer, a dedicated worker, and is committed to the positive development of young people. Although all teachers are involved in these areas, no other teachers have the results of their work so exposed to the public every week during the football season as does the coach.

Many football coaches know at an early age that they want to invest their lives in the coaching profession. Many have a deep, abiding desire to make a difference in the lives of young people. Many are greatly affected by and feel the influence of their own former coaches. Coaches are respected not only by players but also by the adults in the community, and all of the students usually admire and listen to them.

Many times, football provides individuals who have no real purpose in life an opportunity to commit themselves to something. Because of that commitment, they become successful in the game and then are able to make other commitments in their lives that make them successful in other endeavors. This book could be filled with the names of coaches who have made such commitments throughout the years, and consequently have influenced thousands of people. It is interesting to note how similar most coaches have been in their patterns of development. Most coaches played the game in their younger years, were influenced by the coaches they played under, and became dedicated and committed to the profession as a result of those experiences. Attend a coaching clinic and you will see younger coaches just starting in the profession, coaches in the middle years staying up with trends, and coaches who have survived economic crunches and win–loss statistics to remain in the profession several decades.

A true story will further serve to illustrate the reasons people want to coach. One young man who had played football was in the Marines in World War II. He was making a landing on one of the islands held by the Japanese. When they hit the beaches, the firing was fierce, and the young Marine was hit and fell on the sandy beach. One of his buddies ran to him, dragged him out of the water, onto the beach, looked at this ashen face, and called a medic, who shook his head and said; "I'm sorry, he's dead." However, a chaplain who had begun to administer the last rites had noticed a pulse. Two weeks later, in a hospital, the chaplain came to see the young Marine who was recuperating from his wounds. The young Marine had requested that the chaplain visit. He wanted to thank him. As the chaplain walked into the room, the Marine smiled and said, "Thank you for what you did two weeks ago." The chaplain said, "It was truly amazing. I leaned over your body, and was giving you the last rites, when all of a sudden I noticed a pulse beat on your temple, and called for the medic, who came and said you were alive." The Marine said, "I wanted to meet you and see what you looked like, because in the darkness of that day when I heard your voice, I thought it was my high school coach, and he was saying to me, get up—get up and try again, don't lay there, get up and try again'—and I would do anything for my coach. I was determined to get up."[1]

You have doubtless heard or read similar stories that are true examples of the benefits of the coaching profession. Very few occupations bring such a sense of closeness with a select group of young people as does coaching football. The rapport with developing youngsters and the coach's influence come back to the coach year after year, when they see the young people that they have worked with on the athletic field develop into successful citizens and fine college and professional athletes.

REASONS FOR COACHING FOOTBALL

Individuals become football coaches for many reasons. Some never really think about the motivating reasons until their first losing season! If you were to ask most undergraduate physical education students why they want to coach, their reasons would probably be similar to the following list obtained from our students.

1. I have always been active and interested in sports and I want to have a profession in which I will be involved in sports.
2. One of the persons that I admire most is a coach.
3. I like to work with people, especially kids.
4. I think coaches can help build physical and moral character.
5. I want to continue to be involved in athletics when my playing days are over.
6. I want to teach young people the things they need to know concerning fortitude and character, which I feel come through athletic participation.

Being a football coach gives one a sense of pride and satisfaction. You have pride in your team and your work with the athletes in your charge. Challenges arise daily and you gain immeasurable personal satisfaction from solving each problem systematically. Your players admire and respect you, and overall, you hold a prominent place in the school and community. You will have many opportunities to interact with your players and to help them solve their personal problems. You will laugh and cry with your athletes, and these experiences will positively enrich your life and help both you and your players mature. These are a few of the intangible rewards of coaching.

There are, however, some very tangible rewards: Your players' individual accomplishments, your team's accomplishments, the satisfaction of seeing your game plan develop into a winning combination, your additional pay for coaching and, in many cases, material benefits such as a house, gifts from your players and their families, sometimes a car, club memberships, and other "perks."

Many coaches will tell you, however, that they do not stay in the coaching profession for the tangible or financial rewards; they stay in coaching for the many intangibles. This decision is one that each coach must make as each new football season rolls around.

CHARACTER BUILDING

It is a common practice to state that football builds character. And indeed it can. Paul "Bear" Bryant illustrates the point well when writing in his book *Building a Championship Football Team:*

> Football, in its rightful place, can be one of the most wholesome, exciting and valuable activities in which our youth can possibly participate. It is the only sport I know of that teaches boys to have complete control of themselves, to gain self-respect, give forth a tremendous effort, and at the same time learn to observe the rules of the game, regard the rights of others and stay within bounds dictated by decency and sportsmanship. The most advantageous and serviceable lesson that we can derive from football is the intrinsic value of winning. We are in a position to teach these boys intrinsic values that cannot be learned at home, church, school or any place outside of the athletic field. Briefly, these intangible attributes are as follows: (1) Discipline, sacrifice, work, fight and teamwork; (2) to learn how to take your "licks" and yet fight back; (3) to be so tired you think you are going to die, but instead of quitting you somehow learn to fight a little harder; (4) when your team is behind, you learn to win the game; and (5) you learn to believe in yourself because you know how to rise to the occasion, and you will do it! The last trait is the most important one.[2]

Coach Bryant's words certainly speak eloquently of how football builds character! Because so many coaches have received their character building from great experiences in athletics, they sometimes have to be reminded that football is only one of many avenues to the total educational development of young people. There are other avenues also; today's coach should realize that football is not the saving grace for all youth. Football does for some youngsters what debate, ROTC, drama, journalism, and many other extra-curricular activities do for other students. The drama teacher works long hours, like the coach, preparing young actors for a performance; the journalism teacher spends after school time working with young writers on the year book and student newspaper. And how about the band director! Talk about hours of work with kids. Thus a word of advice to beginning coaches: Believe that you can indeed build character, but that privilege is not restricted to you, nor to football, alone. Let's turn our attention now to that first coaching job.

THE IMAGE OF THE COACH

Induction into the coaching profession for a first-year coach is an educational experience to say the least! On the one hand, you are new to the school, the system, and the town, and on the other you are expected to present yourself to your players as a well-composed, all-knowing leader. When assuming a football coaching job, a young coach often settles quickly into the general behavior pattern of the older coaches. More likely than not, the older coaches walk, talk, and generally look like coaches, and the younger coach becomes one of the group. The vernacular of coaches is always in the plural—"our system . . ."; "*we* use tackle call blocking . . ."; "one for all, and all for one." Although this "team" philosophy might sound democratic, in athletics there is little room for democracy. As Al Rosen's *Baseball and Your Boy* points out:

> The youngster will get his lessons in democracy-in-action from other sources. Organized sports are not democratic nor should they be. They teach respect for authority, discipline, and the individual's role in a group activity. The manager's job is to make the decisions and he does not poll an electorate.[3]

Whether your rapport with your players will be democratic or not is something that will have to wait until you are in a coaching position to find out. However, you should consider the type of person you will be dealing with. Young people are often faced with two problems relating to playing football: they are too little, or too slow. Nevertheless, many decide that they are going to be the toughest son-of-a-gun that ever stepped on a football field, despite being too little or too slow. These youngsters often will find a place to play. Young people learn many things about themselves. They learn to be hard-nosed and tough, to endure pain, and to parlay the talents and abilities they do have into opportunities to reach goals, achieve success in athletics, and contribute to the team effort.

As people attain levels of success in their profession, the honors and material gains increase. The basic reason for being in the coaching profession should never vary or change, however. Being continually touched and influenced by players and the profession, coaches are motivated to continue to strive for personal and psychological maturity and development.

DUAL COACHING–TEACHING ROLE

Beginning coaches are primarily interested in coaching. However, coaches realize very quickly that they have another major responsibility—that of teaching classroom subjects. As a matter of record, most states certify only teachers and do not have coaching certification programs. Therefore, even if a school district were interested in hiring people to coach a sport, it must employ them in a certified subject area. This teaching–coaching duality is further illustrated by the following salary breakdown:

Base pay for beginning teacher,
no experience with Bachelor's degree: $20,000.00*

Payment above base for coaching duties, $500.00 to $4,000.00

*Salary is used here as an example only. These figures will vary from state to state and district to district.

Thus, out of a possible $24,000.00 starting salary for a beginning teacher, only $4,000.00 might be paid for coaching or for handling other extracurricular activities. The fact that most coaches teach from three to five classes of an academic subject reinforces the reality that coaches are hired to teach as well as coach. When administrators are asked "Who do you hire: coaches or teachers?", the majority, by far, will respond, "We hire teachers, not coaches." However, this statement is not always upheld; generally, coaches will not be fired because of their poor teaching in the classroom (in the majority of school districts) but they may be fired for their win–loss records on the athletic field.

It should be added that most school districts are developing formalized procedures for the firing of teachers for incompetent performance in the classroom. Such procedures include publishing and distributing guidelines to be followed in developing a case for teaching inadequacy and subsequent termination of employment. When asked if these procedures apply to the coaching staff who have classroom duties, the answer generally is in the affirmative. Unfortunately, many state education agencies, school boards, and superintendents allow coaches to shirk their teaching responsibilities so that they can concentrate on their coaching duties.

Education faculties at colleges and universities are also at fault. Ask the students enrolled in a typical "Methods of Teaching Physical Education" class what they want to do when they graduate. The majority of students will respond that they want to "coach." Thus, in the minds of too many undergraduate students, the belief is that they will only coach extracurricular sports and not teach academic classroom subjects. The point to be stressed here is that coaching has the capacity to be the highest form of teaching in the school. However, coaches often have a poor commitment to their other academic teaching responsibilities. They often do not give serious thought to professional education courses such as educational foundations and philosophy, human learning patterns, methods, or the effects of socioeconomic status on learning. Even technical courses in areas such as motor learning and exercise physiology are often used only in relation to athletic skills and not in the realm of physical education class activities.

The above points emphasize the dual job of teaching and coaching to the prospective coach. Although football coaching might be the primary interest of a physical education major graduating from college and seeking a job, one needs to be aware of the classroom teaching responsibilities that go hand-in-hand with football coaching duties.

PROFESSIONALISM AND COACHING

The image of the coach as viewed by townspeople, players, and other coaches is often as varied as the personalities of the players on his team. The players may view him as dictatorial, dogmatic, and demanding. The townspeople may view him as a football genius and miracle motivator (if winning) or a football moron, unable to tell a good player from a hole in the ground (if losing). Although the full impact of this kind of public judgment will not be felt until one is in an actual coaching situation, several preliminary questions might prove helpful for prospective coaches who wonder "Is this really what I want to do with my life?":

1. Will your commitment to the coaching profession allow you to accept public criticism and maintain your self-confidence?
2. Do you possess the quality of being able to modify your plans at short notice (flexibility) while still keeping your sights on your main objective?
3. Are you willing to neglect your wife/husband and children at times, due to your coaching duties? (Are they willing to accept your time away from home?)
4. Do you seek professional advancement, with the ability to exert leadership as well as follow the directions of others?
5. Are you a good organizer, and aggressive enough to follow through with your plans?
6. Do you feel comfortable when people openly criticize you or your program, and do you have the physical and emotional security to remain calm and on an even keel with your life and career goals?
7. Finally, do you possess the physical health (energy level) and appearance to meet the demands of the coaching profession?

No doubt the list can be expanded and lengthened. However, it is important for individuals aspiring to enter the coaching field to question themselves about their own ability to meet the challenges of an exciting, multifaceted lifestyle. Louis Kelly offers additional advice for first-year coaches in an article published in 1992.[4]

Another area of concern for all coaches is the public image that each coach portrays. You should strive to maintain an educated, professional image. How is this done? Important aspects are your dress, your language, and your social habits, which all of us must be aware of and continually strive to improve. Remember that when you write a note to the English teacher concerning one of your athletes, if your syntax is poor and the note includes several grammatical errors, you certainly don't impress the teacher.

As an active person you should be an example of a physically fit individual who does not carry around any excess weight (especially in the abdominal or hip area) and who serves as an example of good health habits. If you feel your athletes should not smoke or consume alcoholic beverages, you should give strong consideration to your own personal lifestyle. Is it right for you to smoke in public (or in private) if you feel your athletes should not?

Do not use double negatives, and avoid repetitive phrases (such as "OK," "you know") to the extent that they distract from what you are saying. You may feel that your life is spent in the gym or on the athletic field. However, the impression people have of you will come from their interactions with you in the teachers' lounge, the halls at school, the grocery store, or at a social event.

While we are speaking of school functions we should also stress that you should make every effort to participate in activities outside of the world of sports.

Coaches should attend PTA meetings, school plays, debate and journalism activities, civic ballet productions, the local theatre productions, and public forums on civic interests. In other words, read, study, and take an interest in things other than football. If you do, you will find that people will be more interested in talking to you and will respect you as an educated individual with whom they can discuss something other than "Well, how's the team looking?" If you make an effort to expand your lifestyle to include these, as well as other cultural and political areas, you will go a long way in moving away from the "jock" stereotype and toward a more professional image.

The opportunity and the responsibility of coaching should not be taken lightly. There are many reasons why those who choose the profession become successful and fulfilled. Successful coaches will be those who have a commitment based on a sound philosophy, fundamental techniques, and an understanding of human motivation and basic psychological principles. It is these coaches who rightly believe that they can contribute to the personal development of young people and their future successes.

CLASS ACTIVITIES

1. State your philosophy about coaching football, including where you feel football fits into the educational process.

2. Visit a football practice, watch one of the coaches and write a review of his actions. Include his behavior before practice, his actions and language during practice, and a summary of positive and negative comments made during the practice.

3. Visit your local school's administration offices and find out what the current pay scale is in your area. Find out what other school districts are paying for coaching duties above the base salary for teachers.

4. Interview a coach and discuss how coaching impacts on his family life. Look at a coach's job pattern for the past ten years, if possible.

NOTES

1. Grant Teaff, Personal Communication, June 1984.

2. Paul ("Bear") Bryant, *Building a Championship Football Team* (Englewood Cliffs, NJ: Prentice-Hall, 1960), pp. 3–5.

3. Al Rosen, *Baseball and Your Boy* (New York: Thomas Crowell Company, 1967), p. 34.

4. Louis Kelly, "Advice to First Year Coaches (and Veteran Coaches, Too)," *Texas Coach* 37 (1992):60–61.

2

RESEARCH AND FOOTBALL COACHING

Chapter Objectives

After completing this chapter, the reader should be able to:

- Define and discuss the differences between the terms *conditioning* and *training* and give examples of each.
- Write down examples of the three energy supply systems using football activities.
- Identify specific conditioning activities that apply to movement patterns involved in football activities.
- List the justification for static stretching and be able to illustrate the technique.
- Organize on paper a fifteen minute period of a practice session to illustrate knowledge concerning conditioning drills.

THE PROBLEM OF COMMUNICATION

After a football coach leaves college he generally gets farther and farther away from the library containing research journals and closer and closer to the so-called "X's and O's" publications. Herein lies a communication problem: researchers at colleges and universities are continually addressing problems that have an impact on sport participants. This research is usually done within the area of exercise physiology, psychology, sociology, or sports medicine. The main avenue to publicize these findings is through research journals and, as previously stated, these research journals are not widely read by football coaches. In a recent personnel survey of over fifty coaches only 15 percent were able to name any research journals, while more than 90 percent were able to name several coaching journals.

The purpose of mentioning a possible problem in communication is not to criticize the coaching journals but to point out that many of the "whys" of conditioning theory, strength concepts, and training procedures are reported in journals which the coach may never read. Examples of the resulting gap in knowledge are numerous and are best illustrated by the number of deaths that occur each season from heat-related illnesses and the number of injuries produced from strength-building programs that disregard flexibility.

This chapter serves as a stimulus for coaches to become aware of the relevant practical research available that could improve the health and performance of athletes. Although many areas of exercise physiology are open to wide interpretation, the basic guidelines presented below are particularly important to coaches and athletes.

CONDITIONING VERSUS TRAINING

Conditioning and *training* are terms that all coaches use frequently. What exactly do we mean by conditioning, and what do we mean by training? Based on current knowledge, conditioning relates to increasing the capacity of the energy-supply systems (explained below) and physiological systems such as the cardiovascular, respiratory, muscular and nervous systems. Examples of conditioning include windsprints and off-season programs. When we add skill-development in the activities, we are actually "training" the athletes without much consideration for the energy-supply or other physiological systems. Examples of training would be specific football drills and specific play practice. Obviously, some conditioning takes place during training. However, these terms should not be used as synonyms because coaches must be aware of the differences when planning their in-season as well as their off-season programs.

In looking at conditioning programs, coaches need to be aware of the energy requirements of the sports they coach. The energy for all muscular movement is derived specifically from the contractile elements within muscle tissue. The human body supplies the energy for these contractile elements from three metabolic energy-supply systems. The ATP-PC system, the lactic acid system, and the oxygen system. Three terms need elaboration before the systems are explained. These terms are *anaerobic, aerobic,* and *metabolism.*

Anaerobic literally means "without oxygen," which indicates that the human body has the capability to move (and have energy supplied for the movement) without the aid of oxygen to complete the chemical processes. For example, when a football player sprints forty yards in 4.9 seconds, the oxygen he is breathing does not have enough time to be transported, delivered, and used by the muscle tissue that is active during the sprint. Thus, the muscle is chemically deriving its energy without the aid of oxygen. This is anaerobic work. When the athlete is sitting on the bench listening to the coach talk, the energy demand is much lower and oxygen can be supplied to the working muscle tissue. This is *aerobic* work. *Metabolism* refers to the many series of chemical reactions that take place within the entire body as well as within specific cells.

The three primary energy supply systems interact like the gears on an automobile transmission. The systems described below relate to the anaerobic or aerobic metabolism that takes place in skeletal muscle to supply the energy for muscular contraction.

1. (Anaerobically)—ATP-PC Systems—Adenosinetriphosphate (ATP) breaks down to liberate energy for contractions. Phosphocreatine (PC) breaks down to supply the energy to resynthesize ATP. This is a very short-lived system (1–5 seconds). The initial movements or burst of movement when a football lineman charges is an example of this system.

2. (Anaerobically)—Lactic Acid System—Glycogen (a simple sugar) is stored in muscle tissue, the liver, and is carried in circulating blood. It can be chemically converted to glucose and broken down to liberate ATP molecules, which the muscles can use for energy when these molecules break down. This is our primary energy supply system for activities lasting from five seconds to five minutes. Most of the activities involved in the game of football utilize this system. The activities are explosive, and last for a very short period of time. Without adequate oxygen, however, the glycogen molecule is not completely broken down, and lactic acid (which is a prime causative factor in muscular fatigue) is built up.

3. (Aerobically)—Oxygen System—Again, glucose is used to synthesize ATP molecules. If adequate amounts of oxygen are available to working muscle tissue, glucose is not converted to lactic acid but is completely broken down into ATP, carbon dioxide, and water. These products, unlike lactic acid which contributes to muscle fatigue and muscle pain, can be used by the muscle for continued work or can be easily excreted. This system is used in long-term activities (those lasting more than 3–5 minutes) or those that are done at a very slow rate of muscle activity. If we look at a typical football lineman's activities during a game we can see the aerobic system being mobilized during the warm-up, with the anaerobic systems coming into play during explosive bursts of muscular effort. The offensive lineman running onto the field following his team's kickoff return, his standing in the huddle, and his movement to the line of scrimmage (LOS) involve the aerobic system. The explosion off the LOS and his block are anaerobic. If the back breaks into the open and goes for a ninety-yard touchdown, the lineman jogging down the field watching the back run would be using his aerobic system. Thus the systems shift back and forth as the energy demands change from moment to moment.

By following this very simplified (and we must state that these are very complex processes) description of energy dynamics you may be able to see that the game of football depends primarily on the anaerobic energy systems, since most activity is done in a very explosive, short-term manner, which is repeated frequently. However, a high level of aerobic conditioning is the foundation for explosive energy production. The better conditioned aerobically-trained athlete will be able to dissipate lactic acid better, and will be able to perform at high levels of energy production well into the fourth quarter.

The game of football is primarily anaerobically driven if you consider the explosive nature of the sport, but the activity periods are so short that oxygen is easily replenished. Football is a game of 5-second "all out" efforts with many rest periods interspersed to replenish the used-up oxygen. Figure 2.1 shows the approximate percentage contribution of the energy supply systems to various sports.[1]

Although both aerobic and anaerobic systems operate during any activity, one system usually predominates depending upon the intensity and duration of the muscular effort during the activity. Supplying ATP and oxygen are the primary concerns of an athlete who wants to be able to give 100 percent in the fourth quarter.

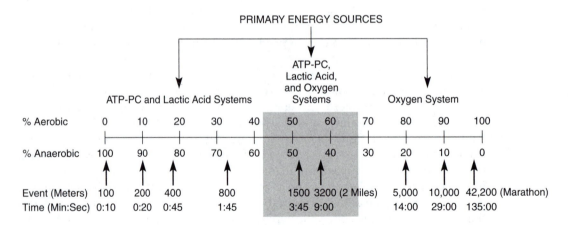

FIGURE 2.1

SPECIFICITY

Football coaches should know how players get the energy for playing, because physiological research has shown that humans are conditioned in very specific ways. Thus the concept of specificity is a necessary consideration in conditioning any athlete.

To illustrate this concept, consider a representative study that used a bicycle ergometer (stationary-resistance loading bicycle) and a motor driven treadmill.[2] One group of subjects trained on the bicycle while the other trained on the treadmill. Both groups were tested for their ability to transport and utilize oxygen (maximum aerobic capacity). Testing was done before and after the conditioning period. Those conditioned on the bicycle showed smaller improvements in aerobic capacity when tested on the treadmill and larger gains when tested on the bicycle. Thus, those trained for bicycle riding only showed performance improvements when tested specifically on the bicycle. Why was this so? The reason is that muscle tissue, as well as the energy supply systems, specifically conditioned in one type of exercise do not have the same efficiency when doing another activity.

This concept of conditioning should be understood by all coaches. The human body conditions muscle fibers in a given muscle to perform in a specific range of motion and speed of movement. Alter the range or speed of motion and those muscle fibers cannot contribute to the activity with nearly as much efficiency. Thus when an interior lineman performs a bench press, the triceps, deltoids, and pectoralis major muscles will be strengthened in the specific movement pattern of that activity. How this applies to on-the-field performance can be analyzed in terms of how many times that lineman will use the bench press motion in game situations. This is not to say that gross strength is not a contributor to athletic success. However, whenever possible a coach must condition the athlete by replicating the exact movements to be performed in actual game conditions.

There are a few individuals who have the genetically endowed capability to perform in a wide range of physiological demands. A good example is Gayle Olinekova (Olinek).[3] This female athlete was a successful body builder as well as a national performer in the 900-meter race and marathon. Jackie Joyner-Kersee and Dan O'Brien are other examples. These athletes compete in events that are at opposite ends of the spectrum of energy requirements, as shown in Table 2.1.

TABLE 2.1

	ATP-PC	Lactic Acid	Oxygen
800 meters	30%	65%	5%
marathon	5%	5%	90%

Once every ten to twelve seasons you may get an athlete who can play all sports for you and do well. But keep in mind that these individuals are exceptions, and your training methods should not be designed only for them.

Drills that you design should serve as a form of interval training to better condition both the aerobic and anaerobic systems. Thus the short intervals of work, followed by a rest or relief period (while waiting), serve to maximize conditioning of the anaerobic systems as well as the aerobic reserve.

Although many coaches turn to skill training exclusively during the competitive season, attention should be drawn to the decline in muscular strength over the duration of a football season. Coaches should stay abreast of current trends by reading national and/or state coaching journals such as *Texas Coach* or *Scholastic Coach and Athletic Administrator*.[4] Figure 2.2 shows the decline of muscular strength and endurance following intensive training (such as occurs following the off-season) and the need for a once-per-week strength stimulus for retention.[5]

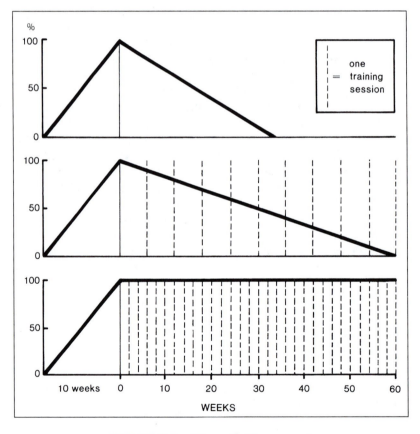

FIGURE 2.2   Strength Decrement

As Figure 2.2 illustrates, football coaches should ensure that their athletes do at least one set of weight training activities of one repetition maximum load once per week during the competitive season. Common practice today finds most teams doing 3–5 sets of 4–8 reps at least once, and preferably twice per week. This seems to stress enough of the musculature and overload the muscle tissue enough to maintain strength levels and motor unit recruitment patterns during the season. Attention should be given throughout the season for signs of staleness or what seems to be a drop in any players energy level/performance.

PRESEASON (OFF-SEASON)

What is done with your athletes during the preseason period has a crucial impact on in-season performance. However, past history has shown that football coaches often place too much emphasis on strength development, neglecting other components that greatly contribute to high levels of performance.

With this in mind, let's consider what we should do in the area of conditioning. Appendix A contains an off-season program that has been shown to improve significantly the anaerobic power of athletes. In addition, a typical off-season college conditioning program is illustrated. We recommend that all coaches set up programs that are reliable and that have been shown to improve the capacity of their athletes. Appendix A also contains several activities to increase power as well as several recognized tests that you can use before (pretest) and after (posttest) any conditioning period to ascertain whether specific energy changes have taken place. Since all coaches conduct off-season conditioning programs, those activities which have been shown to alter the physiological systems used in football should be the ones stressed during this period. Before going on, let's elaborate on a concept basic to all phases of the conditioning program, that of static stretching, which also concerns injury prevention and muscle trauma rehabilitation.

STATIC STRETCHING

A detailed discussion of the physiological bases for static stretching (holding) is not within the scope of this text.[6] It has been documented by reliable research that static stretching activities are far superior (for injury prevention and trauma rehabilitation) to the jerky bouncy stretching exercises that have been so typical of football warm-up activities in past years. However, this discussion continues today, especially in relation to injury prevention, preparation for activity, and effect on muscle function. Attention to research can keep the coach up to date on many concepts applicable to football performance and the controversy that surrounds many concepts.[7]

Observe any animal that has been asleep and leisurely wakes up. How does it stretch? It stretches by slowly extending a muscle and holding that position for several seconds. When we slowly put a muscle on stretch and hold a position at which we feel tension for at least six seconds, the muscle releases its natural tightness, relaxes, and is stretched. Not only has this been shown to be the best method for getting muscle tissue loose, but it has also been shown to aid in the prevention of muscle strains as well as in the rehabilitation of injured muscle tissue. The following suggested activities comply with the recommendations for conditioning major muscle groups. Note that all exercises listed below are held for a given time period. This holding (or static) portion of the exercise is the key to warm-up and increased flexibility. The length of time one should hold the muscle on stretch has not been conclusively identified by research. Most coaches and athletic trainers using this method have the athletes hold from ten to sixty seconds in the stretched position. Practically speaking a 15- to 20-second hold in all exercises seems beneficial.

STATIC STRETCHING EXERCISES

Upper Trunk Stretcher

1. Prone (face down) position, hands under shoulders
2. Keep pelvis on floor
3. Extend arms

Lower Trunk Stretcher

1. Prone position
2. Grasp ankles from behind and pull
3. Hold head up

Lower Back Stretcher

1. Sitting-up position, knees locked
2. Legs extended, toes pointed
3. Grasp outer borders of feet and pull head downward

Upper Back Stretcher

1. From supine (face up) position, bring knees to chest and raise legs up and over head
2. Rest extended toes on floor above head
3. Leave hands and arms flat on floor
4. Return to starting position

Toe Pointer

1. Sit on feet, toes and ankles stretched backward (passive plantar flexion)
2. Raise knees from floor slightly
3. Balance weight with both hands on floor just behind hips

Shoulder Stretcher

1. From standing position, bring right hand to upper back from above
2. Bring left hand to upper back from below and hook fingers of the two hands
3. Repeat to other side

Trunk Lifter (abdominal curl)

1. Supine position, have partner hold feet
2. Hands behind neck, lower legs flexed at knee, feet flat on floor
3. Raise head and chest vigorously, hold

Leg Lifter

1. Arms down at side, prone position
2. Raise both legs off floor about six inches, return rapidly
3. Partner hold shoulders down

Trunk Bender

1. Sitting up, legs apart and straight (extended)
2. Hands behind neck
3. Bend trunk forward and downward, attempt to place elbows on floor, hold
4. Keep back straight

Trunk Rotator

1. Arms extended laterally
2. Twist trunk to left and then to right

Gastrocnemius Stretcher (wall push-up)

1. Feet 2½ to 3½ feet from wall
2. Keep body straight, place hands on wall
3. Keep feet parallel and *heels on floor* (very important)
4. Lean forward
5. Repeat with one foot in front of the other (leave back foot heel down).

Notice from these activities that the exercises require a position that will put the muscle in a passive stretched position, beyond its normal resting state. Then by slowly stretching the muscle even further, a static stretch is obtained. Athletes can do most of the standard calisthenic stretching activities without the bouncy movements if the coach will give simple verbal commands and demonstrations of the movements. The exercises are the same traditional ones, but the emphasis is different—don't bounce.

DO'S AND DON'TS OF WARM-UP

Many coaches stress a few minutes of group stretching prior to each practice. Many times such a period is viewed by the players as a waste (especially since they have been running, passing, and kicking the ball for 15 minutes already). A few pointers on how to avoid this feeling of wasted time are given below.

1. Before the players touch a ball have them go through the series of static stretching activities described above. As this becomes part of the established routine, the players will soon look more seriously on this aspect of each practice.

2. Any bounding or ballistic motion is NOT the way to stretch a muscle. Coaches should eliminate all bouncing, jerky movements during any warm-up period that strives to loosen muscle tissue. This is a hard task since we have been so long accustomed to bouncing.

3. You must closely supervise your players to stress the stretch-and-hold procedure. The holding period can seem like an eternity if you are putting a muscle group (the hamstring muscle group for example) on stretch and you are feeling a burning, tight sensation. But this process is *essential* for proper warm-up. Any standard warm-up exercise can be done statically. Those included in this section or a basic muscle group stretching series can be done. These are designed to work the major muscle groups that produce motion at major joints.

BUDDY DRILLS

What to do with various players as they come onto the field for practice is always a consideration. The coach generally should not work only one to two of the offensive guards for instance, because those working might feel singled out, or the other linemen slighted. A possible scheme to resolve this is buddy system activities. Although many activities could be developed, those presented below suggest a possible scheme. Their purpose is to develop agility, fitness, and a competitive spirit. These drills, performed as the players come onto the field prior to the actual start of practice, give them something constructive to do other than standing around waiting on the official time to start. This is an excellent time to have players involved in conditioning and training activities that can be fun, too. Several suggested activities are given below and you might consider a similar system to fully utilize your players' time. Players should always stretch statically *before* participating in these drills.

Ten stations are located around the practice field. A player and a partner from the same position (or of comparable size) compete against one another over the course.

1. *Successive long jumps.* Players standing side by side on goal line start on a player's command of "go," long jump successively to ten-yard stripe, and return to starting position. Repeat three times.

2. *Sidestep over lying dummies.* Players face one another, start over first of four dummies with step over, use crossover in between, and circle back to start. Repeat three times.

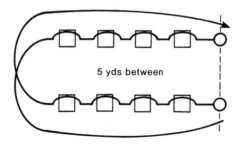

5 yds between

Side Step Over Dummies

3. *One-quarter turns.* Players face one another astride yard stripe. On "go" players turn to right one-quarter turn, placing both feet on yard stripe, back to start, then to left, back to start, one-quarter turn to face away from start and then back to start. Repeat three times.

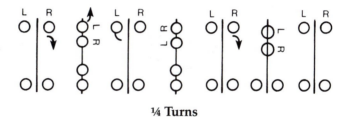

¼ Turns

4. *Side shuffle.* Partners face one another standing between five-yard stripes. On "go," sidestep to one side, touching hand and same foot outside line across to other line and back to center position. Repeat three times.

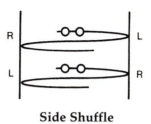

Side Shuffle

5. *Goal post circle.* Players face one another between goal post on end line. On "go," players circle post to the right, around opposite post and back to start. Repeat three times.

6. *Sideline touch.* Players face one another over sidelines—five yards back, helmet resting between feet. On "go," players run to right yard stripe touching line back backward to helmet, touch, then to left and back to helmet. Repeat three times.

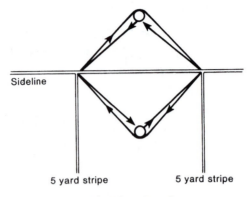

Side Line Touch

7. *Helmet pick-up.* Players place helmet on yard stripe, lie on back, head on yard stripe ten-yards away. On "go," get up, retrieve helmet, and return to start. Repeat three times.

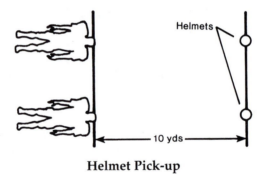

Helmet Pick-up

8. *Cone-run.* Players run in and out of boundary cone markers (helmets can be used) set five yards apart, then back to start, and backward. Repeat three times.

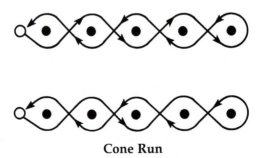

Cone Run

9. *Board run and crawl.* Two planks—12 inches wide by 12 feet long—are placed under a crossbar suspended hip high between goal posts. Players crawl on all fours under bar, over board, turn at end, and return over board with wide stance run.

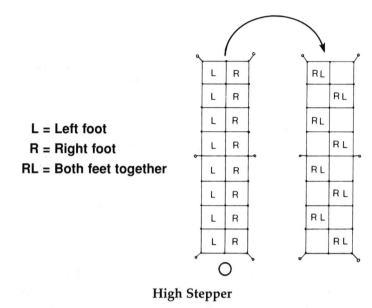

L = Left foot

R = Right foot

RL = Both feet together

High Stepper

10. *High-stepper.* Thirty feet in length. Players run over bars and return, hopping on both feet in alternate boxes (the old tires or rope technique).

These drills should be competitive, and players should keep a running tally of their "win–loss" record on each activity.

TEAM CALISTHENICS

The formal practice follows buddy drills and often begins with team calisthenics. Many teams go through slow carioca, slow high stepping, slow lower leg kick running, as a method to warm and stretch muscles through movement before formal calisthenics. The most widely used calisthenic formation is one in which the entire squad lines up on the yard lines at five-yard spacings facing a coach (or leader) who stands in front of the group. Some coaches align their players according to teams, with first team members being on the first-yard stripe, second team members on the next stripe, etc. This team procedure is not recommended for younger players, because (1) it segregates the team and (2) there will often not be complete first and second teams.

A circle formation can be used with the leader in the center of a formation similar to that shown in the following diagram.

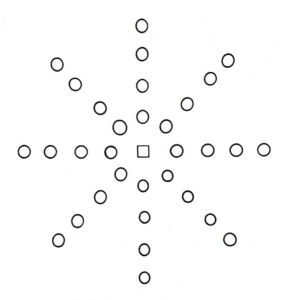

Circle Warm-up Formation

The calisthenics period should be supervised by the coaching staff. Circle formations allow the coach to see all participants, whereas when players are arranged in lines, those at the back often get neglected. In addition, it should be remembered that when a coach is doing calisthenics, he cannot supervise what his players are doing. It is extremely important to stretch the ligaments and tendons prior to a workout. Moreover, doing calisthenics in a team setting many times serves as a psychological lift to get players in the proper frame of mind to practice and work as a team. Activities for the formalized team calisthenic period need not be detailed here. Everyone should be familiar with the standard exercises of trunk rotation, side straddle hop, push-ups, and so on. Although elaboration of these activities is not given, it should be stressed that this period is crucial since the first five minutes of formal practice activity can be the most dangerous. This is because players are exerting themselves at top speed with muscles and joints that still may be stiff and immobile and should be warmed up.

CADENCE AND STARTING SIGNALS

To conclude this section on research and football coaching, an illustration of the research dealing with cadence and starting signals seems appropriate. Although this material relates primarily to offensive players, these illustrations will hopefully add to the reader's knowledge as well as stimulate an interest in keeping abreast of physiological findings that affect football success.

To be most effective, offensive players should start quickly and in unison. Although there are many variations in the auditory starting signal they can all be reduced to two general types: rhythmic and nonrhythmic signals. Disagreement exists among coaches in this respect as some feel that a rhythmic cadence allows players to anticipate the "go" signal better while some feel that a nonrhythmic signal allows greater unison of movement. There is no right way. However, the reader is directed to research in this area to help in this decision.[8] Even though the data were collected some years ago, the bulk of this evidence agrees with current findings, which seem to indicate that rhythmic signals are better if speed of movement is the main concern. It has been found that the rhythmic cadence results in slower starts but fewer offsides than the nonrhythmic cadence does. The optimum rate for rhythmic signals seems to be about 0.6 seconds between sounds, while 1.0 second between sounds has been found to be the best interval for nonrhythmic cadences. In addition, research has shown that the "go" signal should be given within two to four seconds after the players have assumed their set positions.

Examples of rhythmic cadences are shown below. *The spacing between digits or words indicates the time interval between each sound.* Each of these represents what the quarterback would say after all players are up to the LOS (Line of Scrimmage) and ready to start the play.

1. Rhythmic digit

   "Ready—1–2–3"

2. Rhythmic word-digit

   "Down—Blue 28—Hut-one-Hut-two-Hut-three"

3. Nonrhythmic digit

   "Set—1—2–3——4

4. Nonrhythmic word (color)

   "Ready—Hut-Hut——Hut"

Time should be spent with all the quarterbacks so that they call the starting signals loudly, clearly, and with the same consistency. The consistency, of course, is extremely important only if a team uses a rhythmic cadence.

FACING THE PROBLEM

How can coaches stay up to date with current research findings? One way is to become aware of the research summary publications produced by the American Alliance for Health, Physical Education, Recreation and Dance (AAHPERD). This association publishes a series of easy-to-read and very complete pamphlets that collect the research information on a variety of sports.[9] In addition, you will find the titles of several publications which can give specific research papers in the physiology of sports medicine that help the coach make intelligent decisions on training and conditioning procedures.[10] In spite of overloaded teaching and coaching schedules modern coaching requires a football coach to become aware and keep abreast of current research findings, which can be applied to football success. It is hoped that this chapter has assisted in that process.

CLASS ACTIVITIES

1. List several activities of football players that are examples of the aerobic and anaerobic systems.

2. Lead the class in team calisthenics; stress static stretching whenever possible.

3. Take turns evaluating class members' stance position and firing-out techniques.

4. Lead the class in a drill emphasizing conditioning.

5. With groups of six (five linemen and one quarterback) have the unit get set and fire off the LOS. Emphasize holding your position, and everyone releasing at the same time. Rotate quarterbacks.

NOTES

1. Edward L. Fox, Richard Bowers, and Merle L. Foss, *The Physiological Basis of Physical Education and Athletics* (Iowa: Wm. C. Brown Publishers, 1989).

2. George Percher, William McArdle, Frank Katch, James Maget, and John DeLuca, "Specificity of Cardiorespiratory Adaptations to Bicycle and Treadmill Training," *Journal of Applied Anatomy* 36 (1974):753–756.

3. Dan Levin, "Greatest Legs to Ever Stride the Earth," *Sports Illustrated* 54 (1981): 46–58.

4. See, for example, M. Brzycki, "Strength Training: On the March," *Scholastic Coach and Athletic Director* 64 (August, 1994):28–30.

5. See Richard Berger, "Optimum Repetitions for the Development of Strength," *Research Quarterly for Exercise and Sport* 33 (1962):334–338; Barry Syster and George Stull, "Muscular Endurance Retention as a Function of Length of Detraining," *Research Quarterly for Exercise and Sport* 41 (1979):105–109; and, Robert Waldman and George Stull, "Effects of Various Periods of Inactivity on Retention of Newly Acquired Levels of Muscular Endurance," *Research Quarterly for Exercise and Sport* 44 (1969):393–401.

6. For such a discussion, see Herbert deVries, "Evaluation of Static Stretching Procedures for Improvement of Flexibility," *Research Quarterly for Exercise and Sport* 33 (1962):222–229; and Herbert deVries, "Quantitative Electromyographic Investigation of the Spasm Theory of Muscle Pain," *American Journal of Physical Medicine* 45 (1966):119–134.

7. Examples of such research include: Susanna Levin, "Overtraining Causes Olympic-Sized Problems," *The Physician and Sports Medicine* 19 (1991):112–118; Lucille Smith, Mark H. Brunetz, Thomas Chenier, Michael McCammon, Joseph Houmard, Mary Frankiu, and Richard Isreal, "The Effects of Static and Ballistic Stretching on Delayed Onset Muscle Soreness and Creatine Kinase," *Research Quarterly for Exercise and Sport* 64 (1)(1993):103–107; Robert Singer and Dapeng Chen, "A Classification Scheme for Cognitive Strategies: Implications for Learning and Teaching Psychomotor Skills," *Research Quarterly*

for Exercise and Sport 65(2) (1994):143–151; and D. Willoughby, "Delayed Onset Muscle Soreness: A Possible Physiological Etiology and Practical Implications for Coaches," *Texas Coach* 35 (August 1990):34–35.

8. See W. R. Miles and B. C. Graves, "Studies in Physical Exertion: Ill Effect of Signal Variation on Football Charging," *Research Quarterly for Exercise and Sport* 2 (1931):14–31; Clem Thompson, Francis Nagle, and Robert Dobias, "Football Starting Signals and Movement Time of High School and College Football Players," *Research Quarterly for Exercise and Sport* 29 (1958):222–230; Jack A. Owens, "Effect in Variation in Hand and Foot Spacing on Movement Time and on Force of Charge," *Research Quarterly for Exercise and Sport* 31 (1960):66–67; Robert Paige, *The Effect of Pre-Foreperiod Preparations and Foreperiod Duration on the Response Time of Football Linemen* (Ph.D. diss., Indiana University, 1969); and A. D. Dickson, "The Effects of Foot Spacing on the Starting Time and Speed in Sprinting and the Relation of Physical Measurement to Foot Spacing," *Research Quarterly for Exercise and Sport* 5: supplement I (1934):12–19.

9. For example, John Cooper, ed., *What Research Tells the Coach about Football* (Washington, DC: AAHPERD Publications, 1973).

10. See, for example, Richard Strauss, ed., *The Physician and Sports Medicine* (New York: McGraw-Hill, 1995); and D. Mark Robertson, ed., *Medicine and Science in Sports and Exercise* (Wisconsin: American College of Sports Medicine, 1995).

3

SCOUTING

Chapter Objectives

After completing this chapter, the reader should be able to:

- List the things a scouting report should tell a coaching staff, identifying the major aspects of the report.
- Evaluate the strengths and weaknesses of various play-by-play data collection forms.
- Scout a film or an actual game, and develop a coaches scouting report on the team observed, giving all pertinent offensive and defensive tendencies.
- Prepare a player's scouting report similar to one that would be handed to your players.

IMPORTANCE OF SCOUTING

Even at the college level the amount and depth of scouting may be curtailed by the size of the coaching staff, the budget, and conference regulations. At the junior high school level, there is seldom a budget for scouting and the "staff" many times is only one person. This fact should be kept in mind when beginning a section on scouting, recognizing that the procedure of gathering information about opponents from watching them play other schools is vital to a coach's week-to-week preparation for games. Where defensive alignments and stunts are consistent throughout a district, the coach knows what to expect. If the district is small or if the same coaches have been at the schools several years, a coach also knows what to expect when playing a particular team. There will always be the special plays and occasional surprise formations. On the whole, however, once a coaching staff settles on a particular offense and defense they usually become consistent and develop reliable tendencies from which a rival coaching staff can predict what its opponents will do in a given situation. A coaching staff should know the following minimal information about the upcoming opponent:

1. What are their basic offensive formation(s) and best run and pass play(s)?
2. What are their basic defensive formations both mid-field and goal line?
3. Who are their best offensive and defensive players and what are those players' strengths and/or weaknesses?

This information can be gathered from personal conversations with coaches who have recently played your opponent or film exchange arrangements between you and your opponent or between you and people who have played your opponent. When you can't scout a team you will be playing you can use any of these methods to get the basic information listed above. Of course, you can always call the opponent's coach and ask him these basic questions as a last resort. However, when you can personally observe the team you will be playing, you can go to any depth of data-gathering procedures you wish. This chapter attempts to give an example of an ideal scouting procedure. As in most cases of coaching, you will do the best you can with the resources you have available.

In most situations, the junior or intermediate school coach will do the scouting for the high school. If he is not scouting his own opponents, he will be scouting for the high school varsity. Most systems use the non-varsity coaching staff to scout on Friday nights for the varsity team as these people's games are generally played the day before the varsity contests. Thus the head varsity high school coach will, during the month of August or before, assign the non-varsity coach or coaches to serve as a scouting team. These same coaches will generally scout an opponent together throughout the season. This is important as the members of the scouting team will have to familiarize themselves with each other's abbreviations and verbal cues used during the course of a game. To scout with someone who does not know what is meant by "slot I-tandem," for instance, can cause a coach to miss a lot of the action while explanations are given.

In preparing to scout, coaches should purchase a good set of binoculars before they begin their first job. The glasses should be small but powerful (if, by some chance, a coach gets high up in the pressbox, he will need to see the whole field, and it is difficult to see the five-yard line with some lighting systems!). Extra wide-angle glasses (7×25 mm or 10×50 mm) have been found satisfactory for this purpose.

PREGAME INFORMATION

There is no way to learn about scouting until one scouts. The adage that "experience is the best teacher" cannot be argued in this area. Imagine a scouting team sitting on the top row of bleachers, in the rain, umbrellas in one hand, pencils in the other, awaiting the kickoff. They have already gotten to the game forty-five minutes to one hour early in order to get the following pregame, warm-up information:

1. Names and numbers of starting players (positions, height, and weight)
2. Snap count (favorite number, rhythm); go from up or down position
3. Kickoff man (position, distance, height)
4. Extra-point kickers
5. Punters (distance, height)
6. Center's ability and accuracy on kicks
7. Weather and wind conditions

They have also used this time to talk with other coaches or the people standing around about their perceptions of the strengths and weaknesses of the team being scouted. From the program, they have compared the printed weights with what they think the players' actual weights are and have all charts, forms, and materials ready for use. They can also use this time to collect any information or observations concerning injuries.

COLLECTING AND ORGANIZING INFORMATION

The teams have come back onto the field and they are lined up for the kickoff. One member of the scouting team is looking through the binoculars calling out the numbers and positions of the players while the other scout is recording the following information:

1. Kickoff team (alignment, coverage) or
2. Kickoff return team (alignment, type of return, type of blocking, runback distance).

Then begins one of the most hectic activities for a football coach—collecting play-by-play information throughout the game. The high school coach will have a system to record all this pregame information, but the sample form shown in Figure 3.1 should give the reader an idea of the basic format of a scouting sheet.

Once the ball is put into play on the kickoff, the scouts must clear their minds except for the task of charting the action on the field. For the first-time scout or the young coach, this task will be one of the hardest things he has ever done! The

Punters

Name	No.	Type	No. of Steps	Distance from Line	Speed of Kick	Ability

Passers

Name	No.	Type of Pass	Ability and Characteristics

Receivers

Name	No.	Speed and Ability	Remarks

Extra-Point Kickers

Name	No.	Speed	Ability	Holder

Kickoff Man

Name	No.	Tee	Flat	Height	Distance	Ability

FIGURE 3.1   Pregame Warmup Summary Sheet

following is a list of the information that the scouting team is trying to find out about the team it is observing. Scouts should gather information on the following points:

A. *Running Offense*

1. Major formations (those few which are used most frequently)
2. Minor formations (those which are seldom seen)
3. Pre-snap shifts
4. Standard plays used (field position, down, yards gained, time in game) and corresponding defensive alignments
5. Special plays
6. Concentration of running attack (holes most frequently used)
7. Best outside running plays and runner
8. Best inside running plays and runner
9. Particular offensive blocking (crossblock, double team, trap, pulling linemen)
10. Goal line plays, favorite formation, most successful plays, favorite two-point play, who carries the ball

B. *Passing Offense*

1. When they pass (down, field position, type of pass)
2. Play action passes and patterns (blocking protection, completions, interceptions)
3. Straight pass patterns (blocking, protection, completions, interceptions, backfield patterns)
4. Most successful patterns, clutch patterns
5. Favorite receiver (speed, favorite moves)
6. Does passer run when trapped, "eat the ball," throw in desperation, or throw out of bounds?
7. What is the passer's major strength?
8. Can passer be intimidated?

C. *Punting Game*

1. General formation used (depth of punter)
2. Distance and direction of punts
3. Punt coverage
4. Who is easiest (and hardest) to block
5. Who made tackle
6. Snap from center (good, slow, fast)
7. Time taken to punt
8. Fake punts or passes
9. Any punts blocked (how, where)

D. *Punt Returns*

1. What alignments do they use against the punt?
2. What punt-blocking tricks do they use?

3. Can we run or pass from deep punt formation as a result of the above?
4. How do they attempt to return punts (man-for-man blocking, crisscross blocking)
5. How successful were they in returning punts? Did backs attempt exchange? (type of return, blocking-wall, up the middle)

E. Defense (This aspect is the hardest to organize)

1. Defense used against each alignment
2. Specific situations when each defense was used (down, field position)
3. Type of secondary rotation
4. Type of pass defense (zone, man-for-man, combination, bump and run)
5. Reaction to flankers, men in motion, spreads
6. Do they stunt (when, how, who)
7. Successful defenses (basic, short or critical yardage, goal line)
8. Who are weak and strong defensive linemen, linebackers, and halfbacks against run and pass
9. Anticipated adjustments to our formation

F. Extra Point and Field Goals

1. Basic alignment
2. Do they run, kick, or pass for extra points
3. Distance of kicker from center
4. Speed and accuracy of center's snap
5. Success of kicks
6. Trick formations/plays

G. General Information

1. Team spirit
2. Team reaction when scored upon
3. Team reaction when they score
4. Team reaction when behind; when ahead
5. General physical condition
6. Substitutions (when made and number made)
7. Injuries (did player return to game)

H. Postgame Information

1. General impression of opponents (are they superior or inferior to us, by how many touchdowns)

In looking over this list, the coach may be struck by the enormous quantity of information that may be required. In addition, note that an individual can "look at a football game," and then he can "LOOK at a football game." The specific methods used to gather information are as varied as head coaches. This text will examine two commonly used scouting forms. It should be remembered that the forms are constructed so that the scout can get all pertinent information recorded before each play starts and also draw a record of each play. One scout can give the oral report as he sees the team line up while the other records. Sometimes scouts split these jobs on offense and defense.

COLLECTING PLAY-BY-PLAY INFORMATION

The most effective manner in which to take the play-by-play during the game (assuming you are not using computer scouting software) is on a form that contains space(s) for drawing the formation and outcome. Figures 3.2 and 3.3 are samples of such sheets.

The only drawback to these forms is the time involved in compiling the information after the game is over. For example, if a coach wants to know what a team's favorite play is on first down, it is necessary to go through every sheet and find all the first down plays, then chart these to find any tendencies. To combat this problem the "key sort" card was devised. Samples of this type are shown in Figures 3.4 and 3.5.

Hash Mark L-M-R _____
D & D _____
Field Position _____
Gain _____

Hash Mark L-M-R _____
D & D _____
Field Position _____
Gain _____

○ ○ ☐ ○ ○   ○ ○ ☐ ○ ○

Hash Mark L-M-R _____
D & D _____
Field Position _____
Gain _____

Hash Mark L-M-R _____
D & D _____
Field Position _____
Gain _____

○ ○ ☐ ○ ○   ○ ○ ☐ ○ ○

FIGURE 3.2

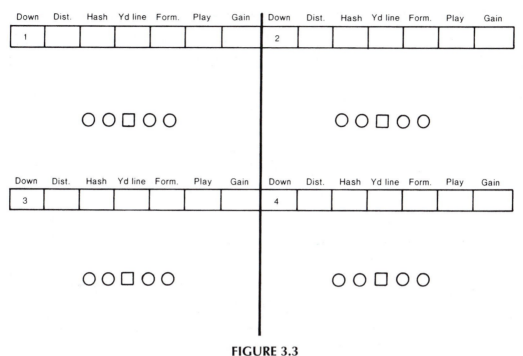

FIGURE 3.3

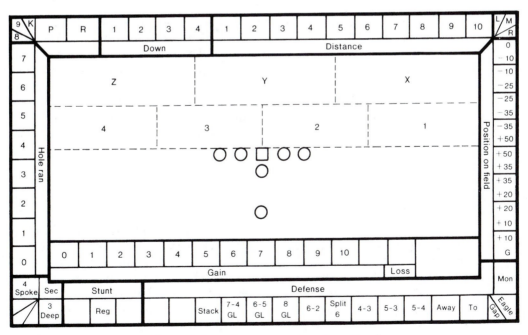

FIGURE 3.4   Defensive Key Sort Card

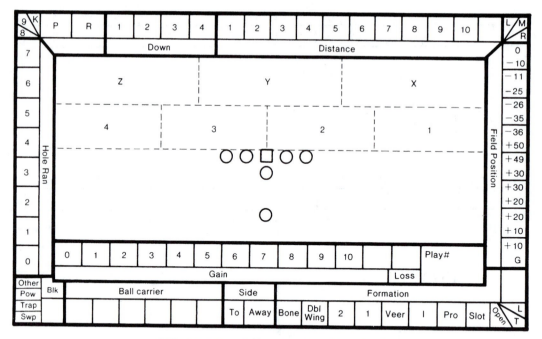

FIGURE 3.5   Offensive Key Sort Card

All of the necessary information needed for the offensive and defensive stages of the scouting procedure are listed around the four edges of the card. The drawing of each play, to be filled in at the center of the card, illustrates formations, sets, blocking or pass patterns, and the like. This procedure is identical to most types of recording sheets. The offensive plays are labeled according to your own system so that terminology will be common. Many teams utilize a card that contains both offensive and defensive information. (Again, if you are using some form of computer scouting software once inputed you can get specific down, distance, % run/pass, holes hit most, etc.)

POSTGAME ORGANIZATION

Immediately after the game, the scouts use a hole punch to notch out all sections of the edge they marked during the game. When ready to begin compiling information a long ice pick or knitting needle can be used to isolate specific cards (that is, to find what the team likes to run on second down with one or two yards to go). The needle is pushed through the second down hole, the coach shakes the cards and all second down plays fall out. The space designated for short yardage is located and the procedure is repeated. Now all cards recorded for second and short situations are together.

After the game the scouting team has the responsibility of reporting back to coaches and players what they have found. The other members of the coaching staff might get the most out of the report if the following type of format is used:

1. Title sheet (game scouted, etc.)
2. General summary and recommendations
3. General remarks (Offense and Defense)
4. Personnel (Offense and Defense)
5. Formation and field position; hit charts (holes ran most often)
6. Tendency sheets

    a. Formations
    b. Plays run on specific downs

7. Diagrams of all runs versus our defense (indicate expected blocking patterns)
8. Diagrams of all passes versus our defense (indicate expected blocking patterns)
9. Diagrams of all trick plays versus our defense (indicate expected blocking patterns)
10. Basic defense should include:

    a. Adjustments or stunts
    b. Goal line and short yardage
    c. Secondary coverages
    d. Prevent or long yardage
    e. Down and field position tendencies

11. Punting game
12. Kickoff game

As can be seen from this list, the scouting team will have to examine, sort out, organize and study all of the information gathered at the game in order to present a concise picture to the rest of the coaching staff. Plans of attack, practice emphasis, and stress points, in preparation for the next opponent, will be discussed by all coaches based on this report. The scouting team will generally have one night plus portions of a day to get its information organized. Some form of master sheet or summary sheet will need to be prepared by the scouting team as the first effort at organizing the bulk of the material collected. These forms mainly attempt to organize all offensive plays and all defensive plays together so that a general impression of the team's performance can be formed. Figure 3.6 shows a sample offensive master sheet. Basic information included on an offensive master sheet might include:

1. Number of play (in sequence)
2. Down
3. Distance
4. Hash Mark
5. Field Position

6. Formation (equated to our terminology)
7. Play (equated to our terminology)
8. Defense (equated to our terminology)
9. Outcome of Play

Specific tendency sheets can be developed from this master sheet. The body of information that the scouting team will use comes from the specific tendency sheets. Usually separate sheets are constructed, one for the defense, one for the offense, and one for the kicking game. Sample forms of such sheets are shown in Figures 3.7, 3.8, and 3.9.

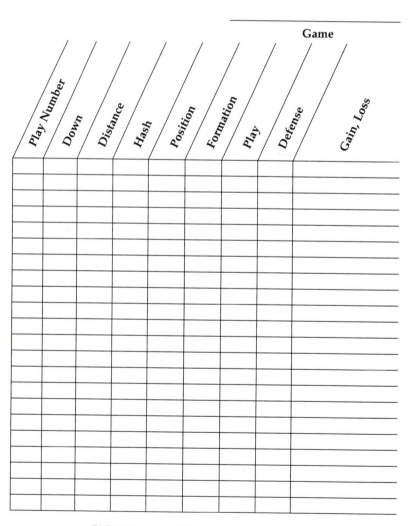

FIGURE 3.6   Offensive Master Sheet

Starting Lineup (by Numbers)

Pos.	Name	No.	Wt.	Ht.	Yr.	Description/Ability
LE						
LT						
LG						
C						
RG						
RT						
RE						
QB						
LH						
FB						
RH						

FIGURE 3.7   Offensive Lineup

Date:_____

Scout: _____

Team Scouted:_____

Game: _____

City: _____

Weather:_____

Wind: Direction and strength: _____

Condition of Field: _____

Remarks:

  1.

  2.

  3.

Score: _____

FIGURE 3.8   Football Scouting Report

40 _____ 40

35 _____ 35

Kicker _____ No. _____ Distance _____ Ht. _____

   Direction _____

Ball Holder _____

Possibility of short kick _____

Do men rush hard all the way _____

Does anyone stay back _____

Do ends guard sidelines _____

Fastest man down field _____

Who made the tackle _____

Additional information _____

_____

Remarks:

Receiving Kickoff

40 _____ 40

50 _____ 50

40 _____ 40

30 _____ 30

20 _____ 20

10 _____ 10

G _____ G

FIGURE 3.9   Lineup When Kicking Off

THE SCOUTING REPORT

The information taken from these sheets plus the play-by-play tendency analysis constitutes the body of the scouting information. What the staff will give to the players, in both quantity of information and form, varies greatly depending on the level of coaching. With younger players, simple verbal instruction and on-field demonstration often suffice. Beginning with the junior high level and higher, in addition to film/video study and on-field demonstration, some sort of written report may be handed to each player. When the offensive and defensive teams are two separate entities, as they are at many high schools and most college and professional levels, separate scouting reports are prepared: a specific report on the offense is given to the defensive team, and a specific report on the defense is given to the offensive team.

Junior and senior high schools often prepare a combination report to give to the entire team. The format of this report can be as follows:

1. Title Sheet
2. Personnel (Offensive and Defensive)
3. Formations (basic)
4. Favorite runs versus our defense
5. Favorite passes versus our defense
6. Basic defenses (regular and goal line)
7. Punting game
8. Kickoff game

One need only examine the differences between a high school scouting report and a college scouting report to get an insight into the kind and quantity of information given to the players. At the junior high school level, the maturity of the youngsters and the type of football played do not warrant a complex scouting report. However, as previously stated, junior high coaches need to have a working knowledge of the ingredients of a comprehensive scouting report. A typical college-level report, particularly one at a major college, approaches the ultimate in quantity of information, and one wonders if even a college football player can find time to digest all of the information handed him on Monday before the game on Saturday! Appendix C contains a sample of the type of report that might be handed to junior or senior high players.

COMPUTER SCOUTING

A final note should be added concerning the use of the computer in scouting. Just as the key sort-needle punch idea came in as a fad, so has the use of computer-programmed scouting. Various individuals knowledgeable about computers have developed systems whereby a scout may use a punch card similar to that shown below to record play-by-play data (see Figure 3.10).

The card shows a convenient method of computer scouting that allows a team to get defensive and offensive information. The scout simply marks with pencil the appropriate data. This card allows the scout to use combinations of numbers to indicate specific items of information. For example, under the "Defense" column the scout might fill in "4 deep," "Zone," and use the numbers "5-4" in both columns to indicate the defensive alignment. It could be that a particular scout would use a "1" or "2" in the left defensive column to indicate an odd or even defensive alignment and then use a number in the right defensive column to indicate a particular stunt or linebacker arrangement. Any combination is possible. After the game, the scout simply submits the deck of machine-readable cards to the computer center. No punching is required. After coding and entering information into the

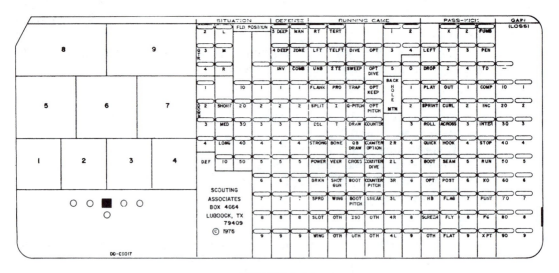

FIGURE 3.10

computer scouting format the final analysis is printed out in verbal and graphic form.

It takes about fifteen minutes to one hour (depending upon the computer backlog and operational conditions) to receive a printout that gives the scout more detailed information on a team than he can usually utilize. But a quick singling out of important data saves the scout considerable time, which is a strong point of computer scouting. These systems range in amount of information available and price to produce a printout.

A final word on scouting methods should mention the fact that, for economy, many teams use films or videos of their opponents to get all the necessary information. Certainly, these media allow repeated close examination and viewing of a team's performance. However, films do not give precise positional sets (because of the frequently poor camera angles), nor does film give the scout information concerning team morale, injuries, cadence, or any pregame in formation.

All undergraduate majors who aspire to become football coaches should get as much practical experience as they can. Most of this type of involvement is on a voluntary basis. But schools actively seek young men who are preparing to be coaches to assist them in their programs, especially in the area of scouting. These experiences can be invaluable!

The answer to the question "Why scout?" can be stated very simply: so a coaching staff can look at a team's tendencies, predict what it will do in a given situation, and plan its strategies accordingly.

As in all areas of football, the "human element" that becomes a crucial factor during the game itself will ultimately determine who wins and who loses. However, remember to balance the two locker room sayings: "Success is when Luck meets with Preparation" and "Hard work and preparation are no guarantee of success."

CLASS ACTIVITIES

1. Assign groups of three (four at the most) to scout a local junior or senior high school game. From the collected data, develop a coaches' scouting report and a players' scouting report.

2. Have class members talk to local coaches and discuss scouting assignments and scouting procedures.

3. Obtain past scouting reports from colleges or high schools to use for class discussion.

4

BASIC OFFENSIVE CONSIDERATIONS

Chapter Objectives

After completing this chapter, the reader should be able to:

- List the major changes in offensive strategy over the last seventy-five years.
- Give the major considerations for deciding on an offensive system.
- Identify the reasons for changing (or not changing) an offensive system.
- Illustrate current offensive formations.
- Discuss the various rationales for huddle arrangements.

OFFENSE-OFFENSE-OFFENSE

The enormous variety of offensive attacks make any chapter on this topic an open-ended book (and many times a "can of worms"). The reader need only attend a coaching clinic session and listen to several coaches discussing the advantages and disadvantages of their offense to get a glimpse of the varied world of offense. Such terms as "I," "Wishbone," "Veer," "Power I," "Tandum Slot," "Wing T," "Pro Set," and "Straight T" are often heard, and the list goes on and on.

As with defense, however, each offensive formation tries to make the best use of the available personnel: "We don't have the quarterback to run a veer," "We'll be passing with our quarterback and split end combination," "We're too little to run over people, but we have the speed to run around folks." Personnel considerations dictate the type of offense you run.

Consistency also plays a vital role because the coach wants young players to feel confident about their offense and be familiar with it. The classic example is the "Powerhouse" football team that is the product of a one-high-school town fed by one or two junior high schools. Each junior high school runs the same offensive attack (that is, formation, numbering, plays) as the high school so that by the time the players reach high school they know and can execute the entire system. Changing from year to year disrupts this type of continuity. It also upsets the confidence the players have in both the coaching staff and the system itself.

HISTORICAL CONSIDERATIONS*

A concise overview of the development of the game of football may give the reader a better insight into the strategy of offensive play. From its meager beginning in 1869, the game of American football has undergone many changes. The first "football" game between Princeton and Rutgers saw twenty-five players on each side, without any protective equipment, play a hard-fought physical game that Rutgers won 6 to 4. Since running or throwing the ball was banned (by English Association rules), scoring was by field goals only. The ball could be snatched in mid-air or on the first bounce for a free kick. To give the reader an insight into how offensive strategy developed, the following chronological sequence of major events may be helpful:

1872 Princeton drew up American football's first written set of rules.

1874 Rugby-style football, in which a dead ball was placed between the two teams for a "scrimmage," was developed.

1876 The American Intercollegiate Football Association was formed (Harvard, Yale, Princeton, and Columbia). A rugby-style game was adopted with fifteen players to a side.

This was also the year when the first formal uniforms were worn by teams from Pennsylvania and Princeton. Running with the ball, rather than just kicking it, was gaining popularity.

1880 Field size was reduced (from an original 500 by 300 feet to 110 by 53 yards). Rugby-style play was adopted, so that a quarterback was chosen who could receive the ball (which was "heeled" back to him) and maneuver it to other rushers to kick or run.

Walter Camp convinced the Football Association that eleven men per team would be better than fifteen.

*Adapted with permission of Scholastic Magazines Inc., from *100 Plus Years of Football*, by Jerry Brondfield, copyright 1975.

1882   The Football Association adopted Camp's recommendation that the attacking team be required to advance the ball five yards in three tries (or downs) or give it up. This produced the first striped or marked fields. This year also produced specific names for positions (seven forwards, one quarterback, two halfbacks, and one fullback). A typical formation and field alignment is shown in Figure 4.1.

The first eligibility rules were established (players could only play for five years).

1883   Virtually every college was switching from a kicking game to a running game. Walter Camp devises the first numerical scoring system: one point for a safety; two points for a touchdown; four points for a try-after-touchdown; five points for a field goal.

1884   The flying wedge was popularized by Princeton. Although there existed specific rules against running interference for the ball carrier, officials became lax, and by 1884, violations for this infraction were not called (though the restriction remained in the rule book, until 1906).

1886   First game played on college grounds (Princeton versus Yale).

1888   Tackling as low as the knees was allowed.

1890   Centers could snap the ball back with the hands (instead of the heel of the foot). The first snap signals were devised. Due to the flying wedge and momentum interference, injuries skyrocketed. Many deaths occurred. Wide criticism was issued by college administrators and the public.

1894   Rule change banned all mass-momentum play. No more than three men could start in motion before the ball was snapped and these men could not be more than five yards behind the ball.

Amos Alonzo Stagg became the first paid college coach with faculty status (University of Chicago). Thirty years later Knute Rockne stated that all

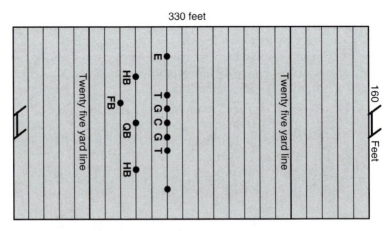

FIGURE 4.1   Football Field Marking Typical Formation

modern football came from Stagg. This statement is exemplified by the innovations created by Stagg.

A. Originated end-around plays, reverses, box formation defensive secondaries.
B. Developed criss-cross plays and double handoffs.
C. Revised place-kicks, man-in-motion plays, and onside kicks.
D. Invented the tackling dummy.
E. First coach to put numbers on jerseys. (Also led in developing the forward pass, after its introduction in 1904.)

1896–1899 Major rule changes were introduced as a result of the increasing brutality of the game. College conferences were established (Western Conference 1895—later known as the Big Ten—became the first formally organized league, composed of Chicago, Michigan, Illinois, Wisconsin, Northwestern, and Minnesota).

Varsity player eligibility was limited to three years; no "tramp" athletes, no freshman eligibility.

Uniforms were standardized. Piling on the ball carrier was banned and at least five men were required on the line of scrimmage when the ball was snapped. No offensive man could take more than one step without coming to a stop before the ball was snapped (1896).

Touchdowns were valued at five points, equal to a field goal; a safety was worth two points, and a point after touchdown was valued at one point.

Eastern schools no longer dominated football play. (Sewanee College, Sewanee, Tennessee, stunned the nation by winning twelve straight games over Georgia Tech, Georgia, Tennessee, Texas, Tulane, Louisiana State, Mississippi, Auburn and others. Five of these games were played in six days.)

1901 Michigan defeated Stanford 49–0 in the first Rose Bowl game. Michigan, coached by Fielding H. ("Hurry-up") Yost, was the first to use the tailback formation to utilize speedy running backs.

Nine-man defensive fronts yielded to seven-man lines as running backs became more adept at breaking past the line of scrimmage.

1904 Forward pass was legalized. The field goal was reduced from five points to four points; this was the first time the touchdown ranked over the field goal.

1905 Eighteen players were killed in college games since mass play, kneeing, and slugging were common as teams were still required to make five yards in three tries.

President Teddy Roosevelt threatened to abolish football if colleges did not revise the game.

The quarterback was allowed to run with the ball so long as he crossed the line of scrimmage at least five yards from where the ball was put into play. The marked field took the look of a large rectangular checkerboard as lengthwise stripes were added to the cross-stripes (thus the name "gridiron").

Columbia abolished football (not to resume until 1915).

1906   Representatives from sixty-three schools met and established the American Intercollegiate Football Rules Committee. The forward pass had to cross scrimmage line five yards out to either side of center snap. An incomplete pass could be recovered by either side if it had been touched. Pass caught behind goal line was touchback, not touchdown. Many critics thought the pass was too unsound. Throwing the squat, oval ball and catching it meant new skills. In addition to putting in the forward pass in 1906, the new rules committee further opened up the game by requiring the offense to advance ten yards in three tries for a first down instead of five yards, which previously had been a great inducement for bruising, battering line play from which no form of mayhem was barred. Under the new rules, the quarterback now had to gamble with wide end sweeps and other wide open plays.

To further discourage mass play, at least six men were now required to be on the offensive line. (This still permitted a tackle or guard to take a position behind the line and enter an interference pattern, or an end to be part of the ball handling act.)

Hurdling, formerly cause of many serious injuries, was banned. Roughing penalties were added.

1910   Mass play was completely banned by requiring seven men on offensive line. The restriction which allowed the quarterback to run only if he went five yards to the right or left of the center snap was removed. Lengthwise stripes disappeared from the field. The ball had to be thrown from at least five yards behind scrimmage, but now it could cross the line at any point rather than being restricted to five yards to either side of center. No back could be aided by pushing or pulling, and the game was divided into quarters instead of halves.

The distance of the pass was now limited to not more than 20 yards from the spot where the ball was put into play. For the first time, something was done to protect the receiver. "Interference" would be called if the offensive player were tackled, pushed, or prevented from attempting to catch the ball.

1912   Field was reduced from 110 yards to 100 yards, with an end zone behind each goal line. Kickoff was to be from the 40-rather than the 55-yard line and a touchdown was now six points instead of five. (The field goal had been dropped from four to three a few years earlier.)

A fourth down was added. The offense now had four opportunities to gain ten years and make a first down.

The forward pass also got new impetus when the 20-yard limitation was removed. The ball could now be tossed for any distance beyond the scrimmage line. Ends with speed were now in great demand to outrace the secondary defenders. Previously, a forward pass caught over the goal line was a touchback and the other team got the ball. This rule change legalized a touchdown on a pass caught in the end zone.

1913–1925   Oklahoma is unbeaten (10–0, 1915). Glenn Scobey (Pop) Warner develops the double wing, roll blocking, and a 3-point stance while at Carlisle Indian School (Jim Thorpe), Carlisle, Pennsylvania. After introducing an unbalanced line double wing, Coach "Gloomy Gil" Dobie at Cornell had unbeaten seasons in 1921, 1922, and 1923, scoring 1070 points to opponents 81.

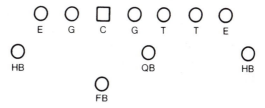

Double Wing Formation

Knute Rockne becomes head coach at Notre Dame (1918). His career will span thirteen years until his death in 1931; career record 105–12–5.

Rockne's influence on offensive football is best summed up by one of his famous quotes: "Victory goes not only to the strong and brave but to boys who think. Football is played with the arms and legs and shoulders—but mostly above the neck!"

Rockne introduced a modified T Formation with a rhythmically shifting backfield. This formation allowed the offense to shift quickly out of set positions, giving the defense no chance to read the formation as to whether it was square, V, Z, flanker or even if the quarterback would handle the ball first.

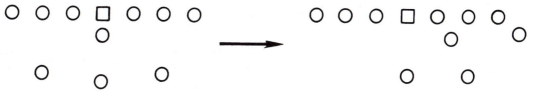

Notre Dame's Pre-snap Shift

Notre Dame's famous backfield of Miller, Layden, Crowley, and Stuhldreher became the "Four Horsemen" (behind the "Seven Mules") who posted a 9–1 season in 1923 and a 10–0 season in 1924. This foursome using the now famous and controversial shift scored 560 points to the opponents 91 in these two years.

Red Grange (whose number 77 was retired by Illinois, the first number ever to be so honored by any college) saves a struggling professional football league by signing for a series of games with the Chicago Bears (1925).

Michigan's quarterback-end combination of Benny Friedman and Benny Oosterbaan became the only forward passing duo ever to make All-American two straight years (1925–26).

The point-after had previously been from the 5-yard line at the spot opposite where the runner had crossed the goal line. In 1922, it was still spotted on the five, but in front of goal posts, doing away with wide-angled tries.

In 1925, in an effort to cut down injuries, clipping (blocking from behind) was made illegal and penalized 15 yards.

1926   Alabama's Crimson Tide became the first Southern school to play in the Rose Bowl (where they defeated Washington). Southern Methodist University, coached by Ray Morrison, began a fifteen-year pass-oriented offense which became nationally known as the "aerial circus."

The forward pass was restricted by 5-yard penalty and loss of down for two incompletes in the same series of downs.

1927   Goal posts were taken off the goal line and placed at the rear of the end zone, affecting field goals dramatically.

1929   The game lost some familiar drama with a new fumble rule. When recovered by opponents after hitting ground, the fumble now could not be advanced past the point of recovery.

1930–1950   The 1930s gave the game a new look. The ball was restyled—slimmer and more pointed—to help the passer, who got further aid by elimination of a penalty for two incompletes in the same series of downs.

1934   Columbia became the first eastern team in fifteen years to win the Rose Bowl on the famous bootleg play:

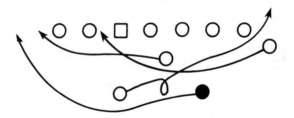

The Single Wing Bootleg Play

1940   Stanford coach Clark Shaughnessy used the T formation, transforming a 0–10 team into a 10–0 Rose Bowl winner in one year. Shaughnessy learned the formation from Ralph Jones who developed the formation while working for George Halas and the Chicago Bears.

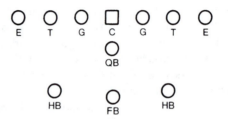

The Full House Backfield T Formation

In the late 1940s Orrin (Fritz) Crisler introduced the concept of two-platoon football and also developed what would become his hallmark—the buck lateral and spin-buck single wing attack:

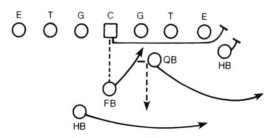

Single Wing Buck Lateral Attack

In the buck-lateral, the fullback, instead of blasting into line, sometimes would hand off to the quarterback before going in; the quarterback would pitch laterally to a hindback going wide, or pass. The defense didn't know which was coming. On the spinbuck, the close man would receive the snap, and spin to give it to the man coming across. Often he would fake, complete his spin, and in the same movement smash back into the line.

1947–49 Southern Methodist quarterback Doak Walker ran and passed his way to three consecutive All-Americans. Coach Don Faurot of Missouri develops the "split" T and the "option" play.

1950–1960 Oklahoma's coach Bud Wilkinson utilized the Split T formation shown below to facilitate making every wide running play and every pass play an option. This formation would produce undefeated seasons in 1950, 1954, 1955, and 1956, and national championships in 1950, 1955, and 1956. (Upon retiring in 1963 Wilkinson's record was 145–29–4.)

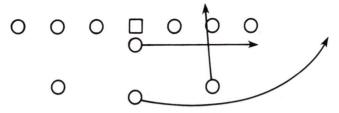

The Split T Formation

1953 Unlimited substitution was discarded and players again had to play both ways.

Coach Woody Hayes used a ball-control ground game to take Ohio State to fame (1954, 1955, and 1957 Big Ten Winners; 1954, 1957, and 1968 National Champions).

1957   Notre Dame broke Oklahoma's win string at 47 with a 7–0 victory.

1958   Rule makers added the two-point conversion, the first scoring change in 46 years.

   Paul (Bear) Bryant became Head Coach at Alabama. (Career record 1958–1982, 323–85–17.)

1959   The goal posts are widened from 18.5 feet to 23 feet 4 inches.

1964   Unlimited substitution (and two-platoon football) was restored. The wing T Formation (see p. 54) is popularized by coaches David Nelson and Forrest Evasheski.

1965–66   Michigan State's Duffy Daugherty uses a multifaceted T-attack to become undefeated Big Ten Champs (Michigan State was defeated by UCLA in the 1965 Rose Bowl).

1969–70   The University of Texas, under Coach Darrell Royal popularizes the Wishbone formation:

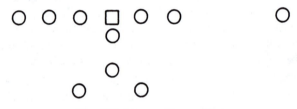

The Wishbone Formation

At the same time, Coach Bill Yomen at the University of Houston was employing the veer formation:

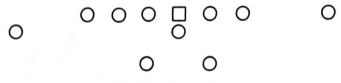

The Veer Formation

   These two formations utilized the concept of (1) a ball carrier being closer to the line scrimmage for quicker handoffs and (2) the isolation of a defensive man for option purposes. This allowed the offensive blockers to have a numerical advantage over the defense since one defensive man was not being blocked.

   At about the same time Coach John McKay at the University of Southern California was using a formation he saw while at Florida State in the early sixties. This was known as the "I" formation:

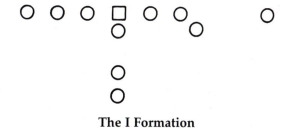

The I Formation

This offensive set placed the tailback seven and one-half yards behind the line of scrimmage so that he would have time to "pick his hole" as the blocking developed. McKay had a back who could do just this. His name was O. J. Simpson.

We can see that over the years rule changes and innovative coaches have determined the offensive strategies that have prevailed. In most cases, however, personnel dictated the formation. For example, you need an exceptional athlete to run the tailback position of the single-wing formation. You need an exceptional athlete in the quarterback position to run the veer or wishbone option offense. And you need an exceptional tailback to run the I formation.

OFFENSIVE SETS

Over the last twenty-five to thirty years, however, the T, veer, wishbone, and I offensive sets have remained the major formations. All began with the basic full-house backfield set. Let us first quickly look at this basic offensive alignment as shown below and then examine some of the more common offensive sets and the strategy for using them.

T Formation Full House Backfield

T formation

This is the straight T formation, developed in 1940 by Coach Clark Shaughnessy (Stanford) and Don Farout at Missouri in the 1950s, and later modified by Coach

Bud Wilkinson (Oklahoma) by widening the splits, making it a "Split T." As mentioned earlier, the T formation allowed a balanced attack while spreading the defense out. Better blocking angles were created by this splitting technique, the quarterback action required a sliding motion, down the line, and an overload situation could be created easily by putting a man in motion.

There are many deviations from this standard set. Below are various other offensive formations and the different labels given to players where they deviate from the standard set shown in the previous diagram.

Power I

The Power I formation spreads the alignment of the running back wider, but also places a tailback behind the fullback. A split end or wide receiver (8–12 yards wide) also spreads the defense out more (at the same time weakening the offensive blocking front). In this alignment the tailback is seven to seven-and-a-half yards behind the ball. If he is a very quick player he can follow the block of the fullback and break for daylight when the hole opens. The wide receiver adds the passing dimension to this formation. If we take the running back and spread him wide opposite the wide receiver we can produce a typical run–pass oriented alignment.

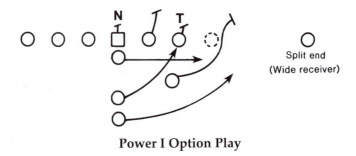

Power I Option Play

Coach John McKay (USC) used the I formation very effectively with O. J. Simpson. Soon, however, many other coaches found that by the time the tailback reached the line of scrimmage (seven-and-a-half yards away), the hole had closed and a big linebacker was waiting (of course, they didn't have O. J. Simpson at tailback!).

Wishbone

The wishbone formation (p. 50) uses the basic backfield alignment of the T formation but alters the positions of the backs. Whereas the running backs in the T formation line up four-and-a-half yards behind their offensive tackle, the wishbone running backs line up approximately three yards behind their offensive guard, or in the guard–tackle gap. The fullback (FB) is still between the running backs behind the quarterback (QB) but he is moved up very close to the quarterback. (His feet are generally four to four-and-a-half yards behind the ball, but when he assumes a four-point stance he is approximately two-and-a-half yards from the ball. He generally is able to reach out and touch the quarterback. This alignment was developed specifically to attack the outside. The following diagram illustrates the typical option play with the isolation of the defensive end and the numerical superiority of the offensive blockers (four blockers, or five with the on-side halfback, attacking three defensive men).

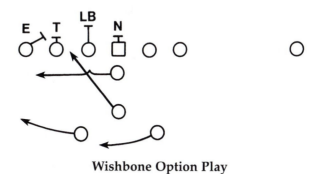

Wishbone Option Play

Both the T and the wishbone are based on a run philosophy. They both require an intelligent, quick-thinking quarterback, a tough, hard-nosed fullback, and speedy running backs.

Veer

Coach Bill Yoman (University of Houston) took the fullback out of the wishbone, spread the defense more, and called the formation the "veer." The diagram below shows the basic veer formation and option play development from this set.

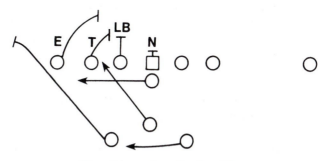

Veer Formation Option Play

The veer, wishbone, and I formations have been the more popularly used offensive sets for the last several years. Generally, a team with a more developed passing component will show a more widely spread offensive alignment. It is also

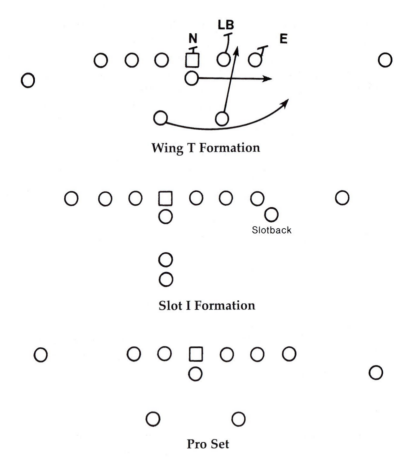

Wing T Formation

Slot I Formation

Slotback

Pro Set

generally agreed that outside running can be facilitated with slot or wing sets. Thus, the following deviations from the above two sets have evolved.

A final note about the run or pass controversy. Although personnel and physical development will govern school-age players, the observations of Duffy Daugherty should provide food for thought:

1. If you throw more than twenty times per game you'll probably lose.
2. All during my twenty-six years at Michigan State, a passing team never won a conference championship.

Although these comments are founded on the college game we might surmise that the running game should be stressed before a lot of time is devoted to the passing attack. It should also be noted that there are risks involved in relying too heavily on either the run or the pass. A one-sided offense is easy to scout and easy to defend.

Looking at formations may give you some idea of the variety of ways players can line up. Other considerations a coach may use when deciding on an offensive system are:

1. Coaching staff competencies
2. Tradition, or the alignment the team has been familiar with
3. Defenses to be faced

A typical offensive system and its description will now be considered.

OFFENSIVE FORMATIONS AND LINEUP POSITIONS

A coach should start with a basic formation, such as the I formation. Such a basic formation could be called a "B-Right" formation:

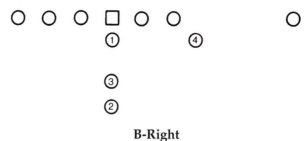

B-Right

This basic set can be adjusted to achieve the following variations:

- adjust the tailback before the snap

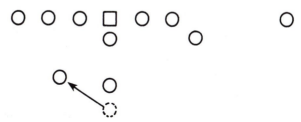

B-Right Walk Left (or Right)

- shift the split end to the left

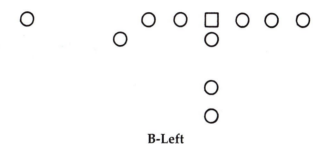

B-Left

- create a power type formation by moving the wingback into a running back position

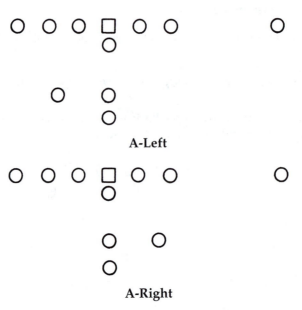

A-Left

A-Right

HOLE NUMBERING AND BACK NUMBERING

Offensive hole and backfield numbering is another area where no set standard is found. However, the possibilities can be narrowed down. The next three pairs of diagrams show the more common methods of numbering both the hole (running lane) and the offensive backfield.

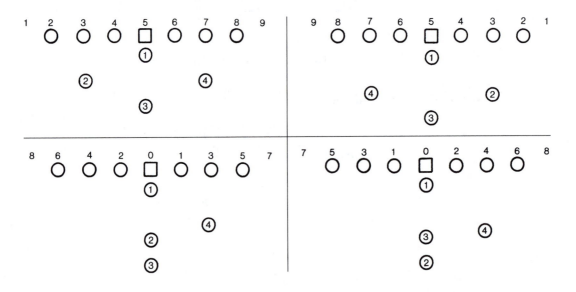

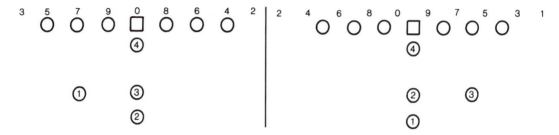

The reason for hole and back numbering is to give directions as to who will carry the ball (2 back) and where (4 hole). Thus, a call in the offensive huddle might be "38 on 2." This says that the "3" back will carry the ball through the "8" hole and the center will snap the ball on "2." No matter what system is used, the first digit usually indicates the back carrying the ball and the second digit the hole. The diagram below denotes a typical Hole and Back Numbering System. The hole numbers and backfield numbers will remain the same regardless of formation changes.

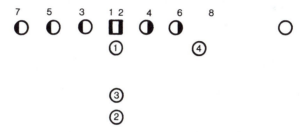

Hole and Back Numbering System

THE OFFENSIVE HUDDLE

Different huddles are shown in the following diagrams. Most teams have the center form the huddle five to eight yards back from the LOS. All diagrams below have the LOS at the top of the page.

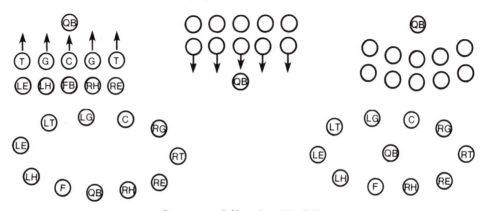

Common Offensive Huddles

Personal choice and philosophy dictate huddle formation. Consider the following offensive huddle:

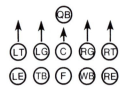

This huddle is considered to be the best for younger age players for the reasons listed below:

1. All offensive players are facing the LOS except the quarterback. As they break out of the huddle all players are still facing the direction they were when the play was called.
2. Both ends are located at the extreme ends of the huddle so that they can leave the huddle quickly and early if needed.
3. It is relatively easy for all players to see the quarterback.

At any level of playing, it is the quarterback who can best remember the play and direction with his back turned to the LOS. All other players need to be facing the LOS so that they can conceptualize their responsibilities as the play is called.

PROCEDURE FOR PLAY CALLING AND HUDDLE BREAK

Once the huddle is formed, players must be taught to remain quiet and look at and listen to the quarterback. Huddle discipline is very important and should be stressed throughout the season. Players may talk to each other before the moment that the quarterback steps into the huddle, but from then on there must be silence.

Teams may have one designated player (usually the quarterback) call the formation, play, and snap signal (for example, B-RT, 38 Sweep on 2). Other procedures delete or add to what is said in the huddle.

1. Formation is dictated by the play called: "38 counter on 2."
2. Formation and line blocking are called in the huddle: "Green Right—George Blocking—32 Trap on 1."
3. Simply Play and Snap: "25 Dive on 3."

The complexity or simplicity of this procedure will be determined by the coaching staff. For younger players, the simpler the better. Following the call in the huddle one or several players (such as, center and split end) can leave the huddle early to get to their positions, or all players can break to the LOS at the same time. Most teams today use an offensive formation that employs split ends or flankers, and at younger age levels it is often helpful to let the center get the ball arranged before the rest of the team gets up to the LOS. For these reasons, we recommend that these players leave the huddle early. This will allow the quarterback to repeat the formation, play, and the snap count for the rest of the team.

Huddle mechanics and discipline rank among the most often ignored phases of the game. Any coaching staff should put much thought and preparation into the system of play calling to be used as well as the placement and organization of the offensive huddle.

THE OFFENSIVE RUNNING AND PASSING GAME

In developing the total offensive attack, at any level of coaching, it is generally recognized that the first approach is to develop a sound middle attack that is based on straight dive plays into the line, sweeps, and play action passes off these. These types of plays are the bread and butter of the offense. If a team can move the football by running up the middle, it will cause (1) the defensive linebackers to stay "at home," and (2) the defensive lineman to play run rather than think pass.

After a middle attack is established the next step is to develop plays designed to attack wide. These involve the sweep and quick pitch plays, again with pass options developing from these. Bootlegs, reverses, and maybe an occasional "trick" play keep the defense honest and hopefully make the bread and butter plays more effective.

Finally, a word on objectives. To set them too high may be discouraging to your team, but without them you may not have consistent, usable goals. The following are offered as possible suggestions for offensive goals. The specific numbers and percentages can be adjusted to the level of play you are coaching.

1. Win
2. Average twenty-four points per game.
3. Average 400 yards per game.
4. Score on two or more drives over fifty yards.
5. Run forty-seven plays per game.
6. No turnovers on our side of the fifty.
7. Score from inside their twenty-yard line (80 percent).
8. Convert 60 percent of third down situations.
9. Score on first possession of 2nd half.
10. Complete 57 percent of passes.
11. No quarterback sacks.
12. No interceptions.

Chapter eight will illustrate playbook material on which standard discussions concerning offensive techniques can be based. As with the defensive material this is presented as it would be if you were distributing it to your players.

CLASS ACTIVITIES

1. Find the origin of two offensive formations.

2. Construct a large poster depicting the major dates that offensive trends, rules, or factors began (for example, center-QB snap, lineman must be set, forward pass made legal, etc.).

3. Visit a local school and observe the offensive alignment. Analyze why this setup is used and make any suggestions for changes.

4. Have each class member draw and label three offensive numbering schemes.

5. List the key personnel needed to run the wishbone versus the I formation.

5

THE OFFENSIVE LINE

Chapter Objectives

After completing this chapter, the reader should be able to:

- Demonstrate both verbally and by on-field performance basic offensive blocks.
- Execute a mechanically correct and fundamentally accurate snap to a deep receiver as well as a quarterback under.
- Draw appropriate blocking patterns for all offensive linemen for offensive plays against both odd and even defensive fronts.
- Identify correct and incorrect blocking techniques (reasons for poor execution) for the basic line blocks.

THE CENTER SNAP TECHNIQUE

Perhaps the keystone of any offensive play revolves around the ball exchange between the center and quarterback. The techniques covered below are used by centers when snapping to a quarterback who has placed his hands in the center's crotch for the snap:

1. *Stance.* The center should align his feet shoulders' width apart, toes pointing straight ahead, usually no greater than a toe–instep stagger. Weight is forward (but not leaning on the ball) since the center must be able to move quickly straight ahead, or to either side. The ankles and knees are flexed and point straight downfield. The hips should be elevated to keep the quarterback from having to bend down or squat too far. The back is as parallel to the ground as possible and the shoulders are parallel to the LOS. The neck is extended enough to allow the center to look straight downfield.

2. *Snap* (for a right-handed center). QB under using perpendicular hand placement (see Chapter 6).

    a. The ball should be directly under the center's head just to the right of midline.
    b. The right hand is placed on the top toward the front of the ball (with laces up). The thumb is on the left side of the laces.
    c. Tilt the back end of the ball up slightly.
    d. The left hand can do one of several things:

        (1) Place left hand on top of rear part of the ball to act as a guide.
        (2) Drop the left hand to the ground under the left shoulder for support of a wide base (between left hand and two feet).
        (3) Rest the left hand on the left thigh

    e. Snap the ball back to the quarterback's hands vigorously, rotating the ball about 30 degrees (a natural inward rotation of the lower arm) keeping the elbow locked. This rotation places the ball into the quarterback's hands with the middle or fat part facing the quarterback with the laces up. The quarterback must follow with his hands to ensure a clean snap. The center must not carry the ball with him during his first step forward. The snap comes first, but in actuality the center snaps and steps at the same time.
    f. Drive off the line after the snap.

FIGURE 5.1   Typical Center QB Exchange Position

FIGURE 5.2   Deep Snap Follow Through

3. *Deep snap procedure.* Generally speaking, the average junior high school boy can be expected to accurately snap the ball only about ten to twelve yards.

  a. Stance is identical with the exception that the ball may be a little more forward and not directly under the head.
  b. The laces are turned down.
  c. The right hand is placed toward the front of the ball, in a passing grip (fingers on laces).
  d. The left hand is placed on top to guide the ball.
  e. Look back through the legs at the target.
  f. Vigorously snap both arms back through legs with hands and arms following through low (Figure 5.2). This follow-through is very important. Weight is not on the ball (this will cause the weight to end up on the heels after the snap. This is a poor position to block with).
  g. Drive off the line after the snap.

DOWN LINEMEN'S BLOCKING TECHNIQUES

A half dozen or so basic techniques account for most of the blocking used in both the running and passing game at the junior/senior high school level.

Head-on (1, 2, 3 Blocking, Base Blocking).   This is the block considered basic by interior linemen. The lineman should concentrate on his first two steps, keeping his eyes on the target point (depending on the play call). His primary job is to neutralize the defender's charge, achieve proper leverage and position, seal off the defender from the ball, and hopefully drive the defender backward or away from the ball. The feet must be in a position to maintain a wide base with the hips under the body. The hands should be brought up and contact the defender right below the chest plate of his shoulder pads. Care must be taken not to hold or twist the defender's pads or jersey. Contact is often made with the armpits of the defender;

COACHING POINTS: Head-on Blocking

- Eyes open at all times. Bull neck.
- Keep feet at least shoulders' width apart.
- Don't position step (a lateral step to get into a better angle or position prior to the charge). Your first step is directly at the opponent, at the appropriate angle.
- The second step must be on the ground before you make contact in order to create movement.
- Don't leave your legs behind you; move your feet like triphammers! Keep your hips under your body.
- Stay after your man until the whistle blows, maintaining contact with him until the play ends. (If you lose him, hustle to block someone else.)

---

however, the blocker must guard against the tendency to grasp the jersey or pads, hold on, and twist or turn the defender with this motion. If the official sees the defender's jersey twist or be pulled a holding call will usually be made against the offensive blocker (this is particularly true when the offense is in the red zone or within their opponent's 10 yard line).

Head-on Block

Load Block or Cross Block.   Many times two linemen will block the man lined up over the man next to them. This is done to improve blocking angles. A decision must be made as to who goes first. A general rule is the man blocking the down lineman goes first; if there are two down linemen then the defender closest to the ball has to be blocked first.

Load Block   **Cross Block**

Scramble Block.   The lineman strikes the opponent in the groin area and attempts to drive his head between the legs of the opponent. Many times the head will drive to the outside leg and the body will hook the defender. The lineman then scrambles on all fours keeping his head between the defender's legs or

COACHING POINTS: Load or Cross Blocking

- The man going first must drive hard and take his legs with him.
- The second man must drop step, keep his shoulders down and quickly move right off the first blocker's hip and attack up *into* the hole.
- The blocker attacking the down lineman must drive his man off the LOS and must not be driven back.
- Both blockers must explode into their blocks.

hugging the outside leg. This block is useful in stopping a defender's lateral movement.

COACHING POINTS: Scramble Blocking

- Drive the head vigorously between the opponent's legs or to the outside leg—don't position step.
- Keep the eyes open at all times.
- Don't leave your legs behind.
- Don't let the defender push you down to the ground.
- Keep the feet at least shoulders' width apart—four-point scramble. Don't go to your knees.
- Stay with your opponent until the whistle blows. Maintain contact.

Reach Block.   The lineman steps with the near foot and drives his facemask to the outside shoulder of the defender. This phase is crucial as the blocker must cut off the penetration or lateral movement of the defender who is lined up to his outside.

Play direction

Reach Block

The blocker makes contact with the defender's outside shoulder then drives with his legs, bringing his body around to seal off the flow of the opponent toward the ball. This block differs from the scramble block in that the blocker attempts to swing his body around the defender and "post" him, gaining leverage with his body.

COACHING POINTS: Reach Blocking

- Don't position step. Step with near foot toward the target area.
- Drive facemask to outside leg, arm shiver to control defenders upper body; try to turn the opponent with this maneuver as you swing your body around.
- Don't go to your knees. Drive with a solid hand shiver maintaining a wide base.
- Stay after your man. Maintain contact until the whistle blows.

Double Team.   This block involves two offensive men blocking one opponent in a coordinated manner.

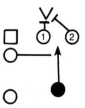

Double Team Block

Notice that the guard (1) is attacking the defender head-on or square. This man is the "post man." It is his job to fire out, neutralizing any penetration of the opponent. His leg action really does not start until his partner, in this case the offensive tackle (2), makes contact with the opponent. The tackle is called the "drive" man in this case since it is his job to step with the near foot, drive his hands/shoulders into the hip region of the opponent, and get hip-to-hip with the post man if possible. When these things have been done both men drive the opponent backward and away from the LOS.

COACHING POINTS: Double Team Blocking

- Post man makes a good hit to stop penetration. Eyes open, extend the legs; wide blocking base, shoulders parallel to LOS.
- The drive man achieves hip-to-hip contact as quickly as possible. The opponent can *never* be allowed to split the drive and post man.
- Both men must drive hard, with short, choppy steps, feet at least shoulders' width apart, maintaining contact with the opponent until the whistle blows.

Pulling and Trapping.   The trap block can be developed for efficient use by older players but is seldom used at younger age levels. This is due to the lack of neuromuscular development, quickness, and agility of younger players. About once every three years a youngster may come along who has the ability to trap block, or pull, and has the quickness and agility to lead the play and turn up the field. Success can be improved if the players work on the techniques of pulling at every practice. The following diagrams show a lineman pulling and trapping as well as one pulling to lead a sweep.

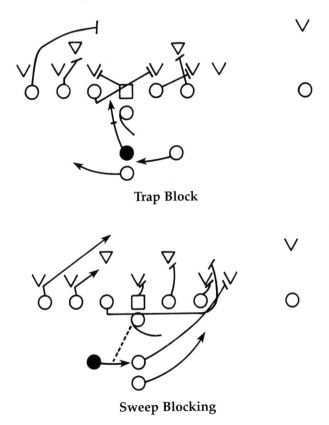

Trap Block

Sweep Blocking

There are two basic methods used in pulling out of the LOS: the cross-over step and the pivot and step.

1. *The crossover step* (pulling right). The crossover technique is probably the easiest as it resembles simple walking. From the basic stance the pulling lineman pushes off with the finger tips on the ground and pivots on the right or near foot in the direction he is going. He then crosses over with the left foot as he takes a normal running stride. From this position the legs are driven quickly and forcefully to achieve maximum speed and distance covered.

2. *The pivot and step* (pulling right). From the basic stance the pulling lineman pushes off with the down finger tips and pivots sharply on the toe of the left foot. This spins his body towards the direction he is going. At the same time the right arm is thrown backward sharply with the lower arm flexed ninety degrees at the elbow. This assists the lineman in getting his shoulders and hips in the right direction and helps in clearing any teammates in his path. The player then takes a short step (6–12 inches) with his right foot in the direction he is pulling. This step is approximately forty-five degrees from the original stance on traps and ninety degrees on sweeps. The body is driven forward by extending the left leg as the normal driving run to the target is started.

The proper pulling technique is something that must be reviewed daily if it is to be used. Getting turned and away from the original position is only the first problem for the pulling lineman. He must stay low and always drive in the direction of the defender's original lineup position. His route must be on inside-out paths. On close traps he uses short, choppy steps as he approaches the opponent but must develop enough "coiled" power to unload on the defender, facemask to the defensive side (driving the man away from the play). This block requires a tremendous amount of speed and power, especially in the legs, which have to develop enough momentum to start from zero and go about two to three yards, strike, and drive through a mass of 200+ pounds. The drive or head-on blocking technique is utilized in this situation. With daily practice and emphasis the motor patterns of pulling can be mastered by young players. The following diagrams show the incorrect and correct path for a pulling lineman.

Incorrect

Incorrect Banana Path

Correct

Correct Inside-out Path

COACHING POINTS: Pulling and Trapping

- Never point, turn, or lean in the direction you are going prior to the snap.
- Don't jump up in the air to get your feet in position to move down the LOS. Pivot and step or crossover and step.
- Stay low. Dip you head and shoulders just prior to contact.
- Bring your legs with you. Keep those legs working and under your body. The ball carrier will trip over them if you "leave them in the hole."
- Explode through the defender. Aim at his midsection and keep your eyes on him. Hit with a two hand shiver or shoulder, and wide blocking base.
- Stay with your man. You *must* drive him *out of the hole*. A stalemate is worthless.

In pulling to lead a sweep or a play around the end, the lineman's path will be more of a banana shape, since he needs depth so he can turn up the field and meet any blockers, especially coming from the inside. He will try to use a head-on block to take the defender inside, but if he can't he will take him any way he can and hope the back will "read" the block and run the appropriate path.

Because the lineman must take a more circular path on these types of plays, junior high school age players do not often possess the speed to "turn the corner" before the backfield men get to the LOS.

The blocks discussed above illustrate the major blocks used by linemen in both the running and passing game at the junior high school level. The reader should be aware that many other types of blocks are possible. A sample listing might include:

1. Reverse Shoulder Block
2. Running Shoulder Block
3. Hook Block
4. Long Body Block
5. Reverse Body Block

ADVANCED BLOCKING TECHNIQUES

Once the basic blocks are learned, the coach and players can begin to use additional blocking attacks if and when the skill level of the players develop.

Crossbody or Shield Block.   This block is used *only* after initial contact has been made above the waist, and downfield contact needs to be maintained. Normally the offside tackle and end will release and go downfield in an attempt to clear the way for the ball carrier after he breaks past the LOS. For the crossbody block the blocker attempts to get as close to the defender as possible and then starts the raise as if he were going to use a high block. If blocking to the right side, the blocker would shoot his right hand across the defender about chest level and contact him with the right hip. The blocker would then drop into a crablike motion on all fours, scrambling on the ground to tie up the defender's feet or roll to cut the defenders

COACHING POINTS: Crossbody or Shield Blocking

- Always stay between the ball carrier and the defender.
- Don't leave your feet too soon on the crossbody block.
- Don't hesitate before making contact.
- Scramble or roll—keep moving—keep contact. If you feel you are losing contact, begin to roll towards the defender. Roll at least three times in an effort to knock the defender off his feet.

legs out from under him. If you are using the shield block simply use the head-on blocking technique, staying between the defender and ball carrier.

Pass Protection Blocking.   The blocking for the passing game is the same as used in the running game most of the time in junior high school. This is true since most teams who do throw use a sprint out or roll out type of "play action" pass rather than the straight drop back pass typical of professional football. A roll out pass typical of the junior high school level is shown below.

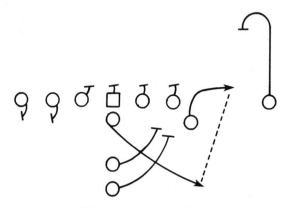

Play Action Pass Play

The blocking for such plays for onside linemen (the side of the line that the play is going to) is always "aggressive," and they would use the same techniques as in a run (hopefully they don't go downfield). Offside linemen (linemen, past the center, away from play direction) will usually block "passively" or use a delay (or turn back) type blocking, employing any of the techniques already described.

Often the backside or offside linemen are called to "cup protect." This is the type of blocking used on all straight drop back passing plays (and the kind all professional teams use). Notice in the diagram below that the linemen are "dropping back" to block. This procedure creates a "cup" around the quarterback, thus the name *cup blocking*.

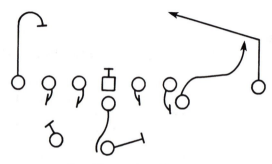

Cup Protection Blocking

Cup Protection Blocking. From the normal stance the blocker can drop back and quickly set up in a hitting position (bull neck, wide base, hips dropped, arms generally up and ready to extend) and wait for the defensive man to come to him. When the opponent is within striking distance the blocker delivers a jolting blow to the opponents breast plate by extending the arms. Explode through the defensive man and stop his charge. After this hit, maintain a base with head and shoulders back. The objective is to keep separation from the quarterback. The lineman must keep good body leverage at all times.

Junior high school quarterbacks generally lack the ability to throw long passes. Therefore, the drop back pass is not used frequently, if at all. With the passing game limited, the basic fundamentals of the running game need to be stressed. The blocking methods described here form the keystone of an effective offensive attack and any coach (at any level) must spend many hours in drill work on these fundamentals. The following list illustrates the type of general information sheet regarding blocking handed to the Wolverines (our "example" team used in this text).

Good Blocking Rules on Running Plays

1. Get contact and keep it until your assignment is accomplished.
2. Keep your eyes open and your feet moving at all times (remember a good base).
3. Keep your body between your opponent and the path of the ball carrier.
4. When your first job is done, don't relax, go on downfield; as long as the ball is alive keep looking for an opponent to block.

Pass Protection Blocking Guidelines

1. This type of block is a test of lineman's desire. It's a dog fight.
2. On cup protection step back quickly, keep balance with as low a position as possible.
3. Give defender outside path if possible.

COACHING POINTS: Cup Protection Blocking

- If the opponent is on the LOS and rushing hard, you may have to deliver a blow immediately. If the opponent is playing further off the LOS drop back about a yard, and set up quickly, always checking the inside lanes.
- Always bull your neck and keep it bulled. *Eyes open* at all times.
- Drive your hands into the pads of the rusher and try to straighten the rusher up.
- The rusher will try to grab you and turn or throw you. Do not let him get his hands on you. Knock them away with quick outward flicks of your arms if he tries to hold your shoulder pads. Use your hands to control the rusher (without holding!)
- Always keep feet at least shoulders' width apart, taking short, choppy steps. Wide base.

4. When opponent commits, drive hard with hands into his numbers. Keep head up, eyes open.
5. Strike a blow, but remember—position is 90% of protection. Position is being perpendicular to the rush lane of defender. Tackles are generally responsible for the width of the pocket while guards and centers are concerned with reducing the depth of the pocket.
6. Never give up. If opponent breaks loose chase him and continue to seal him off on the outside.

A BLOCKER'S CODE

The player who wants to improve his blocking does these things:

1. He studies the technique of blocking.
2. He practices hard and regularly, establishing good blocking habits with drills on the dummy, in scrimmage, and whenever opportunity affords.
3. He works to improve his speed and mobility by taking starts, by running hard in windsprints, and working hard in appropriate exercises and drills.
4. He keeps himself in condition to absorb hard hits by observing some good eating and sleeping rules and by wearing the protective equipment issued to him at all times.
5. When the time comes to take an opponent out of the touchdown trail, he explodes. Beating the other fellow to the punch is essential.

BLOCKING SYSTEMS

Probably one of the most complex and dynamic aspects of offensive football coaching is deciding what type of blocking system to employ for the running and passing game. This problem is largely solved if the opponents played from week to week run the same defenses the entire game. In this instance, offensive linemen know who to block on each play called because the defender is always lined up in the same position. However, if teams play different defenses and several defensive alignments during one ball game, telling the offensive blockers who to block becomes more of a challenge.

To prepare a team effectively the coach should have some system that is simple and easily applicable to most of the defensive alignments that will be encountered during the season. To accomplish this teams use some type of "rule blocking" or "area blocking." Rule blocking is a system in which certain offensive players are given specific blocking assignments on each play. Whatever play is called by the quarterback in the huddle automatically tells each man what to do. The rules are written so that a team can run several backfield patterns through a given hole with the blocking pattern staying essentially the same. In addition, the rules are written so that the same rule will apply against several different defenses.

Rule Blocking

The simplest rule blocking approach is the numbers system. No matter what defensive alignment is presented, the offensive men number off the defensive men starting with any man playing over the offensive center on or off the LOS. The following diagrams show this system against a variety of defensive sets.

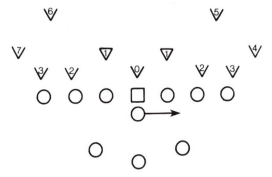

5–4 Defense; "50 Defense"; "59 Defense"

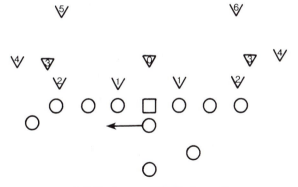

4–3 Defense; "27 Defense"

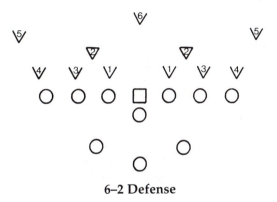

6–2 Defense

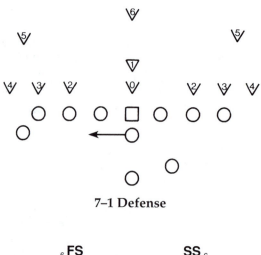

7–1 Defense

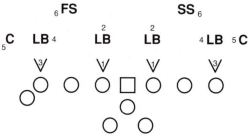

4–4 Stack Defense

As can be seen, the defensive secondary is numbered consecutively depending upon which direction the play is going. Also, when there is no man playing over the center there is no "0" man.

The application of this system is illustrated in the following diagram, which shows a basic dive play utilizing the same blocking rules against two defensive sets.

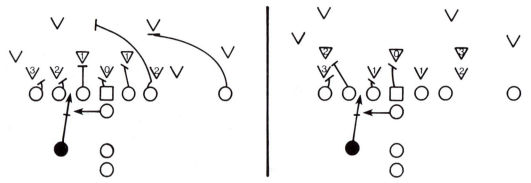

Rule Blocking against an Odd and Even Defense

The blocking rules for this play might be as follows:

Position		Blocking Assignment
Split End	(SE)	Downfield
Onside Tackle	(ONT)	#2
Onside Guard	(ONG)	#1
Center	(C)	#0
Offside Guard	(OFG)	#1
Offside Tackle	(OFT)	#2, Downfield
Tight End	(TE)	Onside-#3, Offside-Downfield

Area Blocking

The coach might instead want to use a system of "zone" or "area" blocking. In this system, instead of assigning numbers to specific men, the offensive linemen recognize the position of the defensive man and apply a basic technique according to the play called. In order to use this system the offensive men must know specific terminology or patterns of communications. An example of such basic terminology is as follows:

On—A man playing directly in front of you, on the LOS.
Over—A man covering any part of you, but not head-up, on or off the LOS.
Inside—A man playing head-on up to the next man towards the center.
Outside—A man playing head-on up to the man away from the center side.
Near (onside) **Linebacker**—nearest your position.
MLB (Middle Linebacker)—Generally found over the center, off the LOS.
Nose—The middle guard or man playing over the center, on the LOS.

These terms are samples. However, any similar terminology or definitions could be used. The illustration below shows the blocking scheme for a basic trap whose rules might be as follows:

Position	Blocking Assignment
SE	Downfield
ONT	Over, Onside LB, Seal
ONG	Nose, Influence, Block near LB
C	Nose, Offside
Off G	Pull, Block 1st man to show on LOS past center
Off T	On, Downfield
TE	Onside—On, Outside
Offside	Downfield

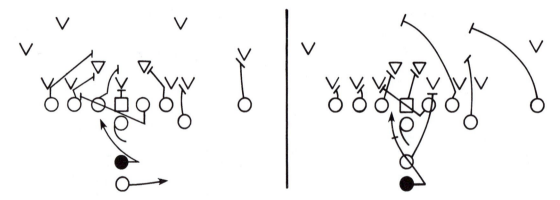

Area Blocking for a Trap Play against an Odd and Even Defense

As the center leaves the huddle and goes to the LOS, he will first check to see if there is a man playing on him, on the LOS ("nose" rule). If so, he blocks him. If not, he goes to his second rule and blocks "offside." These two examples of rule type blocking should suffice in giving the reader a basic idea of what is involved. Most first year coaches will not have the opportunity to be responsible for developing the offensive running game and its associated blocking schemes. For this they should be grateful! Take a little time to draw several defensive alignments against an offensive set and run the same play against each. A coach will soon find that the rule or rules will not be applicable to a particular defense. This is the disadvantage of rule blocking.

Offensive line blocking can be the most frustrating part of football for both the coach and the player. Strangely enough the height of this frustration arrives on game day. All week prior to the game the coach tells his offensive linemen the various defensive sets they will be seeing. He works running plays where the linemen learn to react to a particular man being in a certain spot. The frustration comes when, during the first series of offensive plays, the linemen find that the other team is using a different defense and that the particular men who were supposed to be in certain spots are not there!

This dilemma is solved in some youth league and junior high districts by requiring the same defense to be played throughout the league by everyone. Other groups have chosen to allow varied defenses as well as defensive shifts during the game. Many coaches have gone to a "player's choice" scheme of blocking where the players themselves call the style of blocking they will use when they get to the LOS. These systems require players who are developed enough to analyze different defensive situations and react accordingly. This is generally not the case with young linemen.

Let's take an example of an off tackle play against a straight "50" defense:

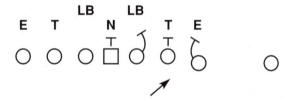

If the defense decides to stunt after we've told our linemen to block specific men they might get confused and miss a block. Instead our lineman should recognize who is onside (play side) and who is offside (away from play side). Play side linemen as well as the center and off guard take a 45° step to the play side and block the defensive man coming into their area:

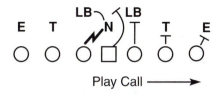

Play Call ———→

The running back now has to see the blocking develop and hit the hole closest to the play call.

The following pages contain the reprint of one article and exerpts from another describing several actual high school systems of call (or area) blocking by offensive linemen. It is hoped that the reader will get some basic ideas so that he will have some type of blocking system in mind should he be in a position to implement such a strategy.

A Blocking Scheme for Offensive Linemen[1]

There have been many approaches to offensive line play down through the years; we don't claim to have an original one, but we do claim to have one that works for Coral Gables High School. Basically, they must be able to answer the vital question "Who do I block at the snap of the ball?"

If you leave on a first count many problems are avoided, because it is more difficult for your opponent to shift defenses and thus confuse your linemen. However, we know that an offensive line will fire out better if they leave on a later count. It better prepares them to get off the line of scrimmage together. So, #1: we use a first count to take advantage of our preshift (up stance) blocking, to catch the defense shifting, and to prevent them from beating us to the punch on our QB's rhythm. #2: we use a second or third count to better coordinate our line fire-out and to take advantage of automatics (audibles).

The problem that occurs is the last minute recognition of changes in defensive alignment that can come when you use a multiple cadence. Your lineman must be able to select his assignment at the split second the ball is snapped. If you will assume your lineman's stance you will notice that he can only see a relatively small area immediately before him, or to either side. Asking him to recognize the whole defensive scheme from his limited angle is an impossibility.

We simply ask him to know three things: (1) Is there a man directly over you on the line of scrimmage? (2) Is there a man in your "frontside gap" (the gap to the side the play has been called)? (3) Is there a linebacker off the line, but over you? Using this approach we attack with our one-to-one blocking techniques. We feel that the entire frontside, and the backside guard, should follow the rule. We can allow the backside tackle and end to "seal" across the face of the man over them and release downfield. Our assignments then are simplified by one rule for backside tackle and end, and one rule for the rest of the line. Frontside: "man over, frontside gap, linebacker," Backside: "seal and release":

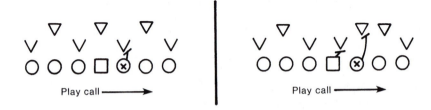

If the man over your lineman shifts to the frontside gap we will consider him to be over and block him. On the other hand, if he is in the backside gap we will ignore him (he is "over" another man) and block our rule. Any straight numbered play—48, 21, 35—we will attack in this manner:

If we wish to change the scheme we will tell the line via a word prefix, in the huddle. Any word can be used that connotes meaning for your linemen and for you. The word "trap" 42 is an example. Double teaming might be called for by use of "blast" 33, "power" 56, etc. Or you might call for "cross blocking" by use of "cross" 77, "exit" 41, etc.

Oral calls by your lineman are necessary, at the line of scrimmage, to cover special situations. Otherwise, you will have to give each man a multitude of exceptions to your rules, and probably confuse him. An example of a need for oral calls would be a sudden shift by the defense to multiple gaps. The tackle finds a man in his frontside gap and also in his backside gap. He will make an oral signal to the men on either side (gap, in, reach, down, etc.). Now all the linemen know to block the man in the gap closest to the center (center will block his rule, frontside).

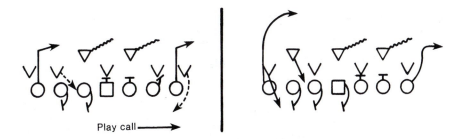

Play call ——→

Obviously, both sides should be making calls, and dummy calls should be used throughout the game, to prevent the defense from loading up. Failure to allow your linemen to "talk" will necessitate the quarterback calling more automatics and the defense dictating to you. Automatics and oral line calls are both necessary.

Our blocking scheme for most action (play) type passes involves fire-out or aggressive blocking to the frontside and pocket type protection on the backside. The uncovered lineman on the frontside has the difficult job of "acting" run and not showing pass. We ask our uncovered man to stay low and slide parallel to the line of scrimmage: using his peripheral vision to pick up stunting linebackers that might try to come through his area. The covered lineman fires-out on the man over. On the backside we give the lineman the rule: "seal and setup." The guard takes a jab step with the foot to the front-side (seals) and then drop steps with the opposite foot (sets-up) to pick up the first man on the line of scrimmage away from the center. The tackle "seals" in the same manner and sets-up on the second man on the line from the center. The center fires-out on the man over, if there is not a man over him, he seals and sets-up, looking for the first loose man to the backside (may be a firing linebacker or an end, depending on the defensive alignment.

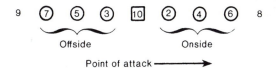

Obviously, both sides should be making calls, and dummy calls should be used throughout the game, to prevent the defense from loading up. Failure to allow your linemen to "talk" will necessitate the quarterback calling more automatics and the defense dictating to you. Automatics and oral line calls are both necessary.

We must keep in mind that the offensive lineman has the basic job of blocking an opponent and that the less confused he is, the more likely he will fireout and get the job done. We believe that he'll be less confused with simply worded, yet technically accurate, rules. Try looking at the offensive lineman's job from his point of view. You should be able to tell him his assignment with a minimum amount of words, and then spend your time on techniques and execution. Remember the "old timer" understands easily, but what about the "rookie"? Can he pick it up fast? He might have to play for you right now!

Simplifying Full Zone Blocking for High School Success[2]

An offensive lineman must know a few things

1. Am I onside or backside of the point of attack?
2. Am I covered or uncovered by a down lineman?
3. Is the man inside of me covered or uncovered? #3 is only for onside and covered linemen.

If he knows these three things he will know what blocking scheme to use on the snap of the football. No matter what defensive front is presented, these three things become automatic knowledge.

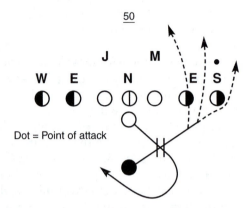

Rt. TE: "I'm onside, covered by a DL and the man inside of me is also covered."
Rt. OT: "I'm onside, covered and the man inside of me is uncovered."
Rt. OG: "I'm onside, uncovered."
OC: Same as Rt. OT
Lt. OG: "I'm backside, uncovered."
Lt. OT: "I'm backside, covered."
Lt. TE: "I'm backside, covered."

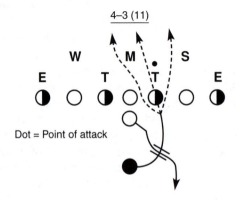

Rt. TE: "I'm onside, covered and man inside of me is uncovered."
Rt. OT: "I'm onside, uncovered."
Rt. OG: "I'm onside, covered and the man inside of me is uncovered."
OC: "I'm onside, uncovered."
Lt. OG: "I'm backside, covered."
Lt. OT: "I'm backside, uncovered."
Lt. TE: "I'm backside, covered."

During walk-thrus I will set up a cone defense and make each player recite these 3 things out loud when I stand in front of them. Then I will have them tell me what blocking technique they have. Onside players only have two types of blocks, either a drive-option or a team block. If they are covered and the man inside of them is also covered they have a drive option. If they are covered and the man inside is uncovered, they have a team block. If they are uncovered they are *full zoning* to the playside working in on the team block.

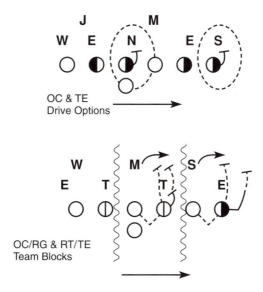

OC & TE
Drive Options

OC/RG & RT/TE
Team Blocks

Blocking schemes are numerous and are continually discussed.[3]

CLASS ACTIVITIES

1. Depending upon class size, units of four (backfield), seven (half line) or eleven (full team) should practice specific assignments on each play.

2. With a quarterback designated, have him call a play in the huddle, break from the huddle, say all of the cadence on the LOS, and run a play.

3. Have class members identify crucial blocks necessary for successful play execution.

4. Observe a football practice and make notes concerning the offensive system used (formation, play sequence, etc.).

5. Scout the offense of a team during a regulation game. After the game attempt to develop offensive tendencies and favorite plays.

NOTES

1. Nick Kotys and Garry Ghormley, "A Blocking Scheme for Offensive Linemen," *Scholastic Coach* 33 (1971):12–13.

2. Phil Pettey, "Simplifying Full Zone Blocking for High School Success," *Texas Coach* 39 (1994):42–46.

3. See, for example, B. Mountjoy, "Playside Blocking," *Scholastic Coach and Athletic Director* 64 (Sept. 1994):68–69; and M. C. Willeford, "A Sweep Slice Base Running Series," *Scholastic Coach and Athletic Director* 64 (Nov. 1994):82–83.

6

THE OFFENSIVE BACKFIELD

Chapter Objectives

After completing this chapter, the reader should be able to:

- Illustrate the proper hand placements that can be used in taking a snap from center.
- Give a basic understanding of the impact of field position on play selection.
- List at least three things a quarterback should observe about the defensive alignment.
- Perform several successful ball exchanges with another player illustrating the correct arm placement for receiving the handoff.
- Work with two or more other players to perform a smooth, coordinated offensive running play.

THE QUARTERBACK

Perhaps no aspect of a coach's work is more observable to the spectators in the stands than the coordination of the center, quarterback, and backfield. On these players' shoulders lies the responsibility to initiate the action, run well-timed patterns, and execute ball exchange maneuvers. Thus, much coaching time is spent with these players and many hours of individual backfield unit practice is under-taken. Coaches can become more well versed if they have a well-grounded under-standing of the mechanics involved in these positions, as well as the importance of working with these individuals as a unit. Many feel that the quarterback should be the best athlete on your team. Therefore, our discussion will begin with a consideration of this position.

Quarterback Characteristics

Ask anyone to name the local starting team and coaching staff in any town and the order of knowledge will go something like this:

1. Head Coach
2. Their own child (if they have one playing)
3. Quarterback
4. Star Running Back
5. Defensive Lineman (or any standout all-state player)
6. Punter (kicker)
7. Assistant Coach (maybe)

Aside from that of the head coach the quarterback's name is on the lips of most hometown folks. He's either a stalwart of the offense or the cause of "our failure to move the ball." It is not necessary to elaborate on the importance of the quarterback, but suffice it to say that just as the linebackers are the best athletes on defense, so the quarterback is usually the best athlete on offense.

The quarterback should be the master of the offensive team. He should be confident (some say even cocky), possess good hands, be taller than average but not too tall to be awkward in his movements, and above all have the ability to expand his football sense past his own responsibilities.

In the huddle he should be forceful and especially confident. If he wants to give a special word to a lineman who will perform a key block, O.K. Special phrases: "Let's get this first down!", "Hold on the ball," are often said. His play calling, if he does it himself, should be liberal some of the time, bold all of the time, and done with a knowledge of the down, distance, and type of defense he is likely to be facing.

Volumes could be written about the quarterback. For additional and more complete information concerning ideal characteristics of quarterback, the reader is referred to two sources written with the college quarterback in mind.[1]

Stance and Hand Placement

The quarterback's typical stance is one with the feet slightly wider than the shoulders, with either the feet even or with one foot in back of the other in no more than a toe–heel relationship. (Teams that use pulling guards sometimes have the quarterback place the foot nearest the pulling lineman back so that there will be less congestion in the lineman's path.) Weight is on the balls of the feet, lower legs flexed at the knees, and a natural flexion of the upper body at the waist to place the quarterback in a good position to receive the ball from the center.

There are two methods of hand placement for the quarterback to receive the snap, (1) the side-by-side placement and (2) the perpendicular placement. The instructions given the center earlier in chapter 5 were designed for the perpendicular arrangement. This type of hand placement will be discussed since most teams today use this method, and it is considered to be the most effective.

The quarterback's right hand (for a right-handed quarterback) goes under the center in the middle of the crotch, so that the natural break of the hand at the wrist follows the curve of the crotch. The hand makes contact with the center, with the knuckle of the middle finger applying the greatest pressure upward against the top of the spine. The heel of the left hand makes slight contact with the heel of the right hand, palm away, fingers spread and pointing almost directly towards the ground. The two thumbs touch so that the knuckle of the right thumb fits into the groove of the left. The left hand serves as a trap to stop the ball and both hands form a cup into which the ball is forcefully snapped by the center. Figure 6.1 shows the perpendicular hand position while Figure 6.2 illustrates the side-by-side position.

If the quarterback must take the snap from different centers he should alter the flexion at the knees, so that he can adjust the height of his body to maintain a

FIGURE 6.1   Perpendicular Quarterback Hand Position

FIGURE 6.2   Side-by-side Quarterback Hand Position

comfortable, relaxed stance with head up and back straight. The center–quarterback exchange should be practiced thoroughly throughout the season, and intensely at the beginning of the season. In addition, each quarterback should work on the exchange with each center. Three basic items that need constant stress involve (1) having the quarterback not pull out too quickly before the snap reaches his hands, (2) maintaining hand pressure up against the center's crotch, and (3) having the center complete the snap before he moves forward to block. It must be remembered that the center has the job of snapping the ball backward and moving his body forward at almost the same time.

The center should always take a step forward as if to block during every exchange. The quarterback should generally pull the ball into his stomach upon receiving the snap. This will be altered if, for example, in an option style attack he quickly extends the ball back to the fullback and "rides" with the fullback up to the line of scrimmage. At that point he pulls the ball out or gives it to the fullback. He then pushes off and goes into his pattern of steps for the play.

The junior high school coach should instill in his players the basic fundamentals of each position, so that they will carry over these skills to high school and beyond. This is especially true of the junior high school quarterback. The following section is a sample of the type of booklet to give to developing quarterbacks in an effort to acquaint them with the responsibilities of their position. This booklet contains things all coaches want their quarterbacks to attend to, from youth football to the NFL, and junior high coaches should not expect junior high school youngsters to be able to remember all these things in a game. But there is no better place to teach youngsters the right way to do things than in junior high school. With these concepts in mind take a look at the "Quarterback's Notebook" to get some idea of the scope of this position.

Quarterback's Notebook

In order to do a good job of running the team on offense you must:

1. Know your coach. Know exactly how he feels about all situations. You should have a good idea of what he'd want you to do under any circumstances.
2. Have confidence in yourself.
3. Have the confidence of the team.
4. Know scouting information thoroughly.
5. Have a very good general understanding of football.
6. Know thoroughly all of the plays you have to work with including:
   a. Which of your plays are basic.
   b. Plays which are complementary to these basic plays (plays that work best when a certain defensive man is doing a certain thing).
   c. Special plays (plays that require a certain buildup and that aren't good until the defense is doing certain things). Examples: draw, screen.
7. Know the full meaning of your constant tactical factors (a) score, (b) time, (c) down, (d) yards to go, (e) position, (f) weather and field conditions.
8. Record and remember what happens as the game progresses.
9. Develop your powers of observation, and know how and where to get information on the things you cannot observe yourself.
10. Have a will to win and a readiness to take advantage of anything that will help you to win.
11. Learn everything you can about your opponents in advance and add to this knowledge as the game progresses.
12. Be ready and able to recognize the need for change in strategy as the game progresses.
13. Have the courage to carry out your ideas.
14. Have the ability to coordinate and tie together the above points without hesitation on your part.
15. The coaches can consult with you and lay out a general plan in advance of every game, but no matter how well this is done, no game can be accurately forecast and once the game begins, you are largely on your own.

Field Position

Everyone on the team needs to know the value of field position, but you in particular must keep the following things in mind at all times.

1. If we must give the ball up to our opponents, we must make sure they have fifty yards or more to go for a touchdown.
2. The average team will score 40 percent of the time with less than fifty yards to go for a touchdown.
3. The average team will score only 5 percent of the time with more than fifty yards to go for a touchdown.

Division of Field (Does Not Apply Late in Games When Behind)
1. Inside our five-yard line—(Danger Zone)—If run is used avoid ball handling plays: Give to back least likely to fumble.
2. Our five-yard line to our ten-yard line—Two downs to make ten yards. Run sound basic plays, limit ball handling, generally don't throw the ball. If you have a third down situation, with more than two yards for a first down, kick on third down.
3. Our ten-yard line to our twenty-yard line—Three downs to make ten yards. Run sound basic plays, limit ball handling, generally don't throw the ball.
4. Our twenty-yard line to our thirty-yard line—Three downs to make ten yards. Run sound basic plays, limit ball handling, careful throwing the ball. Always kick on fourth down, regardless of yardage left for first down. Good quick kick area.
5. Our thirty-yard line to our forty-yard line—Three downs to make ten yards. May pass if defense is crowding—long passes. Always kick on fourth down regardless of yardage left for first down.
6. Our forty-yard line to opponents' forty-yard line—Three downs to make ten yards. Don't kick before fourth down unless you have a good reason.
7. Opponents' forty-yard line to opponents' twenty-yard line—Four downs to make ten yards. Try to score with trick play or a scoring play you have set up. All passes good—use accordingly. Good fake pass run zone. Sweeps are good. If you must kick on fourth down, kick out of bounds or high.
8. Opponents' twenty-yard line to opponents' five-yard line—(Red Zone)—Four downs to make ten yards. Must not lose yardage. Try to get five yards or more on first down. Remember what plays brought you down here.
9. Opponents' five-yard line to goal—(Red Zone)—Four downs to score. Give ball to best back. Run best power play. Be in front of goal on fourth down if field goal is feasible. Generally don't trap in this area.

General Instructions
1. Know your own teammates thoroughly—their strong points and their weaknesses.
2. Put strength against opponent's weakness.
3. Have a reason for every play you call.
4. Repeat successful plays.
5. Make opponents respect your basic plays before using your tricks.
6. Do not reverse or counter to the wide side of the field all the time.

Opponent's Defense
Everything our team does has some effect on the defense:

1. A succession of wide plays will cause the defense to spread out.
2. A succession of inside plays will cause them to close up in the same way.
3. A succession of passes will cause the secondary to loosen up.
4. A succession of deceptive plays will cause the defense to become overcautious.
5. A succession of direct, hard-hitting plays will cause the defense to get reckless.
6. A defensive man doesn't like to get caught on the same thing twice. If you go outside a man with success, he'll invariably try to defend that side more strongly, thereby weakening his inside.
7. A defensive man likes to repeat his good plays. Example: Halfback comes up fast and throws ball-carrier for a loss on an end run. This makes it easy to pull him out of position on a well-executed running pass.
8. A defensive man who has nothing sent his way for a long time tends to become careless.
9. Take advantage of defensive tactics. Examples: (a) Run inside, deep penetrating tackles, (b) Wedge soft playing linemen, (c) Trap hard charging linemen.
10. Know who stopped your play and use something against him—trap, screen, bootleg, etc.
11. Run a play on a quick snap over an opponent who is slow lining up.

Down and Distance
1. Under ordinary conditions, you should gain a minimum of five yards on first down.
2. To be successful on a second down in your territory, you should advance far enough so that you have two yards or less to go on third down.
3. Remember passes are generally more effective on early downs. Late passes should generally be thrown short.
4. Second down and two is a good time to pass. If it's incomplete you still have one down to make two yards. Third down and one is generally a poor time to pass, since when you pass only three things can happen and two of them are bad.
5. Always remember: (a) you can punt a long way with the wind, but not very far against it; (b) a wet ball is more dangerous to handle than a dry one; (c) sharp cutting is nearly impossible on a wet, soggy field.

Score
1. Play conservatively when ahead.
2. Gamble when behind.
3. Take necessary chances when score is even, but don't forget that a tie is better than defeat.
4. When eight points ahead, be conservative, let opponents make the mistakes.
5. Ahead six points we need more.
6. Ahead twelve points—we need the clincher.

7. Behind six points or less, unless later in the game, don't get desperate. You still have time.
8. Behind twelve points or more—gamble a little more.

Time Element
1. Know when to press your team: (a) in the scoring zone, (b) with the wind, or (c) when behind in the score.
2. Know when to slow the pace: (a) against the wind, (b) when ahead in the score, or (c) when playing for time.
3. Know how to spend or conserve time: (a) to stall—run line and sweep plays, but don't pass; (b) if behind, sideline pass, or call two plays at once when huddling.
4. Take chances near end of each half—this is an excellent scoring time.

Weather
1. Take advantage of the wind: (a) kick often with the wind (second or third down), (b) think of long pass with the wind, and (c) hold ball against wind.
2. If wet: (a) kick often—let opponent fumble, and (b) try to avoid particularly bad spots on the field.

Our Team
1. Get maximum efficiency from your backs.

   a. Know what everyone does best and have him do it.
   b. Don't use up the best passes in own territory. Maybe save an old standby for a third and short in their territory.
   c. Know whom to depend on for first downs and touchdowns.
   d. Use a "hot back" freely.
   e. If sub is nervous, don't let him carry ball or handle it until he's adjusted.

2. Know best offensive lineman: when you must have a yard or two, go over him.
3. Make them respect you in the huddle.
4. Be sure your players know what the play is.
5. Get information from your teammates when time is out or between plays.
6. Check all subs for information.

When to Punt
1. General rule: the closer to your goal line, the earlier the kick.
2. Remember the possibility of a blocked kick increases with each down.
3. Don't overlook the wind factor.
4. Anticipate kicking situations; be sure the kicker is not too winded and is ready.

General Rules for Quick Kicking
1. Use between your own ten-yard line and mid-field.
2. Kick on second down with more than seven yards to go.
3. Use the quick kick on third down with more than five yards to go.

4. Use it on first down with more than ten-yards to go within our own twenty-yard line.
5. Use it when the wind is favorable and position is more important than possession.
6. Do not destroy a drive with the quick kick.

Defensive Recognition

1. The first thing the quarterback looks for is to see how many men are over the center. (Includes man on line of scrimmage, linebackers, and safety.)

   a. When the quarterback sees his center covered with a linebacker directly behind the middle guard, then there must be a safety for the defense to be balanced. If there is no linebacker behind the middle guard, and there is a safety, then the secondary has rotated. The quarterback must know that the safety and the middle linebacker must be present in the middle zone when there is a middle guard, or both must be missing for the defense to be balanced. One without the other in the middle zone and the defense is not balanced.

   b. If there is no man over the center on the line of scrimmage, but there is a safety, the quarterback knows the defense is a balanced one and there are five men on each side of the line.

2. The second thing the quarterback must do is determine how many men are outside the offensive ends. (A defensive man head-on with the end is considered half outside and half inside.) General rule:

   a. Two men outside end—tough to run against.
   b. One-and-a-half men outside end—can hit quick.
   c. One man outside end—should be able to run against him.

3. The third thing the quarterback looks for is the placement of men inside the offensive ends to see if he can discover a weakness there.

THE RUNNING BACKS

The running backs should be the fastest accelerators on the team. Having mastered the mechanics of a proper stance (Chapter 3) running backs should work on rapid acceleration in any direction. The back will usually have only a second to receive the football and hit the hole on the LOS. After the snap, the back's vision should be on the line blocking at the point of attack. The proper arm position will be discussed later in this chapter, but we should reiterate that it is the quarterback's job to get the ball into the pocket formed by the running back. Thus, the back's attention should be directed toward where he is going. Ball protection by holding both ends of the football with both hands until the back breaks through the LOS should be stressed. The ability of a back to meet a tackler and drive his feet so that he moves forward (rather than being driven back) is the goal of the high contact area on the LOS.

The back must learn to adjust his speed according to the directions of the play. End sweeps, pitch outs, and wide plays will require the running back to time his speed so that he can (1) receive the football in stride and (2) be under control when he makes his cut, accelerating upfield. Drills emphasizing change of direction, ball control, and rapid acceleration following a change of direction should be practiced daily by running backs. Several drills for this purpose are illustrated in Appendix B.

Whether explosive speed can be developed or taught is open for discussion. The consensus is that either a young athelete has speed or he doesn't. But a coach can observe all phases of a back's performance, from stance, beginning steps, handoff technique, leg drive, cutting ability, ball handling, and general cognizance of field position to make coaching suggestions.

It might be noted here that high knee action should be stressed when the back is in heavy traffic, but such action is not needed when the back is in open field or preparing to make a cut. Good backs will seem to glide over the field, keeping the feet close to the ground to assist in change of direction moves. Let us now move to the specifics of a high-risk procedure—ball exchange between the quarterback and running back.

Ball Exchange

The position of the arms of the back receiving a handoff from the quarterback is crucial. It is the job of the quarterback to properly place the ball in the pocket formed by the back, while the back should be looking at where he is going, and at the development of the blocking. It is the back's job to form the correct receiving pocket.

To do this, the back should raise the near elbow on the side of the quarterback to a point at least parallel to the ground. The arm and hand will be across the chest parallel to the ground, palm down, fingers spread and slightly cupped. The far arm should be placed across the stomach, palm up, elbow slightly away from the body, fingers spread in a cupped position.

As the ball is placed in this pocket by the quarterback, the far arm and hand take and secure it against the stomach. The ball is placed under the biceps of the far arm while being protected on top by the near arm. It is good practice to have the back keep the ball in this two-arm hold position until he has passed the high contact zone and secure the ball by firmly grasping the end with the fingers and keeping the ball under the biceps of the carrying arm. Anytime the ball carrier sees he is going to be hit or he finds himself in a congested area he may want to regrasp the ball with both hands as in the receiving position.

Ball carrying must be a personal goal for each back. He has several important thoughts as he receives the handoff:

1. Carry the ball in the boundry (sideline) arm and don't forget the stiff arm.
2. Work hard to maintain control of the ball with a good firm cradle between arm and ball.

3. Move straight towards the goal line unless there is a good reason to do otherwise.
4. Get first down and keep going until you score. The back should be reminded that when the ball is in his possession he has the entire game in his hands. Figure 6.3 illustrates the typical junior high hand positions for receiving the handoff.

Faking

A very important aspect that must be taught younger players is that of faking when you don't have the football. The quarterback needs to carry out his fake after *each* handoff as if he were carrying the ball, and watch the back for a second after the fake. He should hide the "ball" (which he has already given to someone else) on his hip or stomach, drop his near shoulder, and run at least five yards *as if he had the ball.*

The backs should take the hand fake of the quarterback, lower the near shoulder and run as if they had the ball. This is extremely important as the longer the backs can carry out a fake the more confused the defense will be, and the slower they will react to the real ball carrier. Backs making the fake *should* be tackled as if they had the ball and should carry out the fake full speed at least five yards past the LOS. This aspect is something the coach must continually work on and stress

FIGURE 6.3   Proper Ball Exchange Technique

with all backs. There is really no drill per se for this, only the verbal encouragement (and admonishments!) which are given every time a player stops short and does not carry out his fake.

CLASS ACTIVITIES

1. Organize the class into groups of five and assign each to be center, quarterback, and running backs. These units should then practice running several plays (assigned previously).

   a. Rotate positions.
   b. Give the unit a specific down and distance and have the quarterback call an appropriate play.
   c. Go over several movements that the running backs and quarterback can make (i.e., option, crossback plays, quick pitches, sweeps, etc.).

2. Have the class take turns in evaluating errors of classmates as they perform the stance, hand-off position, and quarterback techniques.

3. Observe a youth football practice or junior high school practice and list the errors observed in backfield action during the scrimmage or offensive unit play.

NOTE

1. Paul ("Bear") Bryant, *Building a Championship Football Team* (Englewood Cliffs, NJ: Prentice Hall, 1960); and John Ralston and Mike White, *Coaching Today's Athlete* (Palo Alto, CA: National Press Books, 1971).

7

THE RECEIVERS

Chapter Objectives

After completing this chapter, the reader should be able to:

- List five coaching points for receiving a football.
- Illustrate the proper technique for running at least three pass patterns.
- List three considerations for gaining position when running pass routes.

RECEIVERS

At lower levels of play the receiver's biggest challenge is catching a badly thrown ball, so good fundamental coaching is needed greatly in this area. We will also give coaching suggestions for receiver and pass reception techniques (applicable to tight ends, split ends, and backfield personnel) so that the prospective coach can utilize any of the points when needed.

Generally it can be said that each receiver must have the confidence in himself to believe he will catch every ball thrown in his direction. He must have quick feet (to get off the LOS, make stops and quick direction changes, and develop top speed after stops) and he must have good hands. Good hands are something that many coaches feel cannot be developed. An athlete either has the ability to relax the hands (as the ball makes contact, folding the fingers securely around the ball) or he does not. You will soon see several examples of the inability to relax the hands if you throw the ball to your offensive linemen. However, drills in handling the ball with concentration on relaxed hands and fingers, and eye concentration on the ball, will reveal many young players who have the capability to become receivers.

Having found several players who you think will develop into receivers you must decide where to place them. If you decide to use a split receiver (as the Wolverine system does), you will need to consider that you weaken the offensive blocking front by splitting a man out. The split-end type formation is based on the premise that the player will have a greater chance to get open and have more room to maneuver on pass routes against a man-for-man situation. Split receivers must be tough, as they get hit frequently, many times from behind. They also play key roles in downfield blocking. Their jobs are varied but when called upon to run a pass route their primary job is to catch the football and score.

The release from the LOS should vary according to the coverage. If playing against man-for-man coverage, the receiver will use more angle paths, changes of speed, and head and shoulder fakes. But still the most important points are the use of the hands and concentration on the ball. Zone coverage requires a faster take-off from the LOS and a more deeply run pattern prior to the cut. Possessing greater speed allows the player to do more faking and still get into the proper receiving position soon enough to allow the quarterback to throw the ball. From high school to professional football the general limit on pass protection time is approximately four seconds. That is to say no one expects an offensive lineman to hold off a rushing defender longer than four seconds. With this thought in mind every effort should be made to release from the LOS without being held up.

Wide receivers generally take a two-point stance. This allows a more explosive start off the line of scrimmage. However, a three-point stance with the inside foot back might be considered. This may enable the player to get off the LOS faster than a two-point stance (standing) and might allow him to look back into the ball from the down position. His split will vary according to the opponent and the throwing strength of the quarterback. Most coaches teach an explosive outside release. That is to say the receiver takes an outside route to drive the defender wider. Following the first several steps the receiver should come to a more head-up position on the defender in preparations for making his cut.

CATCHING THE FOOTBALL

Although this chapter is brief, the prospective coach should, as always, be reminded that it is not his main job to win ball games, but to develop and instill in all players (especially younger players) the basic fundamentals upon which to build the complexities of more advanced play. Some of the more important ingredients in catching the football are good hand–eye coordination, getting your hands in proper position, and always remembering that to be a good receiver you must learn to concentrate and shut everything out of your mind except catching the football. Concentration in catching the football is a discipline which must be practiced each time the ball is caught. Even when the receiver is just playing catch he must concentrate on every thrown ball and should actually see the spin of the ball and look the ball into the hands. The basic fundamentals of good pass reception can be summarized, both for discussion as well as emphasis and clarification.

The following are key points in catching the football:

1. The hands must be in proper position to catch the ball. The general rule is for a thumbs-together catch for balls thrown at shoulder level or above. For balls thrown below shoulder level, the thumbs should face out. The thumbs-together position is the strongest.

2. Catch the narrow part of the football (gives the receiver a part of the ball to look at) while placing both hands on the ball at the same time. Many balls are missed because the ball is stopped with one hand and the other hand actually knocks the ball away as the receiver attempts to bring the other hand in position to catch the ball. The problem is alleviated when both hands are placed on the ball simultaneously.

3. On hook or curl routes where the receiver turns and faces the passer, the chances of catching the ball are much greater if the receiver will "center up" on the ball. Always shuffle to a position where you are directly in line with the ball. Do not reach to either side to catch the ball when you have time to move your body in direct line of the flight of the ball. This position allows for a more secure catch. It also keeps your body between the ball and any defender who is attempting to intercept.

4. A good rule to follow on passes where the receiver is facing the passer is to always have something moving toward the ball. Your chin, nose, forehead, etc. moving toward the ball help you to keep your eyes on the ball all the way into your hands. When the head turns before the ball strikes the hands it invariably causes the hands to separate and the ball to be dropped. Movement toward the ball keeps you from getting the weight on the heels and wanting to turn and run before the ball arrives. Catch the ball, and then run.

5. On low thrown balls, bend the knees and get your eyes as close to the level of the flight of the ball as possible. One of the most difficult balls to catch is a low ball, particularly when the receiver simply bends at the waist and does not bend at the knees to allow his hands to get in position below the ball.

Tips That Receivers Should Always Remember

1. Anybody can run patterns, but only good receivers can find the open spot and get free.

2. Everybody in a three-, four-, or five-man pass play is eligible; never stop running or break your pattern. In your mind you are always the intended receiver.

3. Always know the yardage needed for a first down. Develop a philosophy that every complete pass should result in a first down or a touchdown.

4. As soon as the pass is caught all remaining receivers are blockers. Go to the ball and block for pass receiver; you might catch the next one.

5. If you see a blitz coming, make sure your are ready to adjust your route and look for the ball in a hurry.

6. Come to the passer when he is in trouble.

7. Always give your passer a good angle. Deviate from your pattern if it will aid the passer. Get your elbows under a low thrown ball.

8. Always know where the sideline is and run your pattern accordingly. Never run out of bounds.

9. If your are to run an outside pattern, concentrate on getting outside of your defender immediately (just the reverse on any inside pattern).

10. Get off the ball as fast as you can. The first three steps in football are the most important. Drive hard with the arms and legs. Anticipate someone holding you up at the LOS and plan your move to avoid or overcome this attempt.

11. If you are running a unit pattern (that is, when you and another player are working in a combination route, make sure one defender can't cover two men.

12. Learn to recognize all types of defenses. Know when you are zoned, single, or double covered. The defense can alter your course. Study the secondary coverage patterns and personnel of your opponent.

13. Your speed is more important than faking when playing against a zone. Find that open spot in the zone, and get to it.

14. When you run against single coverage, make your defender move—then fake. Change of pace and faking are more important than speed against single coverage.

15. If you are running a pattern into a zone defense, pull up and face the passer.

16. The only time you are ever a decoy is when a screen or a draw play is called. Run your best pattern.

CLASS ACTIVITIES

1. Have each member of the class execute five pass patterns stressing correct release and technique.

2. Interview several local coaches and as certain what they do to work on pass-catching technique.

3. List the physical characteristics of a good pass receiver and then check this list with several coaches in your area who can single out the best receiver on their team.

8

A SPECIFIC OFFENSIVE SYSTEM

Chapter Objectives

After completing this chapter, the reader should be able to:

- Draw the basic slot I formation indicating back numbering and hole numbering.
- Show both on paper and on the playing field the blocking routes for all players on all plays against an even and odd defensive set.
- Illustrate several types of blocks that can be used to execute the running plays.
- Show alternate pass routes for both drop-back and sprint-out pass plays.

THE WOLVERINE SYSTEM

Huddle Procedure

```
                    QB
        LT   LG   C   RG   RT
        TE   TB   FB   WB   SE
```

1. The center will form the huddle eight yards from the ball facing the LOS.
2. The five interior linemen will place their hands on their knees.
3. The ends and backs will be erect with hands on hips.
4. All eyes on the QB—absolutely no talking.

Procedure for Calling Play and Huddle Break

QB calls in sequence:

1. Formation
2. Play
3. Snap count

After receiving the snap count, the center and split end will leave the huddle.

4. The QB repeats the snap count, says "Ready Break." Example: "B-right, 33 Pop on Two-B RT 33 POP-on Two, Ready Break."

Line of Scrimmage
1. Linemen will line up in a two-point stance with elbows on their knees. Toes of stance should be even with the heels of the center.
2. The split end (SE) will be in a two-point stance, outside foot back.
3. On the command "DOWN" the linemen will go to a three-point stance, adjusting their splits at this time. The backs will also shift to the formation called at this time.

Line Splits and Lineup

Basic splits are as follows: Guards (LG & RG) split two feet, Tackles (RT & LT) and Tight End (TE) three feet. The split end will line up twelve yards from the ball but no closer than five yards from the sideline. His position may vary to splits ranging from two to twelve yards.

The Fullback (FB) will line up behind the center with his feet three-and-a-half yards from the ball in a four-point stance (see p. 132). The Tailback (TB) will line up directly behind the FB with his feet four-and-a-half yards from the ball in an upright stance, with hands on knees. The Wingback (WB) will line up in a three-point stance (see p. 133) according to formation.

Starting Count

"DOWN"—linemen go to a three-point stance and the backs shift if necessary (pause). All men must be set one full second before the next command. "Color-play called" (Example, "Blue 38")—this is the nonrhythmic part of our count and it also starts our rhythmic count.

Rhythmic Count

HUT ONE-HUT TWO-HUT THREE, etc. The center will snap the ball and all players will move when they hear the "T" of the HUT of the snap count. Our QB will say the following (as an example) at the line of scrimmage:

DOWN—GREEN 26—GREEN 26—HUT ONE, HUT TWO, HUT THREE. . . .

THE RUNNING OFFENSE

Pop Series

A. Onside Linemen

    1. Inside-up to head-on next man
    2. Over-on or off the line
    3. Outside

B. Offside linemen

    1. Over
    2. Outside
    3. Downfield

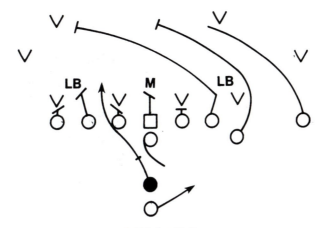

B-Right 33 Pop

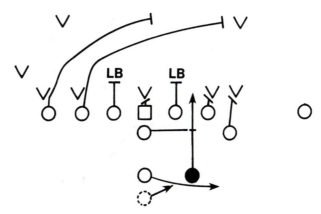

B-Right Walk Right 24 Pop

Blast Series

> TE—Onside-on, outside
>   Offside-downfield
> On T—Inside gap, on, outside
> On G—Nose, on, inside gap
> C—Over, outside LB
> Off G—Over, outside downfield
> Off T—Over, outside downfield
> FB and HB—Lead through hole block near LB

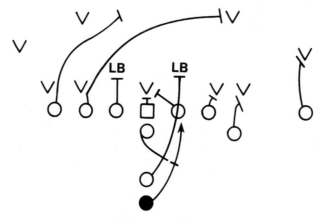

B-Right 24 Blast

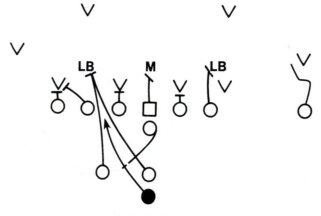

A-Left 23 Blast

Sweep Series

TE—Onside-on, outside
    Offside-downfield
On T—Inside gap, Over
On G—Pull, turn up field blocking first man to show looking to inside
C—On, Onside
Off G—Over
Off T—Downfield

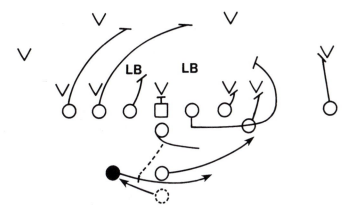

B-Right Walk Left, 28 Sweep

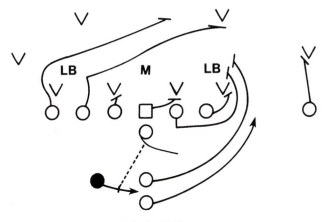

A-Left 48 Sweep

Trap Series

    TE—Onside-on, outside
        Offside-downfield
  On T—MLB, Onside LB, Seal Off
  On G—Nose, Influence, Block Near LB
  C—Nose, Offside
  Off G—Pull-Block first man to show past center on LOS, out
  Off T—On, Downfield

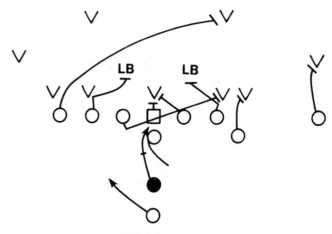

B-Right 32 Trap

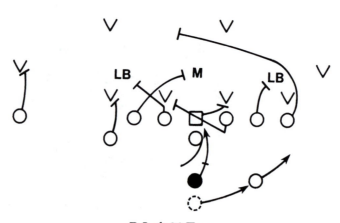

B-Left 31 Trap

Quick Pitch Series

> TE—Onside-on, outside
>   Offside-downfield
> On T—Pull, block first man to show in or out
> On G—On, Near LB
> C—On, Onside
> Off G—On, Near LB
> Off T—Downfield

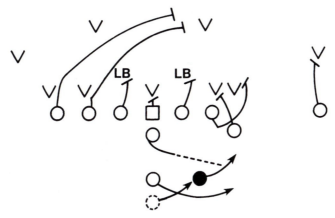

B-Right Walk Right 28 Quick Pitch

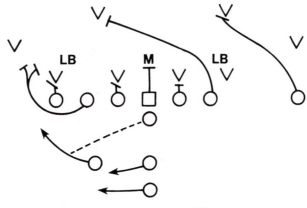

A-Left 47 Quick Pitch

Counter Series

> TE—Onside-over, outside
>   Offside-downfield
> On T—Over
> On G—Over, Near LB
> C—Nose, Over
> Off G—Over, Near LB
> Off T—Downfield
> SE–Downfield

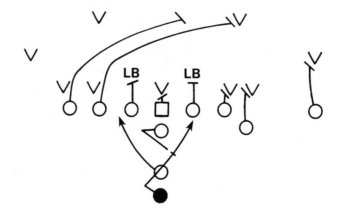

B-Right 24 Counter

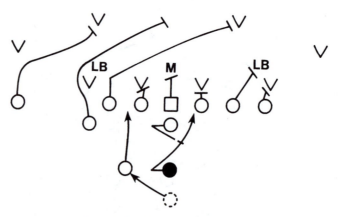

B-Left Walk Left 32 Counter

The plays above represent the basic run offense. The following plays illustrate variations from our basic set to adapt our system from week to week. This can adjust the offensive attack to take advantage of our opponent's weaknesses.

Special Running Plays

B-Right-Walk Right, Z Motion Left-25 Power

TE—Double-team blocks with LT. If DT disappears, blocks LB upfield.

On T—Blocks man on; if the defender loops outside, he must have help from LE.

On G—Sprints to the left playside hip of LB; maintains contact.

C—Reach blocks Nose.

Off G—Sprints to playside hip of LB; maintains contact.

Off T—Releases inside DT; sprints to block downfield (10 yards upfield playside)

SE—Releases inside; sprints downfield to block.

TB—Walk Right, Take ball from QB, follow blocks

WB—Goes in motion behind the QB. On snap, blocks out playside DE.

FB—Lead blocks; aims at outside hip of LT. Looks inside to block LB, looks outside for CB, or runs downfield to block near safety.

QB—Reverse pivots, and carries out bootleg.

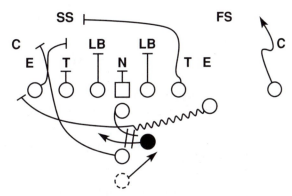

B-Right Walk Right, Z Motion Left-25 Power

B-Right Double Pull 26 Lead

TE—Releases inside; blocks middle $\frac{1}{3}$ or the FS.

ON T—Blocks #2; gets help from the WB or pulling lineman.

ON G—Blocks #1, on or over.

C—If covered, blocks O; if uncovered, backside.

Off G—Pulls playside to the double team. If WB kicks out DE, pulls up inside. If the WB hooks the DE, runs outside.

Off T—Pulls playside read blocks on corner

SE—Releases downfield;

WB—Blocks #3 with ON T; if possible, slides off to help with LB.

FB—Blocks #3 on end of LOS; uses kickout block or log block. If #3 blocked turn upfield.

QB—Reverse pivots deep and wide, hands off to TB, and rolls out playside.

TB—Take two counter steps to the right, plant, take hand off, follow blocks.

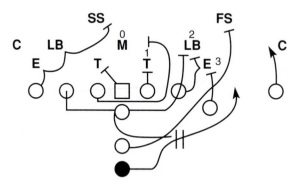

B-Right Double Pull 26 Lead

THE PASSING OFFENSE

88–89 Passes

These passes are our setup passes with the QB dropping straight back or behind the tackle to the side of the call. We will use area or "cup" protection.

    TE—Onside-gap, on, offside-gap (pass route if called)
    On T—On, outside gap
    On G—On, outside gap
    C—On, outside gap, drop to offside
    Off G—Onside gap, on, drop to offside
    Off T—Onside gap, on, offside gap
    SE—Pass route
    WB—Pass route (if not called, same rules as TE)
    FB—Split blocking
    TB—Split blocking

Technique.   All linemen step back quickly and come up to a hitting position. Take on any defender coming through your area. Area protection is passive: *Let defender come to you, then attack.* Do not get beat to the inside. Drive rusher to outside, check to backside, help teammate. Remember you are responsible for a gap not a certain person.

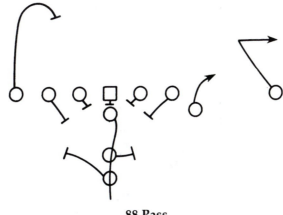

88 Pass

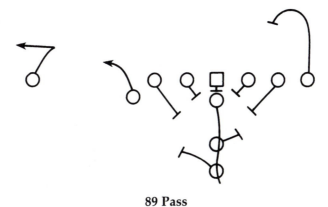

89 Pass

98—99 Passes

These are our sprint-out passes, whereby the QB is putting pressure on the corner. We will use aggressive blocking, meaning that onside linemen will attack and offside (backside) linemen will use area blocking:

TE—Route
On T—On, Outside (Aggressive)
On G—On, Outside (Aggressive)
C—On, Outside (Aggressive)
Off G—On, Check backside, Drop (Area)
Off T—Drop (Area)
SE—Pass route
WB—Pass route

FB—Block first man outside onside tackle's block (Aggressive)
TB—Block first man outside FB's block (Aggressive)
QB—Open step, sprint outside; run–pass option

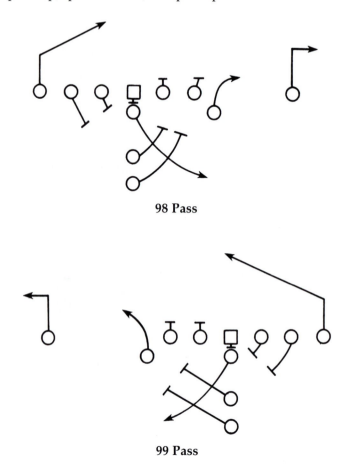

98 Pass

99 Pass

Bootleg Protection

Example: B-Rt, 33-Pop, Bootleg Right

This protection will be used when the backfield action fakes in one direction and the QB moves with the ball in the opposite direction. *Onside* is always *opposite* the play fake and blocks aggressively as the ball will be run or thrown outside the tackle.

TE—Backside (area) protection, pass route
On T—First man on line of scrimmage on or outside guard
On G—Pull and block first man to show
C—Onside gap, on, offside
Off G—Pull as QB escort
Off T—Onside gap, on, outside

SE—Pass route
WB—Pass route
FB—Fake play called and fill for guard
TB—Fake play called (opposite action from QB)
QB—Fake play called, sprint out to run or pass

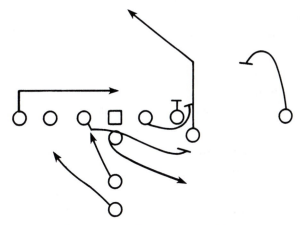

B-Right, 33-Pop, Bootleg Right

PLAY ACTION PASS

Play action passes (passes which develop like a running play but are actually passes) can be developed from any of the running plays included in the playbook. Such plays are always excellent at any level since the defense generally will react to the run and allow pass receivers to get open. A typical example is the pass developed from the sweep, as shown below.

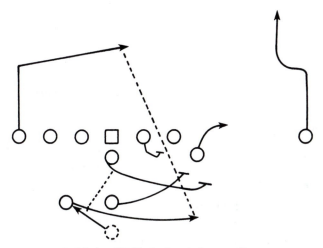

B-Right, Walk Left, 28 Sweep Pass

Of course, this takes a running back that can throw the football. However, many plays can be disguised, allowing the quarterback to keep the ball after faking a run and then drop back or roll out and throw. One such play is the bootleg.

Three additional play action passes from the Wolverine system are shown below:

B-Left Cross Buck Pass

TE(X)—Releases free; runs curl route away from the LB.

On G—Fan protection, blocks out DT.

On T—Fan protection, blocks out DE.

C—Blocks Nose, playside gap.

Off G—Aggressively cup blocks playside.

Off T—Aggressively cup blocks backside.

SE(Y)—Runs post route.

WB(Z)—Aggressively cup blocks.

TB—Fakes crossbuck over Off G; blocks first defender to show.

FB—Fakes buck over NG; releases into the flat. If he stunts, blocks LB.

QB—Flash fakes FB and TB, drops back, and looks to throw to FB in flat, SE or TE.

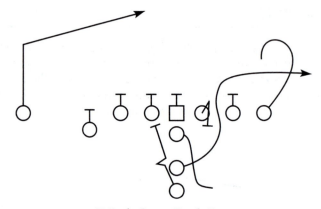

B-Left Cross Buck Pass

A Right 29 Screen Pass

TE(X)—Takes a maximum split; runs a streak route. Playside.

On G—Begins pass protection, waits for C's go call, and sprints weak side flat, angling at a depth of six to eight yards.

On T—Pass protection.

C—Blocks pass protection, counts 1001, 1002, 1003, then yells go. Sprints flat across Off G's face and straight down the line. After passing Off G, gets seven yards deep to block run support defender in flat.

Off G—Blocks pass protection, waits for C to cross face, and sprints to the weak side flat angling at a depth of four to six yards. Looks to block FS or frontside LB.

Off T—Blocks pass protection, locks on, and rides the DE to a depth of seven yards, executes crossbody block with his head to the outside.

SE(Y)—Hooks over middle, looks for ball.

WB(Z)—Runs streak route to offside

TB—Blocks pass protection, attacks strongside B gap, butts up frontside LB if he blitzes, and slips into weak flat two yards behind the LOS and five yards outside the Off T. Looks inside, catches ball; runs off of C's block on run support.

FB—Blocks pass protection RT side

QB—Makes 88 pass set. Looks deep, retreats three to four more yards, and throws to TB in weakside flat.

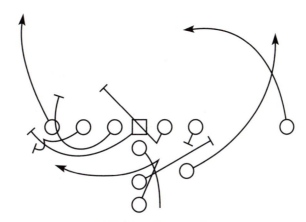

A-Right 29 Screen Pass

B-Right Fake 25 Pass Z Motion Left-post

TE—Runs an out-and-up route at depth of twelve yards.

On G—Blocks man over or outside

On T—Blocks man over or inside.

C—Blocks man over or offside.

Off G—Blocks man over or inside-out.

Off T—Blocks man over or inside-out.

SE(Y)—Releases vertical; after turning upfield, Y times his route to go behind post route by Z.

WB(Z)—Goes in motion. Runs upfield at depth of twelve yards; breaks post route.

TB—Fakes 25 blocks first LB outside-in playside.

FB—Blocks first LB outside-in on backside.

QB—Fakes 25 with TB, drops into pocket after fake, and runs straight back at depth of nine to ten yards. Reads CB on called side. If CB plays run, throws quickly to Y. If CB plays Z, throws to outside shoulder of Y and runs fade route into the numbers or if FS covers X and Z has SS beat to inside throw to Z.

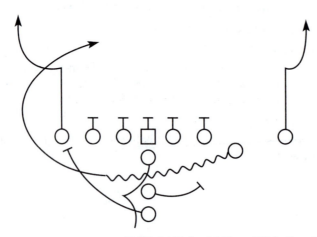

B-Right Fake 25 Pass Z Motion Left-post

The possibilities for additional plays are limitless. Add also the dimension of various formations and one can stay awake all night dreaming up new plays that work on paper. But as we have tried to stress elsewhere in this text, all plays will work on paper; it's how things develop on the field during the game that makes football, as well as all athletic competition, a true test of the determination, desire, and spirit of the athlete.

CLASS ACTIVITIES

1. The class should be assigned two running plays to learn for onfield demonstration. Assign each person two offensive positions.

2. Have the class break up into groups of four (the offensive backs) and have them go over backfield patterns and timing.

3. Divide the class into groups of seven and have them go over offensive line blocking rules for the offensive series.

4. Using bell dummies or hand held dummies, conduct a half-line, half-speed scrimmage with several offensive units going against one set of defensive people.

5. Have the offensive quarterback of a unit call two or three plays in succession to build a cohesive attack.

9

DEFENSIVE STRATEGY AND TERMINOLOGY

Chapter Objectives

After completing this chapter, the reader should be able to:

- Perform the basic stance and football charge techniques used by linemen and linebackers.
- Recognize and draw on paper, as well as perform on the field, the proper alignment for various defensive positions.
- Show the appropriate flow and pursuit patterns of various offensive plays run against the 59 defense.
- Show line and secondary adjustments to at least two offensive sets using a standard defensive alignment. These should be demonstrated on paper as well as on the field.
- Discuss the strengths and weaknesses of at least two popular defenses and be able to draw them against several offensive alignments.

DEFENSIVE BASICS

Introducing football to any group seems to be considered easier when the fundamentals of defense are considered. The reasons for this are several: (1) defense is usually thought of as more of a team effort than is offense, which usually is thought of in terms of the line and the backfield; (2) defensive sets and formations seem to be fewer and less confusing; and (3) defense seems simpler overall than offense—one hears phrases such as "they can't win if they can't score," "offense is thinking and skill, defense is just desire," and "the head-hunter instinct is all you need to play defense." At younger age levels players will frequently play on both offense and defense, but will find that their dual roles are quite different. They will discover that desire and hustle will come into play more on defense than on offense. Desire is that unmeasurable quality that football coaches are always looking for in young athletes. Synonymous with *determination, spirit, intestinal fortitude, will-to-overcome,* or just simply *guts,* the concept of desire is essential to football success on both offense and defense, although it is more evident on defense. Coaches who use athletes both ways should spend a great deal of practice and preparation on defense, since offensive success is very dependent on what is done defensively.

The entire defensive unit has five basic goals:

1. Prevent the offense from scoring.
2. Prevent the easy score.
3. Gain advantageous field position.
4. Get the football.
5. Score.

In order to accomplish these goals, each defensive player must do the following in the order listed:

1. Neutralize the offensive blocker's charge.

   a. By exploding into the blocker.
   b. By disengaging from the blocker.

2. Find the football.
3. Get rid of the offensive blocker.
4. Pursue the football.
5. Tackle the ball carrier.

This chapter will provide the reader (and future coach) with the fundamentals necessary to instruct younger players in how to accomplish these individual defensive goals.

DEFENSIVE TERMINOLOGY

As with any learning experience, an adequate vocabulary is essential. This is especially true when the coach examines the variety of names given to defensive formations and actions. For example, a 5–4 defense may be called "59," "52," "50," "Oklahoma," or any number of other possibilities, although they essentially refer to the same defensive alignment. A note should be given here concerning the figures used in this text. As you may have noted we use the standard method of drawing football diagrams, which has the team you are discussing facing in a northerly direction, or toward the top of the page. For example, if we were discussing a defensive alignment, we would draw the defensive men facing north (top of the page) and the offense facing south (bottom of the page). This system has been used throughout this text and is recommended as a habit to be adapted by anyone who will be drawing football formations.

The following terminology will give the reader a basis for talking defense.

1. *Blitz* (red dog; dogging). The reckless abandon charge of a defensive lineman or, as is usually the case, a linebacker rushing across the line of scrimmage (hereafter LOS) on the snap of the ball.
2. *Combination defense.* The defensive alignment usually utilizing both the odd and even principles (i.e., odd on one side of the LOS, even on the other).
3. *Counter play.* A type of reverse play which comes back against the grain or opposite the main flow of the offensive blocking.
4. *Defensive numbering.* The concept that gives each offensive man and gap a number for positive positioning of the defensive men. The most typical numbering system is shown below.

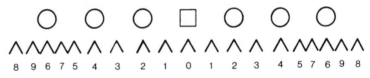

Typical Defensive Numbering

A defense could be called by the numbers, with the first being used to tell the defensive tackle where he lines up, and the second number where the defensive end lines up.

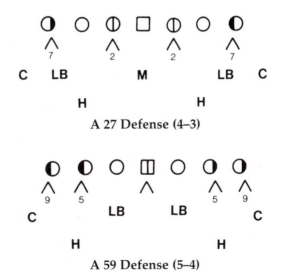

A 27 Defense (4–3)

A 59 Defense (5–4)

5. *Defensive team components.* The defense will usually be composed of three main divisions or groups according to playing responsibilities:

   a. *The defensive line.* Usually the men in a down position (three-or four-point stance) on the LOS. The responsibility of these men is to react to blocks and pursue the football. Their first responsibility is to stop the run and their second responsibility is to rush the passer. The shaded areas denote the position of alignment.

**Offensive Men Have Been Shaded
to Illustrate the Exact Position
of the Defensive Player**

   b. *Defensive linebackers.* Usually the men who line up two to three yards off the ball in a two-point (standing) position. They are responsible for both the run and intermediate areas on pass coverage (sometimes responsible for deep pass coverage).

The Defensive Linebackers

   c. *Defensive secondary.* Usually the men who line up from two to eight yards off the ball in a two-point stance and have pass responsibilities first and run responsibility second.

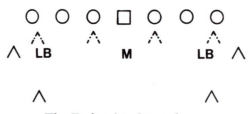

The Defensive Secondary

6. *Three deep.* Pass coverage that utilizes only three secondary men. Usually uses a defensive end or linebacker in the pass coverage, which is zone-type coverage in most cases. A typical three-deep coverage is shown in the following diagram.

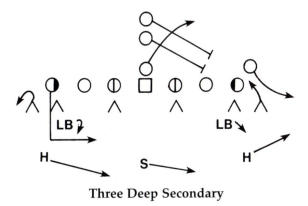

Three Deep Secondary

7. *Four deep (umbrella secondary).* Pass coverage that employs four defensive backs in various types of coverages. May be man-for-man, zone, or combination type coverage. An example of a four-deep zone coverage is shown below.

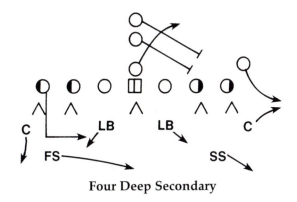

Four Deep Secondary

8. *Eagle position.* When a linebacker and defensive down lineman exchange positions, as illustrated in the following two diagrams:

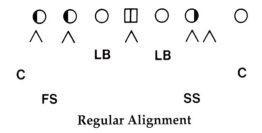

Regular Alignment

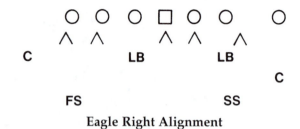

Eagle Right Alignment

9. *Even defense.* A defense is known as even when there is no man on the LOS directly over the center or the middle man on the offensive line. This is also a defensive set with an even number of defensive linemen down on the LOS. Typical even defenses in three variations are shown in these three diagrams:

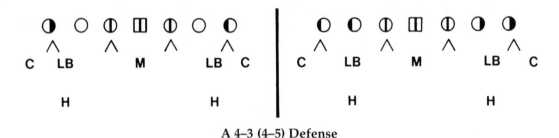

A 4–3 (4–5) Defense

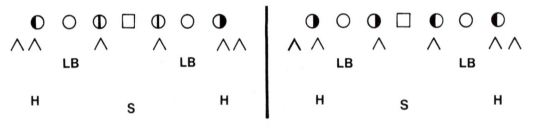

A Wide Tackle 6 (6–2) Defense

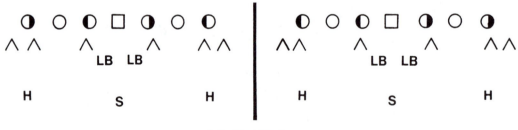

A Split 6 Defense

10. *Flat.* The pass route area, which extends two to three yards past the LOS and the width of the field outside the offensive end:

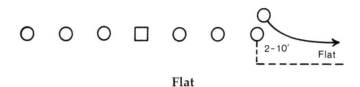

Flat

11. *Forearm (hand) shiver.* A technique used by linebackers (usually to slow a blocker's charge). As the defender steps to meet the blocker, he simultaneously drives the heels of both hands (arms fully extended, elbows locked) into the shoulder pads of the blocker.
12. *Forearm lift (rip up).* When stepping to meet the blocker, the defender flexes his striking arm 90° at the elbow with the fist clenched and held out in front of the chest. This arm is then used to strike the numbers of the blocker in an effort to straighten him up and neutralize his charge. The defender's shoulders are square to the LOS, with feet moving and legs churning.
13. *Gap defense.* A defensive alignment with one or more of the down defensive linemen located in the gaps between offensive linemen. Usually used on the goal line or in short yardage (third down and one yard to go) situations.

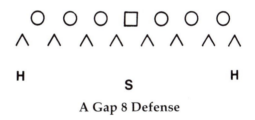

A Gap 8 Defense

14. *Hitting position.* A football position characterized by a bull neck, with the head up, back straight, and hips dropped. The player has a good base, is coiled, and generally has his fists clenched, feet moving, and is ready to strike a blow.
15. *Hook (curl) zone.* That area about eight to ten yards past the LOS where an offensive receiver usually runs a hook or curl pattern. A curl zone is usually wider and deeper than a hook zone, as shown in the following illustration.

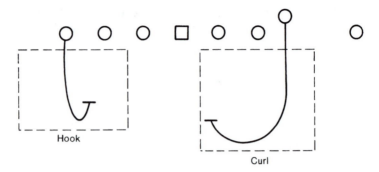

16. *Inside-out position.* (pertains particularly to linebackers). When tackling the ball carrier on the LOS, the tackler should keep an inside position (relative to the center) and tackle while moving to the outside.

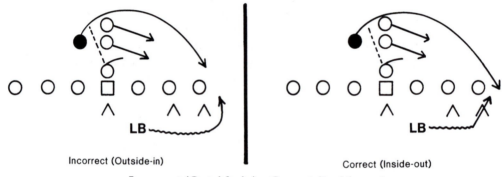

Incorrect (Outside-in)   Correct (Inside-out)

Incorrect (Outside-in)—Correct (Inside-out)

17. *Interior linemen.* Those men playing from tackle to tackle positions on the defensive LOS.
18. *Invert.* A defensive formation usually used with a four-deep secondary alignment in which the defensive cornermen and halfback will change responsibilities and alignments.

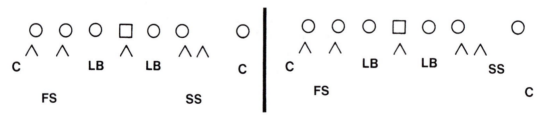

Regular Alignment—Invert Alignment

19. *Key.* To use one or more offensive men as an indication of what the defensive man is supposed to do. A defensive back keys or looks at the offensive end. If the end blocks, he plays as if it is going to be a running play; if the end releases downfield, he plays pass.
20. *LOS.* The line of scrimmage.
21. *Man.* Term used in pass coverage in which one or all defensive backs or linebackers are assigned a receiver to follow wherever the receiver goes.
22. *Mike.* Term given the middle linebacker or the man playing over the center of the LOS and standing in a low two-point hitting position.
23. *Monster (rover).* Usually a defensive secondary man or linebacker whose line-up position is determined by the offensive formation or field position (for example, third down and ten yards to go, ball on the right hash mark).
24. *Nose.* Name given the middle guard or man playing in a three- or four-point stance down on the LOS, usually over the center.
25. *Neutralize.* An attempt to stop the momentum of the offensive blocker with counterpressure and force, while attempting to straighten the blocker into an upright position.
26. *Odd defense.* A defensive alignment with a man lined up over the offensive center (or middle man on the offensive line). A defensive set with an odd number of men down on the LOS. The following three diagram show typical odd defensive alignments in two variations.

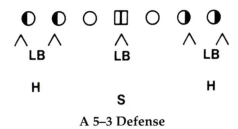

A 5–3 Defense

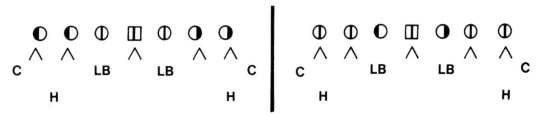

A 5–4 Oklahoma Defense

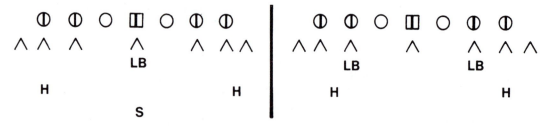

A 7 Man Line Defense

27. *Pursuit.* The angle of chase by the defense that will allow it to cut off the ball carrier for the least amount of yardage gained. Proper angle of pursuit is very important.

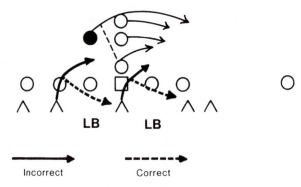

Incorrect   Correct

Correct/Incorrect Pursuit Angles

28. *Read.* To react to the direction that the offensive player leads you. For example, this will tell the defender which way the blocker is trying to drive him.

29. *Shoulder block.* This technique is used when the defender wants to neutralize the blocker's charge by driving his shoulder into the blocker's numbers. The arm of the hitting shoulder is flexed 90 degrees at the elbow, and the forearm is parallel to the ground. This provides a wider blocking surface. The defender should avoid getting "tied up" with the blocker by driving the offensive man into the hole, back into the backfield, or into the ground.

30. *Stunting.* When a defensive man slants (on the snap of the ball) into another position in an effort to penetrate the LOS or confuse the block of the offense.

31. *Submarine.* A move requiring the defensive man to drop low on the ground and get penetration into the backfield (usually between two offensive blockers).

32. *Trap.* A false key by the offense which allows the blocker an advantage (an attempt to blind-side a defensive interior lineman usually with an offensive lineman from the opposite side of the line). The trapper may attempt to drive the defender out of the hole or attempt to hook the defender on a play going to the outside or be blocked by a setback. Two examples are illustrated.

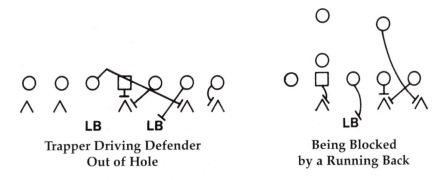

Trapper Driving Defender
Out of Hole

Being Blocked
by a Running Back

33. *Trap reaction.* When an interior lineman is not blocked or is blocked and quickly released, he should suspect a trap and immediately step down with his inside foot, in a low hitting position, if the trapper is attempting to knock him to the outside. If the trapper is trying to hook him to the inside, he should react to this by fighting through the pressure and playing the football as the situation dictates.

TEAM DEFENSE

The terms and specific individual techniques discussed thus far need now to be applied in a basic defensive alignment. Team defense is an effort to maintain a co-ordinated alignment, and to achieve the overall goal of containment. The reader should study the development of this defense and the rationale behind player po-sitioning. Similar detail will be applied no matter what the basic defense happens to be. A basic illustrative defense to use is the 5–4 or "59" defense since it appears to be the consensus defense in many schools.

From youth league through professional football, the players will be exposed to several defensive sets. Most teams will have one basic defense they are able to play consistently and confidently in a variety of situations. The prospective coach should become thoroughly familiar with the positional strategy, problems, and re-sponsibilities of one defense so he can use similar thinking patterns for whatever defense the school is using where he takes a coaching position.

The 5–4 defense was developed in the 1950s to combat the split T offensive for-mation. Bud Wilkinson, then head coach at the University of Oklahoma, originated the defense, which became very effective in stopping the running and passing of-fense of the split T formation. Thus, it has been called the 5–4 Oklahoma defense. This defensive alignment has become a standard in defensive play, being used ex-tensively in all levels of competition. It is a versatile defense, which has been effec-tive against the variety of formations to arise since the 1950s. Recently, the wishbone or veer formation has given all defensive alignments many problems. A section will be devoted to this attack later in this chapter. However, younger play-ers generally are not developed enough physically and intellectually to execute an offensive attack such as the veer, so the 5–4 has remained an effective alignment in youth league, Pop Warner levels, as well as the junior high, high school, college, and more recently, professional levels of play.

The format presented in Chapter 12 is what we would use if we were handing out the material to the players themselves. Most coaching staffs believe that players should receive their respective position assignments and responsibilities from lecture-discussion "chalk-talks" as well as in written form. The problem in this is that the players are students who have lots of other written material to concern themselves with (pertaining to algebra, science, English, etc.). So the coach must keep all such material short, simple, and to the point, but complete enough so the player knows where he is supposed to line up, how he is supposed to line up, what he is responsible for, and how he should react to various offensive alignments. This last will usually evolve from week to week based on what the scouting report says or who the next opponent is. We will reiterate here that a football coach has the results of his teaching on display every Friday or Saturday of the football season.

The task for the reader in this section is to learn the mechanics of each position of a basic defense thoroughly, so as to be able to coach a defensive line, the linebackers or secondary, or perhaps the whole defensive team when he takes his first job. This may contrast sharply with the limited experience of even the best former football player who played only one position but now has to know what everyone must do on defense under various conditions.

Those coaches in the middle or junior high schools probably should be prepared to learn and teach the system used by the high school where their players will be going. This enhances the total program.

POPULAR DEFENSIVE SETS

Below are several standard defensive sets used at all levels of play. They are given simply to show the various alignments so that the reader will at least be familiar with the names and looks of different defenses. It should be noted that spacings, alignments, and general set-ups of the defense hypothetically cover and contain all possible running areas and lanes. Several names are given for each defense to indicate its various titles. There are as many possible names as each coach can dream up. Each coaching staff uses names to suit their situation and philosophy, although those given in the text are standard labels. The reader should be able to draw these defenses against a standard offensive set when discussing football play.

5–4, 59, Oklahoma 5–2, 50

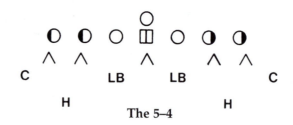

The 5–4

Strengths. Since the 5–4 is a nine-man front (5 down linemen and 4 linebackers) this defense is an excellent defense against the run. It is a good containing defense as well as a pursuing defense. These strengths depend primarily on the two linebackers. You need strong people here. A four-deep secondary in combination with linebackers make the hook and flat area well protected. A strong, quick noseguard puts immediate pressure up the middle of any offense.

Weaknesses. The alignment leaves itself open for angle blocking, double teams, cross blocking, traps up the middle, kick-out blocks on the defensive ends, and runs off tackle. Proper flow of secondary and linebackers is needed for adequate pass coverage.

4–3, 27

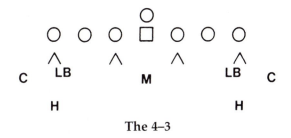

The 4–3

Strengths. Presenting a nine-man front (including the cornerbacks) this alignment is stronger outside than inside. With the corners and two outside linebackers, containment of wide running plays can be easily accomplished. Linebackers can pursue very quickly or drop to pass protection zones. The defense is generally stronger against the passing game than the running game. A great deal of stunting and blitzing can be used and linebackers can flow and pursue easily.

Weaknesses. Quick running plays and traps can hurt this defense. Since three linebackers are positioned off the LOS, running lanes are created inside from tackle to tackle. Slight misalignments of the defensive end and linebacker can make the defense weaker on the corners. Defensive rotation of the secondary to the strength of the formations or flow of the ball is crucial.

Split 6

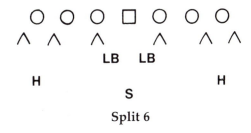

Split 6

Strengths.   This alignment puts four defensive men over the center of the offensive line (three men). The defensive ends are in a good position to contain and the off-tackle play is strong if the defensive tackle is aligned inside the offensive end. This defense puts the maximum number of players into pass defense quickly with the linebackers being able to get to the middle hook zones very quickly.

Weaknesses.   The area between the offensive guard and tackle is weak. With the defensive tackle lined up in an outside position it weakens the inside run position; if the tackle lines up in an inside position, outside run support is hurt. The flat areas for pass coverage are weak and the three-deep secondary can be attacked through the air.

Wide-Tackle 6

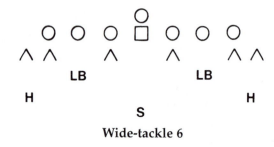

Wide-tackle 6

Strengths.   This defense is stronger outside than inside and prevents the double-team block over the off-tackle area. The defensive guard area is somewhat strong, as is the end area if the defensive tackle has a physical advantage. The defense can hold up the release of the offensive end and is a good defense against delays, and counters.

Weaknesses.   The offense has a numerical advantage over the middle (three versus two). The linebackers must stop the dive play and if the offense takes big splits, the defense is vulnerable to traps and a three-deep secondary makes the middle zone weak.

5–3

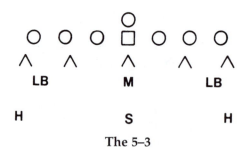

The 5–3

Strengths.   The hook areas are well covered with this alignment, as is the off-tackle area. The defense is a good containing defense for wide running plays, and is ideal for stunting and blitzing. A good noseguard can apply quick middle pressure.

Weaknesses.   The middle area is vulnerable to plays up the middle and to wide plays if the defensive end crashes to the inside. Problems of coverage occur if the offensive line takes large splits. The outside linebacker can be sealed off to the inside easily and if the linebackers stunt, the defense is vulnerable to the passing game in the flat and middle hook areas.

In reviewing these defensive alignments we should keep in mind that they are generally used between the ten-yard lines by most teams. A team will pick one defense as their basic defense and then will develop variations from it. Some will have two types of defenses (odd and even) with variations of each. Coaching staffs must decide on the type of defense to be used as their standard, based on their knowledge of the following:

1. Personnel
2. Opponents' strengths
3. Learning capacity of the players

A team might have two players who have the strength and mobility to play linebackers and one individual who is quick and is a good tackler, but not strong. For this situation a five-man front with two linebackers may be ideal. Another team might have only one lineman who can play well. This might indicate a four- or six-man front with two or three linebackers. These considerations must be decided at the start of each season when considering personnel and developing a defense.

Secondly, a coaching staff must consider that changing the defense a team ran in a previous season requires a great deal of new learning and confidence building by players and coaches. Once players learn to respond to a certain set of situations it is more difficult many times to learn new alignments and responsibilities. This holds true for all levels of football play, but it is especially evident with less experienced players.

Finally, a word on objectives. As with offensive goals setting them too high may be discouraging to your team, but without them you may not have consistent, usable goals. The following are offered as possible suggestions for defensive goals. The specific number and percentages can be adjusted to the level of play you are coaching.

1. Win.
2. Hold opponent to less than 16 points.
3. Hold opponent to three yards or less on first down 65 percent of the time.
4. Stop 50 percent of the time on third and short; 70 percent on third and long.
5. Don't allow any runs over twenty yards or passes over twenty-five.
6. Cause three turnovers.
7. On six possessions by opponent do not allow a first down.
8. Sack quarterback or deflect pass one out of every ten passes thrown.
9. "Oskie" (Intercept) one out of every ten passes thrown.

10. Don't' allow opponent first down when they start inside their twenty-yard line.
11. Give offense field position three times inside the fifty or score defensively.
12. Do not allow opponent a first down after a turnover.
13. Allow opponents less than 295 yards total offense per game.

The following newspaper report featuring Texas Tech defensive back Tony Green and Rice defensive back Randy Piel, is taken from the *Lubbock Avalanche Journal:*[1]

> It was also a game of big plays. One of the biggest was a 72-yard TD bomb from Tommy Duniven to tight end Sylvester Brown and safety Randy Piel took the blame.
>
> "We were in a formation where the safety is up short, covering the tight end, anyone coming over the middle, and the quarterback on a run," he explained. "I expected a curl route and he didn't run a curl. I hung in the middle too long.
>
> "The play was an audible at the line. I caught the audible and guessed, but I guessed wrong. It was a great play by them and it cost us 6 points."
>
> Tony Green, from his strong safety spot, picked up a Tommy Kramer pass and zipped in untouched 42 yards to give Tech a 21–7 advantage; then later in the third period, Tommy Duniven hit Sylvester Brown with a 72-yard bomb for the winning points.
>
> "We were in man coverage and I stepped in front of him. I knew," grinned Green, "that no one was going to catch me after that. . . . A few plays before, we had been in zone coverage and the guy was kinda open. We were in man coverage (on the interception), but we kinda disguised it and I held off until he threw it."
>
> Both backs gambled. One was successful—one was not.

CLASS ACTIVITIES

1. Review football films and identify the type of defensive alignment being used.

2. Have several defensive alignments drawn on large cards and have the class identify each.

3. Go onto the field and align a team into several defensive fronts. Have the class identify each alignment.

4. Have several members of the class illustrate the position and responsibilities of a nose, five, and nine technique on defensive.

5. Observe a high school or college game and have the class chart the defensive alignments during the game.

NOTE

1. Carter Cromwell, "Famed Capers Missing from Rice Locker Room," *Lubbock Avalanche Journal*, November 2, 1975, p. C-1. Reprinted with permission.

10

SPECIFIC DEFENSIVE TECHNIQUES

Chapter Objectives

After completing this chapter, the reader should be able to:

- Illustrate on the field a correct three- and four-point stance giving the important check points for each.
- Illustrate by example the correct defensive lineman moves, and feet position when reacting to head-on, reach, double team, trap, and pass type blocks.
- Identify the correct defensive linebacker positions for two standard odd and even front defenses.
- Describe the responsibilities of the linebacker when playing a standard odd or even defense.
- Illustrate on the field proper linebacker reactions and flow to various blocks and pass action plays.
- Show by example proper tackling mechanics for both straight ahead and side tackling situations.
- List several coaching points that should be stressed when teaching players to use the shoulder, rather than the helmet, as the contact point when tackling.

DEFENSIVE BASICS

The following is a step-by-step sequence of important techniques for defensive play. Although a new coach will be exposed to a variety of ideas and theories concerning which defense is best, there remains a core of fundamentals common to all defensive play no matter what the specific alignment might be. Prospective coaches are encouraged to make the following techniques a part of their knowledge, since these are the basics around which every successful defense is built.

The defensive line will usually have at least one man on every second offensive lineman and will usually have at least four men on the LOS. However, defensive lines can vary from three- to eleven-man lines, since there is no rule limiting the number of men who can line up on the LOS. Regardless of the number of men on the line, several basic techniques will apply to all defenses. Stance is the first technique that needs to be examined.

The basics developed here are for a standard four-point stance, which many coaches feel is the best stance for down linemen on defense. This reasoning is based on the observation that: (1) a four-point stance is more stable than a two- or three-point position, (2) more of the player's weight can be positioned forward of the center of gravity, and (3) most players believe that they can get a stronger forward charge from a four-point stance. In addition, older and more experienced players can get their weight on the balls of their feet and can experience better lateral movement. These factors are beneficial in achieving the defensive player's first responsibility: neutralizing the offensive player's block. The three-point stance is also described and attention is drawn to the fact that both penetrating and nonpenetrating descriptions are given. A defensive lineman can line up according to the technique he is going to play on that specific down.

STANCES

Four-Point Stance

1. The player assumes a position with his weight supported on the balls of the feet as well as the fingers of both hands. *The arms are placed shoulder width apart,* with arms and shoulders in a straight line.
2. *The feet are staggered* no further than a toe–instep relationship, creating a balanced four-point base with hips and knees flexed, and one foot forward (the exception is the middle guard who generally has his feet parallel).
3. *The fingers are spread wide* for better support. Players should be taught that the knees do not touch the ground. It is a four-point, not a six-point, stance! The weight is forward.
4. The head is up enough to see the down hand of the offensive opponent. A young lineman should be taught to look at the down hand or hands of the offensive player as his "key" for movement. Although many coaches believe

that the defensive lineman should direct his attention to the ball, it is felt that a young lineman can get just as good a jump on the offensive blocker when he concentrates on the blocker's down hand. Some coaches teach the lineman to look through the helmet to determine what is going to happen to him (such as pass, reach, drive). Whatever technique is used, the defender will soon learn to see the reaction of the blocker and look through his opponent for action in the backfield. This is known as "split vision." However, not all players can develop this.

5. *The back is straight* with the hips only slightly higher than the shoulders.
6. The weight is evenly distributed on the hands and feet with the shoulders square or parallel to the LOS.

Figures 10.1 and 10.2 illustrate a typical four-point stance of a young player. This stance can be used for all penetrating situations or reading situations when players are in the down position on the LOS.

Three-Point Stance (Penetrating Charge)

1. The inside arm is down and the inside foot is slightly staggered. The free arm rests on the near thigh with the hand in a clenched position. Place the down arm with the finger tips in front of the shoulders.
2. The shoulders are slightly higher than the back.
3. The head is higher than the shoulders.
4. The feet are staggered heel and instep, no greater than heel and toe, outside foot is forward. The foot on the side of the down hand is usually back.

FIGURE 10.1 Four Point Stance

FIGURE 10.2   Four-Point Stance

5. The weight is on the *balls of the feet with very little weight on down hand*. This stance is more effectively used when playing on the LOS in a controlled defense, where the lineman does not penetrate but "reads" the play as it develops and reacts accordingly.

FIGURE 10.3   Three-Point Stance

DEFENSIVE LINE TECHNIQUES

The initial reaction of defensive players to offensive movement is of prime concern to defensive line coaches. Young linemen must be taught to overcome three faults that are very common to defensive play:

1. Failing to *deliver a blow and stay low.*
2. Failing to work the legs and *fight through the pressure* of the offensive blocker.
3. Failing to *find the football and pursue* at the proper angle.

Once a properly balanced stance is achieved, the defensive lineman should be coiled (both physically and mentally) to deliver a blow that will stun the offensive blocker, straighten him up, and ideally, knock him back. What initiates this action is movement of the offensive blocker—the defensive players do not listen to the cadence but move on what they see, not what they hear! In order to master this technique each defensive lineman must deliver a forearm lift or hand shiver in conjunction with a full extension of the legs and body, rapidly bringing his feet with him (moving like pistons). His prime objective is to get contact and quickly lose it (as he finds the football and pursues).

The defensive lineman must work at all costs to stay square to the LOS (that is, keeping his shoulders and hips parallel to the LOS) and not get turned or driven back by the blocker. Contact must be stressed and reemphasized to the defensive lineman. The shoulder charge combined with the forearm or hands lift appear to be the most effective methods of striking a neutralizing blow. However, the forearm lift makes it difficult to disengage from the blocker. Many coaches feel that football games are won and lost during the first ten minutes of a game, when the offensive and defensive players are establishing supremacy of strength, quickness, and ability to strike a blow.

Figure 10.4 illustrates a typical "exploding" stance for a young player. Although the preferred 45° angle, rigid posture is not achieved, the youngster has uncoiled and is in the process of getting his legs into action. Figure 10.5 illustrates a youngster who has taken a step as he hits the sled. This considerably reduces the force he can generate. In addition, the player has lowered his head, and with his feet not in a coiled position has put himself in a very poor position to execute a successful defense against the block. Finally, Figure 10.6 shows the all-too-typical situation in which the blocker has got his feet crossed and his body twisted. This all but eliminates any effective force generation. Simple sled blocking drills should be practiced continually in order to constantly check the blocker's basics of explosion, wide base, body square to blocking surface, and keeping those feet moving like triphammers.

The young defensive lineman must be made to feel that his particular territory is the most important area in the team's defense and that he must protect and gain control of this territory first and foremost. The only time a lineman on defense should move to protect a teammate's territory is when he is *certain* the ball is not going through his territory. To fulfill these obligations, the lineman must find the football before determining his pursuit pattern.

FIGURE 10.4   Two Man Sled Drill, Initial Explosion

In order to protect his territory best, and maintain a position that will not allow the offense to gain yardage, a defensive lineman can (1) drive through the blocker, (2) go over the top of the blocker (swim technique), (3) roll away from or pivot away from the blocker or (4) go under (submarine) the blocker. Although there are some defensive schemes that permit a down lineman to go around a block, the coach must stress again and again that the defender *never, never, never*

FIGURE 10.5   Offensive Blocker Initial Contact

FIGURE 10.6   Blocker Not Keeping Wide Base with Feet

runs around a blocker. If he does, in almost every case, he will put himself in a poor pursuit position, or (worse yet) open his territory to the runner so that he will be behind the runner instead of in front of him.

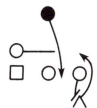

Running around Blocker

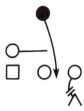

Fighting through Pressure

REACTING TO BLOCKS

Having neutralized the block, the next order of business is to get rid of the blocker and pursue the football. This may be accomplished in the following ways:

Reaction to a Head-On Block (One-on-One; 1-2-3 Blocking; Drive Block)

This is the basic blocking attack every defensive lineman must conquer. The coach should realize that it is extremely difficult for a man who is playing head-on to react and defend a simple dive play and cover both gaps or sides of the offensive blocker.

COACHING POINTS: Reacting to a Head-on Block

- Deliver a blow.
- On making contact, bring your back foot up so that your feet are even.
- Stay square to the LOS.
- Fight through the head of the blocker. Fight the pressure.
- Do not allow the blocker to get under your shoulders.
- Get rid of the blocker quickly.
- Do not let the blocker knock you back.

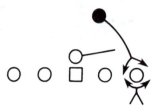   

Head-on Block Reaction   **Head-on Position Responsibilities**

This situation can be improved if the defensive player is moved back from the LOS (up to one yard, for example) so that he can read the offensive blocker's charge, be in a better position to fight the pressure of the blocker, and cover the appropriate gap. The defender should step-up and deliver a shoulder charge or rip-up while maintaining good leverage. He should work the feet and legs to coordinate with the rip-up and drive the blocker straight back or, better yet, into the hole. Whatever he does he must not get straightened up, turned and/or driven back.

Reaction to a Reach Block

Whenever a defensive lineman is playing on the outside or inside gap, or shoulder of an offensive lineman, he should expect the blocker to attempt to shoot his head across the defender's body and "hook" him (or gain position outside by hand control). The maneuver is called a reach block:

   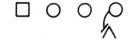

Reach Block   **Reach Block 2**

The defender must read the blocker's head and step into the blocker's pressure. If aligned outside, he should deliver an inside shoulder charge and forearm

COACHING POINTS: Reacting to a Reach Block

- Do not let the blocker get his head or body to your opposite knee or hip.
- Drive hard with your shoulder, staying as square to the LOS as possible.
- Look through the blocker into the backfield and find the football. Head up, eyes open!
- If you get the blocker off balance and turned, extend your arms using a hand shiver to drive him down and away.
- *Do not* get driven back.

shiver to cut off the blocker's angle and drive him back. The legs are worked hard and the hands are used to push the blocker down and away. He must get the trail leg up the field when contact is made with, for example, the forearm lift or arm shiver technique. This will prevent him from getting cut off.

Reaction to a Scramble Block

Whenever the blocker tries to drive his head between the defender's legs and scramble him backwards on all fours, (using the scramble block technique) you should read this move as quickly as possible and use a quick, strong arm extension or hand shiver (getting your pads on his pads) to drive the blocker down into the ground. Step with your back leg and get square to the LOS.

COACHING POINTS: Reacting to a Scramble Block

- Quickly flatten the blocker out by driving him into the ground with your shoulders, arms and hands.
- Don't give ground quickly.
- Keep your head up and your eyes open looking for the ball carrier.
- Pick your feet up and step on or over the blocker to get the ball carrier.

Reaction to a Double Team Block

When two blockers attempt to drive one defender off the LOS, the defender must feel and react to this pressure by driving his head and shoulders between the blockers and driving very hard with his legs. His main objective is to split the blockers, thus gaining penetration and neutralizing the block. The defender must uncoil and drive his body forward by working his legs with authority. He must defeat the post blocker and get his pads under the drive blocker as he turns his pads to split the block.

COACHING POINTS: Reacting to a Double Team Block

- Keep your head up and your eyes open looking for the ball carrier.
- Do not lie on your stomach and leave your feet behind you.
- Keep your legs churning and driving, shoulders square to the LOS.
- After splitting the blockers, get your head and shoulders up, and look for the football. At the same time, *get up on your feet* in a hitting position. Work those feet.
- If you can't split the double team and get penetration "die in the hole"—create a pile-up—but *do not* get driven back!

Reaction to a Trap Block

Although a misdirection play (a play that appears to go in one direction but is coming in another direction) and its blocking scheme may vary, at times the defender will not get blocked immediately by an offensive lineman. In similar situations the man the defender is playing over just gives him a step, uses a rip-up (or forearm or hand shiver) and quickly releases to the inside or outside. This should signal the defensive lineman that (1) someone is coming from the blind side to block or trap him, or (2) a backfield man is going to run through the line and try to knock him into the nickel seats! In either case, he should immediately think trap, look to the inside, step down with the inside foot forward, stay in a low hitting position, and get ready to meet and defeat any blocker with good leverage and timing. His goal is to attack the trapping lineman and squeeze the hole down as much as possible.

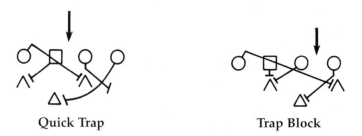

Quick Trap   Trap Block

Reaction to Drop-Back Pass Protection

Although drop-back pass protection or cup blocking is not seen in many younger age division levels (due in part to the quarterback's throwing ability and in part to the difficulty of learning and teaching pass protection blocking) the young defensive lineman may encounter a passing situation of this type.

The blocker will either deliver a short extension-and-retreat blow or just retreat (drop back about a step) and set up in a hitting position. He will then attempt to keep the defender off the quarterback who has dropped straight back about five to seven yards and is set up to pass.

COACHING POINTS: Reacting to a Trap Block

- React quickly. Respond to no pressure or light pressure and release with a step down to the inside.
- Don't follow the releasing lineman with your eyes or your body.
- Keep shoulders and body parallel to the LOS.
- Stay low in a coiled hitting position and meet any blocker with your inside shoulder and arm (or cross the face of the trapper) and try to stuff the blocker back into the hole.
- Don't get knocked back or away from the hole. "Die in the hole"—create a pile-up instead.
- Use a rollout or pivot upfield as a last resort to cut off the ball carrier before he breaks away.

The defender should step up and deliver a forearm lift or hand shiver while driving into and through the blocker. Read the pass (find the football) and attempt to maintain contact with the blocker. Place your hands on the shoulders of the blocker; shove him one way, and then pull him forward as you reach over the blocker with the opposite arm and move past him in the other direction, (swim technique). The defender should attempt to keep the blocker off balance and turned in one direction as quickly as possible so that he can move by him with ease.

COACHING POINTS: Reacting to Drop-Back Pass Protection

- Shove or push (do not slap or hit) at the helmet and shoulder pads of the blocker to knock or pull him off balance. Use feints, the swim technique and quick moves to get by him.
- Keep constant pressure, drive legs and work feet. Get to the passer!
- Don't let the blocker hold you—knock his hands away from you if he does.
- Look through the blocker at your target—the quarterback.
- If the blocker tries to cut your feet from under you, *do not fall over him*, pick up your feet and run over him as he lies.
- Tackle the quarterback high—wrap his arms up (both of them) in the tackle.

BASIC DEFENSIVE ALIGNMENT

Depending on the type of defensive front employed, a down lineman may be positioned in one of several basic positions.

FIGURE 10.7   Head-on Defensive Position

Head-On

This position is the most difficult position for an offensive lineman to block (when the defender is aligned head-up on the blocker). Figure 10.7 illustrates a head-on, or "on" position. The defender is responsible for both running lanes on either side of the blocker and must "read" the initial move of the blocker and react accordingly to the type of block.

Gap

Figure 10.8 illustrates a defender who has lined up in a "gap" position. Now either blocker may have the "angle" on the defender. However, this position allows

FIGURE 10.8   Gap Position

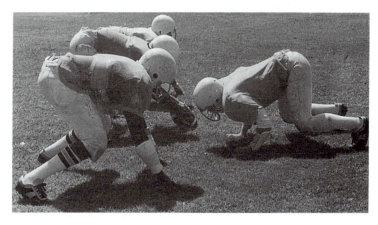

FIGURE 10.9   Goal Line Defensive Charge Position

the defender to penetrate quickly, and if he's not expected by the offense, he can cause trouble for their play development.

Goal Line

A similar gap position is often taken on the goal line. This "frog" position is illustrated in Figure 10.9. The positional play is described in Chapter 12 when the "1" technique is discussed in relation to the goal line defense (6–5 defense).

Inside-Outside Shade

An inside or outside shade position can be utilized by a down lineman in order to cut down on blocking angles or to alter the basic defensive set. Figure 10.10 illustrates an inside shade.

FIGURE 10.10   Inside Shade Defensive Position

FIGURE 10.11   Outside Shoulder Defense Position

An extension of this position moves the defender to the outside or inside shoulder of the blocker. Figure 10.11 shows the down lineman on the outside shoulder of the guard. This position comes close to a gap position, but the defender definitely covers the shoulder of the blocker.

In all of the above positions appropriate adjustments should be made by the linebackers to ensure that all running lanes are covered. Also the shifts are used in reaction to the total defensive alignment scheme.

THE DEFENSIVE LINEBACKER

The linebacker position is one of the most difficult jobs on defense. This is true for many reasons: (1) he must deliver and receive blows from a standing position, one that exposes his blocking surface to a blocker; (2) he is often blind-sided from linemen coming from the opposite side of the line; (3) he is responsible for filling or covering several holes or running lanes, thus he must be very aggressive; (4) he is responsible for lateral movement and must be mobile, with the ability to shed blockers rapidly without giving ground and reach the ball carrier or proper pursuit angle as quickly as possible; (5) he must be an aggressive and skillful tackler who can come up to meet the ball carrier on the LOS; (6) he must defend against the pass as well as the run, thus he must have the speed to get into the flat zone or the hook zone quickly or cover a back out of the backfield deep; and (7) being in an up position close to the LOS, he must be able to read keys, the flow of the ball and offensive movements quickly and accurately. This entails a knowledge of formation, down, distance to go, position of the ball, and score, as well as the strengths, weaknesses, and tendencies of the offense. The linebacker is also in a position to see if all of the defensive down linemen are properly aligned, and to tell them if they are not.

Linebackers, obviously, must possess great versatility. This means equal run and pass responsibility. The linebackers are concerned with an orderly series of preparations and reactions to defend against the offensive play. These preparations and reactions include:

1. Maintaining an advantageous stance
2. Neutralizing the offensive block while reading your key(s)
3. Maintaining position
4. Getting rid of the block
5. Pursuing the ball carrier
6. Making the tackle

The linebackers will usually line up over offensive linemen that are uncovered by defensive linemen, or they will be positioned so that they can cover one vacant area or several vacant areas:

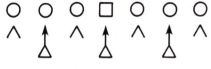

Linebacker Position

Linebacker Run Responsibilities from a Stack Defense

When there are an even number of linebackers (2 or 4) there will usually be an equal number on either side of the middle man in the offensive line. If there are an odd number of linebackers (1, 3, or 5), one is usually placed over the middle man in the offensive line. The others are placed over running lanes not protected by down linemen.

Two Linebackers   **Three Linebackers**

Four Linebackers   **Two Linebackers**

LINEBACKER STANCE

Linebackers should attempt to maintain a low hitting position to minimize the area exposed to the offensive blocker. They line up in a two-point stance, varying the distance off the LOS depending on the situation and/or players ability. A good guide for the closest position is that the toes of the linebacker should be aligned with the heels of the down linemen.

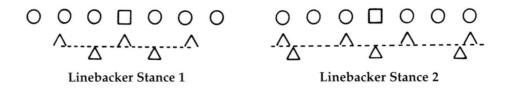

Linebacker Stance 1   **Linebacker Stance 2**

This position is very important and it should be reviewed throughout the season. If the linebacker positions himself closer to the LOS, his lateral pursuit is often cut off if one of the down linemen is blocked and driven back. If he gets farther away from the LOS he may be too late in responding to a play and closing the hole before a gain is made.

The weight should be equally distributed on the balls of the feet, which should be approximately shoulder width apart. The lower legs are flexed at the knees allowing the body to drop and crouch into a low hitting position. The middle linebacker (Mike) should have his feet parallel to the LOS but other linebackers are responsible for getting to the outside and moving laterally down the LOS. Thus, they should align themselves with the outside foot back (away from the blocker).

The position of the arms and hands varies with each player. Essentially, they should be in a position best designed to deliver a blow or hand shiver to the blocker. Whatever feels right for a player to prepare himself to do this should be the proper position for him, unless the coach sees that he is not warding off blockers well. In this case the coach should assist him by changing the player's arm and hand positions. The shoulders should be parallel to the LOS with the head up and the eyes looking through the key on the offensive line or backfield.

Figure 10.12 shows a typical linebacker stance.

FIGURE 10.12   A Typical Linebacker Stance

From this basic stance the linebacker should be ready to meet the pressure of the blocker without allowing himself to be turned or driven backward. His basic tools for doing this are the hand shiver (used mainly on cut-off blocks or hooks), the forearm lift (used on straight-ahead blocks) and the shoulder charge (used in conjunction with the forearm lift when defending a straight-ahead block). This is a last resort because it often gets the linebacker tied up with the blocker.

LINEBACKER TECHNIQUES

Reaction to a Head-On Block

This type of block represents the first and foremost job of a linebacker. As the ball is snapped, the linebacker sees the offensive blocker (back or lineman) charge straight at him. He should step up with the appropriate foot and deliver a good leverage blow (explode into the blocker, hitting him on the rise, with back arched at all times). This is crucial since the blocker has a running start on the linebacker and will drive him backward if not met with a full extension and explosive blow by the linebacker. He must keep his outside arm and leg free (if an outside line-backer), fighting through the pressure of the block looking into the backfield to find the football. His main objective is to neutralize the blocker's charge and drive him back into the hole or down into the ground. He must be cognizant of the proper pursuit angle and move to that position, shedding the blocker as quickly as possible.

COACHING POINTS: Reacting to a Head-on Block (Linebacker)

- Stay tense and react immediately by stepping up to meet the blocker and delivering a blow. Hit him—don't let him hit you.
- Attack the offensive blocker so that your arms and shoulders are lower than the shoulders of the blocker. Don't let the blocker get his hands on you.
- Keep your eyes in the backfield while you are seeing and feeling the blocker. Look through the blocker.
- Don't get turned—keep shoulders square to the LOS.
- Never get hooked or sealed off from the outside pursuit or the pursuit that gives you the best tackling angle.
- Never run around a block—fight through the pressure. Pivot or spin out as a *last resort* to get the outside.
- Do not give ground.
- Do not get caught in the "garbage" (stay clear of linemen's feet when pursuing).
- Your primary key is the football and you will usually be tackling from an inside-out position.

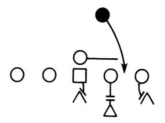

Reaction to Head-on Block

Reaction to a Reach Block

The second most frequent situation that a linebacker must be ready to stop is the wide play to his side. The offensive blocker will try to cut off the linebacker by (1) blocking him high, controlling him with his hands and sliding his head and body to one side in an effort to get between the ball and the linebacker or by (2) hitting him low and trying to knock the linebacker's feet out from under him.

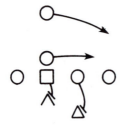

Reach Block by Guard

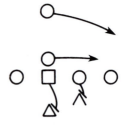

Reach Block by Center

Upon reading a high reach block attempt (and probably a backfield flow to the outside) the linebacker will lead step with the outside foot and attack the blocker with the inside shoulder. Neutralize the blocker while keeping the outside arm/leg free. It should be noted that the linebacker is attempting to keep his shoulders as square to the LOS as possible at all times. Having achieved an outside, or lateral, position, the linebacker should push or throw off the blocker and pursue the ball carrier parallel to the LOS, giving as little ground as possible.

COACHING POINTS: Reacting to a Reach Block (Linebacker)

- Work hard to get the outside position, staying as parallel to the LOS as possible.
- *Feel* the block—*look* into the backfield.
- Get rid of the blocker and pursue the ball carrier from an inside-out position.

Reaction to an Isolation Block

Any time a linebacker does not see or feel immediate pressure from an offensive lineman he should suspect that (1) a backfield man is coming through the line to block him; (2) he is going to be trapped by a pulling lineman or (3) someone missed his block. In the event of (1) or (2) the linebacker should immediately step up into the hole on the LOS and assume a low hitting position in an effort to block the running lane or clog up the hole. Reaction must be quick and the head and eyes should be active in an effort to determine where the block is coming from and where the football is. Keys should be consistent in playing the isolation block: If the back leads then the linebacker fills.

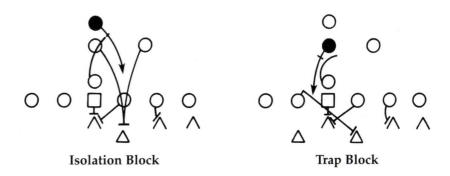

Isolation Block   **Trap Block**

A note should be added at this point to stress some basics concerning linebacker flow down the LOS. The linebacker should key by looking through the offensive down linemen and into the backfield. If no one blocks him immediately and he sees flow, it is possible that the offense will attempt to "cut him off at the pass" or around the offensive end.

COACHING POINTS: Reacting to an Isolation Block

- Step up quickly and deep into the LOS.
- Stay square to the LOS in a low hitting position with feet and legs churning.
- Meet the blocker with good leverage (body extended approximately at a 45°
  angle in a manner allowing you to become rigid when hit). Do not get driven
  back—"die in the hole" as a last resort.

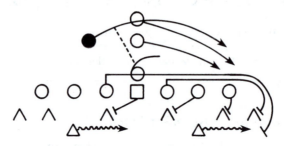

Linebacker Flow to Outside

It is quick reaction time when the linebacker feels no immediate blocking pressure. He needs to read the backfield flow quickly and attempt to determine his reaction and movement. However, he cannot flow too soon. If he does, he will often overrun the ball carrier and allow him to cut back upfield.

The flowing linebacker always steps laterally and slightly back with the outside foot (don't cross your feet) when the lineman he is keying pulls out. Pursuit

COACHING POINTS: Linebacker Flow

- Don't go for fakes. Read keys and find the football, then react quickly and with
  authority.
- Don't attempt to strike a blow too soon because you may get tied up on the LOS
  and be unable to flow laterally.
- If the flow goes away check for counter plays and reverses. Look for faces or
  opposite-colored jerseys. Don't commit yourself too soon. "Stay at home" for a
  split second, then flow. This general rule may be adverse to some defensive
  schemes.
- Always stay about a step-and-a-half *behind* the ball carrier. Remember when he
  turns up the field to close in and deliver a blow from the inside-out position.
- If the flow goes away and the offensive lineman you are covering pulls and you
  see faces coming toward you, *yell* "Reverse–Reverse" as loudly as you can and
  go meet the play.

should always be parallel to the LOS from an inside-out alignment with the feet under the body.

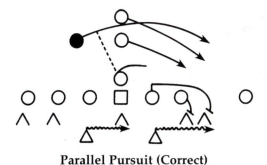

Parallel Pursuit (Correct)

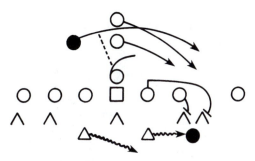

Diagonal Drop (Incorrect)

Reaction to Pass Block

The linebacker should always be cognizant of a possible passing play. When his keys (either the quarterback preparing to pass or "reading" the offensive block) show pass, the linebacker should immediately move to his specific area of coverage, which is usually the hook or curl area. The linebacker should also know where the other defenders are supposed to be covering, the field position, and the possible pass patterns. It is extremely important that the linebackers react quickly to this situation, as they have a critical role in the total pass defense scheme. When the passer sets up to throw, the linebacker should set up: this means getting under control so that he can move to the ball when it is thrown. The feet should be moving constantly and the linebacker should be looking for receivers coming into or across his zone, as well as the passer's eyes, arm, and motion.

In dropping to pass zone area, the linebacker should take an initial step forward and then drop back quickly while using shuffle steps. He should never take his eyes off the passer and never turn his back on the passer before the ball is thrown. Usually the linebacker may, after stepping with his outside foot, cross his inside foot to the outside, running backward, while looking at the passer over his inside shoulder. The job of the linebacker is to get to his zone in the quickest possible time.

Having reached his zone or area the linebacker may encounter several situations. In many instances the offensive linemen may use blocking schemes to make the play look like a pass such as:

1. A *fold block* is becoming more common even though it is difficult for a junior high school player to execute.

Fold Block

2. A *draw play* (fakes—the offense fakes a pass then runs over the area the linebacker has vacated).

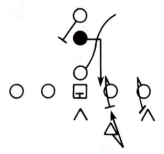

Linebacker Reaction to Draw Play

The defender's golden rule of "fighting through the pressure" applies in this situation. Step up to meet the block while staying parallel to the LOS. The linebacker must be cognizant of keeping his outside arm free but should attempt to drive the blocker back into the hole.

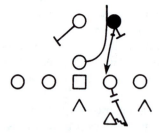

**Linebacker Reacting to Draw Play
by Fighting through Blocker**

A linebacker has several other situations to which he must react and at the same time be cognizant of run possibilities:

3. A *back out of the backfield* is an offensive back swinging out from the backfield into the flat after faking a pass protection block. A back swinging out is not always the linebacker's responsibility.

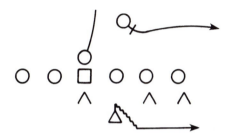

Linebacker Flow to First Back Out

4. A *screen pass*—(fake long pass then pass to the flat with blockers forming a wall, or "screen," in front of the receiver(s).

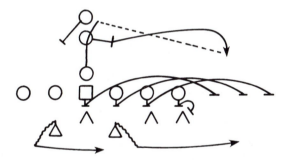

Linebacker Reaction to Screen Pass

COACHING POINTS: Reacting to a Pass Block (Linebacker)

- When you read pass, drop quickly, *staying turned to the outside,* and move to your zone. *Keep the passer in view* and as many receivers as possible in your peripheral vision.
- Always knock down any receiver you can. Just knocking him off stride will upset the timing of many passes.
- When the passer sets, looks, and starts to throw, get under control and break for the intended direction of the ball.
- Watch the passer's eyes and throwing arm.

5. The passer decides to run.
6. Other—if none of the above happens, then the linebacker should continue to watch for receivers coming into his zone and knock down anyone who tries to cross through, come into, or approach his zone (if the ball hasn't been thrown yet). If no receiver is coming and the passer is still looking (because the defensive linemen haven't got to him yet!) then the linebacker should prepare to defend in-depth against a long pass or trick play.

TACKLING

The three basic elements of football, according to most authorities, are blocking, tackling, and running. In considering defense, tackling becomes foremost of these "big three." The ultimate goal of all defensive players is to tackle the man with the ball as quickly as possible following the snap or kick or pass reception. Every defensive player must think that he is going to make the tackle on every play. The proper teaching of tackling is the most tedious job and difficult responsibility of a coach.

The mechanics of tackling are not complicated and the basic fundamentals apply at all levels of the game. However, the coach should be ever cognizant of the fact that successful tackling is much more than a mastery of basics. Desire, instinct, and innate ability all play extremely important roles in tackling.

More good football players have been "run off" in drills involving tackling than in any other activity. A broad statement to make? Not really. In observing football coaches, particularly at the youth football league and junior high school level, we find coaches who line up youngsters ten yards or more apart and command them to run at full speed colliding head-on. The tackler is supposed to put the ball carrier on his back, all the while hearing the coach screaming, "Hit, Hit, Hit"—"Wrap him up"—"Move those feet"—"Drive through him"—"Punish the ball carrier," and so on. Consider the situation. This is no way to teach a youngster anything.

It is not, *absolutely not,* necessary to have full-speed tackling drills, especially with players twelve years old or younger, to teach tackling fundamentals. Instead, run, pass, and even block full speed in practice, but tackle full speed *only* in a scrimmage or game.

Of all the phases of football that take courage, the skill of tackling should head the list. One should begin slowly with young players and work up to half or three-quarter speed in all tackling drills throughout the season. Tackling is something beginners need to do every day, for it is a crucial element of defense. "Men and boys separate at the goal line" because of the ability to hit *and* tackle.

Straight Ahead Tackling

Although a defender seldom gets to tackle a ball carrier squarely head-on in a game, the technique for this situation is the basis for all aspects of tackling. We strongly recommend that coaches refrain from using the terms "head on the numbers," or "head," or "face" in an effort to eliminate using the helmet as a weapon. After sprinting for the ball carrier, the player must break down into a hitting position. This means getting the body under control by dropping the hips, getting the legs under the body's center of gravity, feet chopping up and down, knees bent, head up, and eyes on belt buckle (or other target, such as the number) of the ball carrier. The tackler should be moving into the ball carrier at all times rather than standing still and waiting. The tackler extends his body forward keeping his eyes open. Just prior to contact, the tackler will slide his head to one side and plant a shoulder on the target (football?), as he drives his legs and wraps his arms around the runner and attempts to lock his hands behind the ball carrier. (Some coaches advocate wrapping arms around the thighs of the ball carrier and then lifting). This sequence of movements should enable the defender to (1) drive through the opponent, (2) lift the opponent off the ground, or (3) stop the opponent at that spot and drive him to the ground. Ideally the tackler should end up on top of the ball carrier if the tackle has been well executed. Figure 10.13 illustrates the first phase of a tackler who is contacting the ball while Figures 10.14 and 10.15 illustrate the now illegal and dangerous mistake of tacklers who lower the head and

**FIGURE 10.13   Correct Head Position When
Tackling (Helmet on the Ball Position)**

**FIGURE 10.14   Incorrect Head Position
When Tackling—Potentially Dangerous**

close the eyes or make initial contact with the head or facemask. This can cause serious neck injury and possible paralysis.

Angle Tackling

As any viewer watching Monday night football can observe, most tackles are made from the side. In this instance, the task of the defender is to get his body between the opponent and the tackler's goal line and stop forward progress. The best way to achieve this goal is to maintain an inside-out position. Drive the head and body up and across or in front of the ball carrier, developing as much forceful extension as possible. Lock up the hands or grab hold of any piece of the opponent within grasp. Keep the feet moving with short, driving steps. This maneuver should turn the ball carrier as the tackler continues to twist in the direction of rotation while pulling the ball carrier around and down. If on the sideline, the defender has the choice of trying to knock the runner out of bounds or shooting his body across the face of the runner (to opposite shoulder) forcing the runner to cut back into the field of play (hopefully where help is coming) instead of continuing down the sideline.

**FIGURE 10.15 Potentially Dangerous
"Face in the Numbers" Position**

COACHING POINTS: Tackling

- Keep your head up and your eyes open at all times, especially prior to and at the moment of contact.
- Don't overextend or wait too long to extend your body into the opponent. Time your hit so that you can get the full force of your fully extended legs. Ideally the body should approximate a 45° angle with the ground at the moment of impact.
- Shorten your stride as you approach the ball carrier and use short, choppy steps prior to the hit.
- Drive through the opponent. Run through the opponent. Drive your feet until the whistle blows.
- Your target should be the ball.
- Lock up. Get your arms around the man and lock your hands together or grab his jersey or anything else. A good hit without holding on is worthless.
- Hold on—help is on the way.

Teaching tackling is not difficult, given the proper coaching philosophy and an inspired youngster. You should pay special attention to the applicable drills in Appendix B to examine the suggestions for tackling instruction and practice.

The two instances of tackling given above relate primarily to those tackles made close (±5 yards) to the LOS. As stated earlier, tackling the ball carrier is the job of the down linemen and linebackers. However, there are times (few, hopefully) when your secondary people will have to make an open field tackle on a runner who has broken through the LOS and run past the linebackers. This type of tackle is very difficult in that (1) the ball carrier has built up momentum and (2) there is plenty of room for the ball carrier to maneuver. If the opponent is in the middle of the field it becomes a matter more closely resembling the straight-ahead tackle. Most runners will try to fake out or run around a tackler. Thus it is extremely important for the tackler to keep his head up and his eyes open focusing on the belt buckle of the runner. The decision to tackle high or to attempt to knock the runners feet out from under him is made based on the size, speed of the runner or skill of the tackler. If you don't knock the runners feet out from under him, it is very important to wrap up or grab anything and hold on, if possible.

If the runner decides to run over the tackler it becomes a matter of the tackler hitting an extended blow, grabbing something, and holding on. It will help if the tackler is moving into the runner in a controlled manner. In fact, this is essential because a ball carrier will surely run over a stationary tackler in the majority of cases.

As discussed earlier, if the ball carrier is near the sideline the tackler's main concern is to keep him from continuing down the sideline. The success depends on leverage and proper timing. The drill section will illustrate this procedure more clearly and the reader is referred to that section at this time to get a better picture of sideline tackling.

CLASS ACTIVITIES

1. Have each member of the class fire out against a bell dummy or sled. Have other class members give coaching points or corrective comments.

2. Have groups of four arrange themselves into three offensive linemen and one defensive linemen. Have the defender react to various blocking schemes (walk through the motions).

3. Have students pair up as linebackers in a 52 defense. Have each pair react to movement of an offensive backfield.

4. Have the class observe and evaluate the linebacker or defensive line play of a local high school or college game.

5. Use films and evaluate the line and linebacker play. Rate the players based on their performance.

6. Have each student develop two drills which would help practice or develop defensive skills.

11

DEFENSIVE SECONDARY STRATEGY
AND TECHNIQUES

Chapter Objectives

After completing this chapter, the reader should be able to:

- Give the strengths and weaknesses of a two-, three-, or four-man secondary.
- Perform the stance of secondary players and their reactions to different situations.
- View a game or films and identify the type of coverage.

BASIC ALIGNMENT CONCEPTS

No other phase of defensive football requires the type of coordinated effort that the defensive secondary does, nor are mistakes made by the defense so obvious to the typical fan. Since the individuals who play the secondary are the last line of defense between the offense and the goal line, many hours of practice go into this phase of defensive football. The defensive secondary is a containing unit, with a primary goal of preventing the opponent from either running, or more importantly, passing into their end zone.

This section will describe the general techniques, responsibilities, and situations common to those players and their various positions. We should begin by stating that a secondary unit is just that—secondary. They are a second line of defense that traditionally is expected to be responsible for pass protection. As previously discussed, we position down linemen and linebackers to stop all running lanes and give the linebackers the dual responsibility of playing both the run and the pass. On the other hand, secondary defensive personnel should be initially thinking and reacting to the pass on every snap of the ball. The defensive secondary unit, then, always plays pass *first* and run *second*. As a last resort they should be making tackles on ball carriers who come through the LOS.

Each member of the defensive secondary can be aligned in a variety of positions. Most secondary units will be composed of a three-deep "diamond" secondary or a four-deep "umbrella" secondary. Occasionally a two-deep secondary unit will be found.

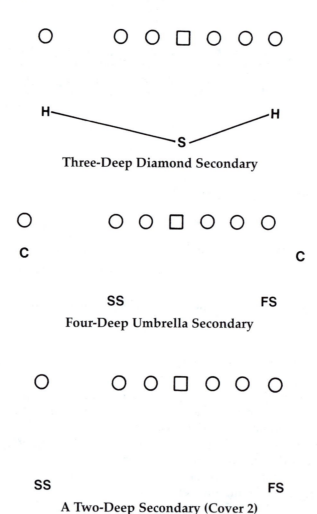

Three-Deep Diamond Secondary

Four-Deep Umbrella Secondary

A Two-Deep Secondary (Cover 2)

These secondary people are the "containing" unit of the defense. If you look back at the other two units of the defense (line and linebackers), you can readily see that the secondary unit's job is made easier if (1) the defensive line puts on an aggressive rush, causing the passer to hurry his throw and limiting the receiver's running time and (2) the line and linebacker knock down or cover all possible receivers.

This, however, is seldom the case, especially with younger players and even in professional football! Some coaches feel at least seven men are needed to rush the passer, or at least seven men should drop back to cover receivers. The general rule is that if four men rush, seven men are involved in pass coverage; if seven men rush, four are back in pass coverage; or if three men rush, eight men are involved in coverage. Any combination is possible, depending on the situation and the players' ability.

OBJECTIVES OF THE SECONDARY

There are three basic pass defenses: zone, man-for-man and combination. All have the same primary objectives:

1. Prevent the long run by forming a pocket when the ball carrier breaks into the secondary.
2. Defend against the pass.
3. Prevent the long pass (long score).
4. Keep pass completions to a minimum.
5. Intercept as many passes as possible.
6. Score.

Defenses, however, can be played differently and there are many coverages within each secondary. Thus, the general category of *zone defenses* includes two-, three-, or four-deep zones; invert zones; revert zones; and others. With man-for-man defenses two-deep, three-deep, and four-deep coverages are used, all of which use linemen and linebackers.

Combination-type secondary units may find the linebackers and ends playing man-for-man while the secondary plays zone. More sophisticated football requires secondaries to go to great lengths to disguise the type of coverage used. Some will line up in one set (zone) and on the snap of the ball revert to man-for-man coverage, hoping to confuse both passers and receivers.

These are advanced techniques, however, and with young players the coach should always "keep it simple." This applies to all areas of the game, especially to the type of secondary coverage the coach will have his players memorize and respond to. In the face of all this, keep in mind that the perfectly executed pass play, like a perfectly executed run, is impossible to stop.

ZONE COVERAGES

In zone coverage, the secondary defenders must stay between the receivers and the end zone, or play as deep as the deepest receiver. The secondary moves as a

COACHING POINTS: Pass Coverage (General)

- Try to know where any help is coming from.
- Line up correctly, keeping proper spacing between you and your teammates.
- Keep adequate cushion between receivers when covering (not closer than one-and-a-half yards before the ball is thrown).
- Always talk to your teammates.
- Always have one defender deeper than the deepest receiver no matter how many men are in his zone.
- Everyone break for the ball when it is thrown.
- Hit with authority at every opportunity.

unit, with all members rotating or dropping back in unison, keeping all receivers contained. The defenders *never* turn their backs on the passer and they attempt to keep all receivers in front of them. "Never" is a big word. If a receiver has beaten the defender, then the defender must turn and run to get the receiver. In addition, when the field is divided into various zones each defender is responsible for *his* zone and does not leave it until the ball is thrown. Communication is crucial when playing zone. When the ball is thrown, all players react directly to the ball and go to it quickly, hoping to intercept the ball, knock the pass down, or dive through the receiver knocking the ball out of his hands or tackling him at the spot of reception.

Advantages of the Zone Secondary

1. Makes better use of average or inexperienced personnel.
2. Adapts better to slower players.
3. It is easier to defend the run when playing zone.
4. Allows more players to break when the ball is thrown.
5. Affords greater safety against the flat and medium seam passes (passes completed in the area between two defenders).
6. Is easier to teach to younger players.
7. It is possible to have a free safety when playing split receivers.

For clarification, we will divide zone coverages into categories of straight and rotational zone coverages.

Straight Zone Coverages

Two-deep Zone.   This alignment has two halfbacks (H) or safeties (S) who align with the inside foot forward, two-point stance, and who are responsible for one-half of the field.

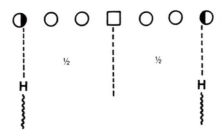

Two-deep Zone Alignment

No matter where the ball goes, the two defenders play pass first, covering any receivers in their half of the field. Generally, these two men align themselves on the inside shoulder of the offensive end and play approximately seven to ten yards from the LOS. Alignment is in halves (that is, two defenders each covering one half of the field). The coverage cannot be on a particular man but on the location of the ball and on the field area that needs to be covered.

Three-deep Zone.   With three defensive men back, the field is divided into thirds with each man covering one-third of the field.

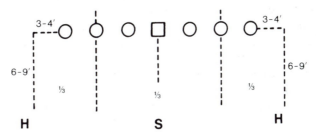

Three-deep Zone Alignment

The halfbacks generally align with the inside foot footward three to four yards outside the offensive end and from six to nine yards deep. The safety aligns directly over the center man on the LOS, approximately nine to twelve yards deep, with his feet parallel. Each man will cover any receiver coming into his zone and will leave his zone *only* when he is sure the ball has been thrown or the passer is running. In either case, the halfbacks' approach is made from an outside-in angle. The safety is just that—the last line of defense. He makes sure the halfbacks have turned the runner in before making the tackle. If the play goes away from the halfbacks, they must stay in their zone until they are absolutely certain it is not a pass. Then they will pursue across the field to intercept the ball carrier.

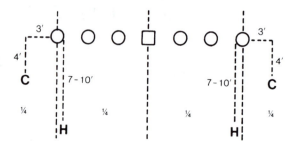

Four-deep Zone Alignment

Four-deep Zone.   The four-deep zone is generally composed of two cornerbacks (C) and two halfbacks or safeties.

The cornerbacks align approximately three yards outside the offensive end and four yards deep. The inside foot is forward, with a two-point stance. The halfbacks align on the inside eye of the offensive end, seven to ten yards deep with the inside foot forward in a two-point stance. Again, no matter where the ball goes, so long as there is a possibility of a pass, the defenders stay in their one-fourth of the field, until the ball passes the LOS.

The secondary defense illustrated in the preceding figure is mainly used against the long pass. Since this is not a great threat in football below the college level more complex pass defense specifics are not expanded on in this text. It should be sufficient to say that the straight zone is simple to teach and does not require excellent athletes to make it work. However, it is very weak (1) in the seams (areas between defenders), (2) against short passes and flat passes, (3) against flooding (more than one receiver in a zone), (4) against diagonal pass patterns run across the field, and (5) against any weakside option play.

Generally one halfback is designated as the "strong safety (SS)" and lines up to the tight end side, or wide side of field or formation or scouting call. The other safety is often called the "free safety (FS)" and generally lines up to the split end side, weak side of the formation, field position or scouting call.

The following diagrams illustrate two types of passes designed to beat a straight zone coverage. It should be remembered, however, that these do not show the human element of defense, or how the players will respond and how quickly. In addition, against any defensive set a coach can draw an offensive play that will beat it—on *paper*!

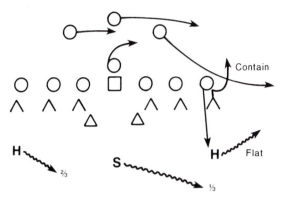

Pass to Beat Straight Zone Coverage (A)

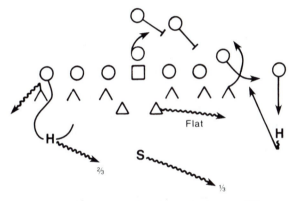

Pass to Beat Straight Zone Coverage (B)

Rotational Zone

This type of defensive alignment attempts to roll with the flow of the ball or toward the strength of the offensive formation. The following material discusses both three- and four-deep zone coverages, with an additional explanation of four-deep zone coverage systems in Chapter 12. Rotational zones require the defenders to leave their zone to cover the next adjacent zone as the play or flow dictates. The diagram below shows the rotation of the three-deep zone to the flow of the ball while the following diagram illustrates a similar rotation to the strength of the formation.

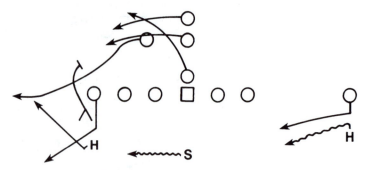

Three Deep Reaction to Flow

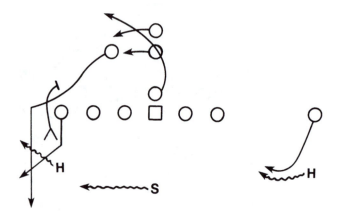

Three Deep Rotation to Formation Strength

In both of these formations, the halfback who is toward the flow of the ball or toward the offensive formation strength comes up to cover the flat while the safety covers the deep, one-third area. The offside halfback (back away from the flow of the ball) will protect the other two-thirds of the field assisted by another player, such as a linebacker. The defensive end nearest the flow can be responsible for containing any running plays while the defensive end away from the flow drops back to cover the backside flat or deep one-third.

Weaknesses in this type of defense are similar to those of the straight zone, with the additional problem of the distance that the offside halfback and corner or safety must travel. The offside halfback must cover the middle third of the field. The onside halfback must move quickly to an area deep outside, leaving the area behind the cornerback covering the flat open. The diagrams below illustrate possible patterns to exploit the weak areas of the rotational zone. The safety cannot react quickly enough to cover the end or the LBer cannot react quickly enough to cover the back out or the backfield.

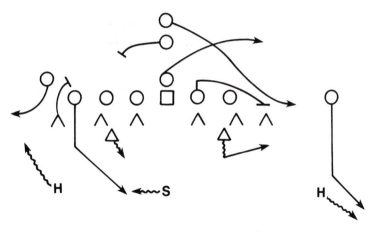

Safety Covering an End

The following diagram shows the end faking a pattern into the flat then breaking back up field.

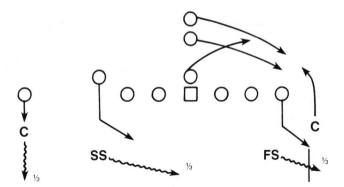

Faking One and Running Another Pattern

An additional drawback to the rotational zone is that once the zone begins to rotate in one direction the backside becomes vulnerable, as illustrated in the following diagram.

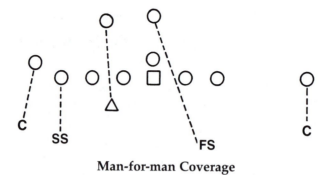

Vulnerable Backside

In the situation above you have a one-to-one coverage with either the defensive end dropping off and covering the flat and the linebacker covering the quarterback or vice versa. Either way, it will be tough to cover the man in the flat. Some teams play so that the rotating zone rotates back with the quarterback.

Four-deep Rotations.   The four-deep zone is generally considered a better balanced defense. Generally one man covers the flat area while the other three rotate to cover any deep patterns. The direction of rotation is determined by the backfield flow, by the strength of the formation, or by a predetermined call (according to down, distance, situation).

The secondary can also play man-for-man defense, as illustrated in the following diagram.

Man-for-man Coverage

COACHING POINTS: Zone Coverage

- On the snap of the ball, secondary men should shuffle back or backpedal several steps to determine their rotation.
- Play each man in your zone as closely and as deeply as possible while he is in your zone. Watch the quarterback and break hard for the ball.
- If the man leaves your zone, yell to the adjacent defender and let him know.
- Cover the deepest receiver if more than one man comes into your zone.
- If two men come downfield on one side, the halfback (or corner) covers the outside and the safety (or halfback) covers the inside.
- Keep a cushion (a space) between you and the receiver. Leave just enough yardage so that you (1) can come up and get with him if the ball is thrown to him in front of you, or (2) can accelerate if he puts on a burst of speed and tries to pass you. As a general rule you can tell an experienced player to allow a three to four yard cushion, but this will vary depending upon the speed of the defender as well as the speed of the receiver.
- Shuffle step looking over your shoulder at the passer and/or the receiver. If you must change directions, open up toward the line of scrimmage, (don't let your feet get tangled up), and change directions as quickly as you can.
- When the ball is thrown, forget everything else and converge on it with aggressive play.

We wish to emphasize again that throwback passes are effective, but they require an effective throwing quarterback and lots of time to develop.

MAN-FOR-MAN COVERAGE

The term *man-for-man* is self-explanatory. Each defender is assigned a possible offensive receiver, and if a pass develops, he covers that receiver (staying between the receiver and the end zone) wherever he goes. The defender will react to whatever his key (or man) does on the snap of the ball. If he releases and appears to be coming downfield for a pass, the defender will play pass. If he blocks, the defender will play run. If he fakes a block and then goes into a pass pattern, the defender is called upon to read quickly enough to change his course and stay between his man and the goal line. The secondary man must be constantly aware of the total flow of the backfield and the play development as he reacts to the fake (probably by taking his initial step back, then moving up and reacting to the run). The diagram on the next page illustrates the possible pass patterns a cornerback might see when in man coverage.

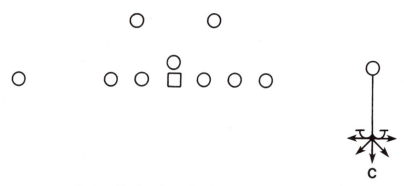

**Corner Backs Covering Wide Receivers Face
a Variety of Possible Pass Patterns**

Professional football probably has made the best impact on people's understanding of one-on-one, open field coverage where you have an excellent split or wide receiver covered by one defensive man, both of whom are isolated from the rest of the team:

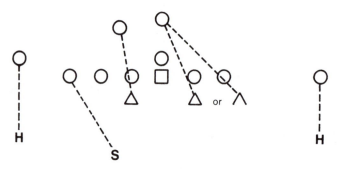

A Typical Professional Alignment

The variety of possible moves combined with the speed of some receivers makes this an exciting aspect of any professional game. However, with younger players, the receivers will not be as fast, and the quarterbacks will not be as effective. Nevertheless, the receiver is still running a pattern that both he and the quarterback know. This gives the edge to the receiver. Fakes are much more effective as a method of getting open (for instance, a head-and-shoulder fake to the outside, by a receiver who plants his outside foot and breaks to the inside. If the defender is playing too close, he may get his body moving to the outside, and it will be tough to change directions and maintain coverage).

The defender leans over at the waist so that the head and upper body are slightly in front of the feet (chin over toes) as the player backpedals, the arms are pumped close to the body and the chin is kept in front of the toes (or in front of knees). *Reach back with the feet, don't push back with the toes,* as this will cause the

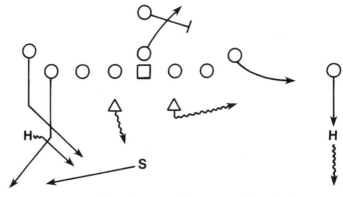

Man-for-man Coverage (A)

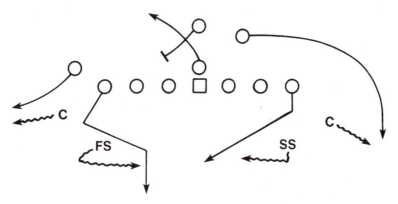

Man-for-man Coverage (B)

shoulders to rise and the head to come up, making it more difficult to reverse or change directions.

Man-for-man coverage, like zone coverage, can be employed by two-, three-, or four-deep secondaries, although it most commonly uses three- and four-deep defensive halfbacks and corners *plus* additional linebackers and/or ends. The diagrams above illustrate the type of assignments that can be used by various sets.

It should be evident that with three or four defensive secondary players, an end or linebacker is needed to cover the other eligible receivers. In addition, if one of the backs who is assigned to a deep defender does not go out into the pattern, that defender can play free safety and assist where needed. Play action passes are used against man defenses because they look like running plays (which bring the defenders up) and then develop into passing plays. These types of plays also hold or freeze the linebackers from assisting in pass defense as they must respect any faking back into the line by staying home. ("Staying home" should tell your players to remain in their position for a few counts before flowing or moving to another position).

COACHING POINTS: Man-for-man Coverage

- Always try to know the speed of the man you are covering, and leave an appropriate cushion.
- Concentrate on the man's belt buckle because that will move the least while he is trying a head-and-shoulder fake. Keep weight well forward and over the center of gravity.
- Don't get your feet crossed, and never turn your back on the passer unless you are beaten and must run to catch the receiver. In this case, try to watch the receiver's eyes and anticipate when you should turn to look for the ball.
- When the ball is thrown you must quickly close the gap between you and the receiver.
- Play through the receiver to get the ball. Time your hit so that you arrive at the same time as the ball.
- Unless you are sure you can intercept the ball, do not cut in front of the receiver to attempt to catch the ball.

Man-for-man coverage is not used extensively with inexperienced players. Because of the lack of maturity of reaction time, coordination, and neuromuscular skills, it is extremely hard for a defensive back to cover one man effectively, especially if the quarterback has adequate time and ability to throw.

With the split receiver formations seen today, it becomes necessary in many instances to play a combination zone and man coverage. The split receiver is taken by a corner or halfback man-for-man, while the rest of the secondary and linebackers play a zone defense.

Players younger than college age need constant practice in man-to-man coverage, and there is no half-speed or individual way to practice. To get the timing for covering a pass receiver as he comes toward the defender, feinting, faking, and finally cutting into his pass route, the receiver and defender should be moving at full speed.

CLASS ACTIVITIES

1. Arrange the class into groups of four. Have four align themselves in a four-spoke defensive secondary and have the unit flow and rotate with a quarterback and the ball.

2. Repeat the same procedure as above except use groups of three and rotate or cover man-for-man using only three defensive secondary men.

3. Have class members cover a pass receiver man-for-man while receiving passes from the quarterback.

4. Attend a local high school or college game and concentrate on the secondary coverage.

5. Diagram and explain two drills (other than those in the drill section) to work on secondary techniques.

12

A SPECIFIC DEFENSIVE SYSTEM

Chapter Objectives

After completing this chapter, the reader should be able to:

- Draw the basic 5–4 defensive formation indicating the basic alignment of each player.
- Discuss the specific responsibilities of each position on the 5–4 defense.
- Diagnose correct alignment and reaction moves of each position on the 5–4 defense.
- Illustrate various defensive shifts from the basic alignment.
- Discuss various secondary coverages and playing techniques.
- Be able to explain the specifics of a goal line/short yardage defense.

WOLVERINE DEFENSE

Defensive Huddle

```
                    RLB
        LE    LT    N    RT    RE
        LC   LLB   LH   RH    RC
            Defensive Huddle
```

Right Linebacker (RLB).   Line up two yards from the ball with your back to the LOS. When the huddle forms, RLB will cup hands and give defensive alignment call and stunts.

Nose (N).   Line up facing RLB, hands on knees, eyes looking at RLB. Huddle begins with N.

Tackles (LT & RT).   Left tackle will line up on the left side of N; right tackle will line up on right side of N; both with eyes on RLB, hands on knees.

Ends (LE & RE).   Left end will line up on the left side of the LT, right end will line up on the right side of the RT; hands on knees, eyes on RLB.

Left Halfback (LH).   Line up directly behind N. Hands on hips. Left half will give secondary coverage (if needed) after RLB has given defensive alignment.

Left Linebacker (LLB).   Line up to the left of LH with hands on hips, eyes on RLB.

Left Corner (LC).   Line up to the left LLB with hands on hips, eyes on RLB.

Right Halfback (RH).   Line up to the right of LH, hands on hips, eyes on RLB.

Right Corner (RC).   Line up to the right of RH, hands on hips, eyes on RLB.

Huddle Procedure
1. N sets huddle. Everyone in place, remaining silent.
2. RLB will cup hands and give the defensive call.
3. LH will call the type of secondary coverage (if needed).
4. RLB will then say "BREAK" with the remaining team clapping their hands once—huddle breaks.

HUDDLE DISCIPLINE IS A MUST!!!

59 Defense

The basic alignment is shown in the following diagram, with running lanes labelled *A, B, C,* and *D*.

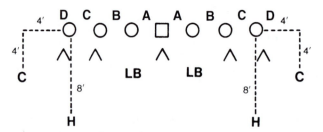

Defense: Basic Alignment

Nose (0 Technique)

Line up head-on the center. Distance from the football will vary depending on the situation. Play the center's head with a quick hand shiver on the snap of the ball.

When you make contact with the center, your feet are parallel to the LOS. If the quarterback goes straight back to pass, the 0 technique is responsible for the draw play—he then rushes the passer. If it is a run instead of a pass play, you will keep the center away from your blocking surface, not permitting yourself to be tied up in the middle of the line. Pursue the ball by taking the proper angle (depending on the type of running play). Play through the center's head. Your prime duty is to control the running lanes on either side of the offensive center (A & B gaps).

Keys

1. If the guard and center double team—fight through lead block.
2. If the center blocks out—fight through his head to far shoulder.
3. If the center drops back for pass protection—rush the passer.
4. If the guard blocks on you—fight through his head to far shoulder.
5. If the guard pulls behind center—step toward other guard and key guard—center block.

Tackles (5 Technique)

Line up on the outside eye of the offensive tackle, with your feet staggered (outside foot back in most cases). On the snap of the ball employ a forearm lift or hand shiver charge into the tackle. As you make contact your back foot is brought up even with your front foot. You have 75 percent off-tackle responsibility, and you should never be blocked in by only one man. If it is a straight back pass, you should rush the passer from the inside-out. If the play comes toward you, neutralize the tackle's block, find the football, and tackle. You must be certain to keep the offensive blocker in front of you at all times—you can be eliminated from the play very easily if you try to go around the blocker. If the play goes away from you, pursue the football. Your prime duty is to keep the offensive tackle off our linebackers and control the running lane over the offensive tackle (C gap).

Keys

1. If the tackle blocks out—fight pressure for inside play.
2. If the end blocks down—fight through pressure for outside play.
3. If the tackle releases to the inside—come to balance immediately and look for trap; if there is no trap—look for the counter and play the football.
4. If the tackle drops for pass protection—execute a hard rush employing pass rush techniques.

Ends

Line up, splitting the outside foot of the offensive end. You should line up fourteen inches off the LOS with most of the weight on your outside foot (which is back). When the ball is snapped, take a short step with your inside foot toward the offensive end, and at the same time deliver a hand or forearm shiver to the shoulder of the offensive end. If the offensive end blocks in and the play comes toward you, immediately look for the near halfback or the trapper, expecting to be blocked by either offensive man. The man playing the end technique must deliver a good blow to the offensive end *on every play* and never get hooked in (blocked or sealed off to the inside). You are responsible for D gap or running lane off the hip of the end.

Keys

1. If the play comes toward you—tackle the quarterback if he is attempting an option.
2. If the quarterback fakes to a back coming over your area—"search" the back first to be sure he doesn't have the ball.
3. If the flow goes away—you are the trailman. Get as deep as the deepest offensive man and watch for reverses.
4. If the quarterback drops straight back as if to pass, rush from the outside in— do not let the quarterback scramble to your outside.

Linebackers

Line up on the outside eye of their respective offensive guards, and read through them into the offensive backfield. This position will be approximately two yards from the ball. Maintain a balanced stance with the inside foot forward, no more than a "toe–heel" relationship.

If the play comes toward you, you are directly responsible for plays coming over your respective guard (A & B gap). On plays going outside your end, you become the second contain man, staying one step behind the ball carrier, tackling from the inside out. If the offensive flow and the ball go away from you, first check any counterplay action (a play coming back to your side opposite the main offensive flow), then shuffle down the LOS and pursue—don't overrun the ball carrier. If the quarterback drops straight back (any place between the offensive tackle's position) to pass, quickly open up to the outside and sprint to your side hook zone. Check the flat. Set up eight to ten yards deep.

Keys

1. Never be hooked by the guard.
2. Keep your outside arm free.
3. Always play the run from the inside out. Do not overrun.
4. Be aggressive at all times.
5. Check the alignment of the down linemen on your side.
6. Watch the quarterback's eyes and react as he looks.
7. Play the blocker's head.
8. Read the block of the offensive guard and key the ball.

Secondary Coverage

The diagram on page 174 illustrates the depth and width of the secondary defenders in the four-spoke defensive alignment when the ball is in the middle of the field (between the hash marks.) All defensive secondary men on the snap of the ball will shuffle-step, chin over toes, (take short, quick steps without crossing or overlapping the feet) backwards two steps and then react to the flow or the ball.

The Defensive Corner.   Line up about four yards wide and four yards deep, crouched in a relaxed stance with arms hanging loosely, feet at a 45° angle to the LOS, outside foot back. Key or read the offensive half back closest to you, and the nearest end. The reaction of the corner man will be determined by his keys (offensive end and near halfback).

Keys

1. If the end blocks in and the backs come toward the corner man—come up and contain the play quickly.
2. If the end or back comes out and does not block and the ball comes—turn to the outside, sprint back eight yards and get set to cover your short one-fourth area (flat).
3. If the end and/or back comes out and does not block and the ball goes away—sprint back and get in a position to cover the outside deep one-third zone.
4. If the end and/or back blocks and the ball goes away, shuffle in place—check counter, drop off and sprint deep.

The corner is the contain man (TE side). It is his job to turn all running plays to the inside. If the corner covers a split receiver run containment will shift to E or LB depending on situation.

The Defensive Halfbacks.   Line up eight yards deep on the outside shade of the offensive end in a 45° angle to the LOS. The outside foot is back. On the snap of the ball, shift your weight, shuffle two steps to the outside while reading the block of the near end and the near back. These keys will help you determine the flow or direction of the ball. If the play comes toward you, force all plays from the outside in. Cover the deep outside or deep middle if pass is indicated. If the play goes away revolve and replace the other halfback, then react to the play. If a drop back pass is shown, move to your one-third zone coverage responsibility on the first indication of pass.

Keys

1. If the end and the back block and the ball comes toward you—come up to the inside and play the run.
2. If the end and the back release and the ball comes toward you—drop off and out quickly to cover deep outside one-third zone.

3. If the end and the back block and the ball goes away from you—shuffle in place for two counts and check for counters and reverses and move to the middle one-third zone.
4. Never let a pass receiver behind you.
5. Think pass play first and running play second.

This defense is a keying and reacting defense. React to your keys. Find the football, and move with the rest of the defensive secondary as a *unit!!!*

ADJUSTMENTS TO FLOW AND FORMATION

Shown below are various offensive sets and flows that might be encountered during a season. Adjustments will be made from week to week depending on who the opponent will be. These figures show the general picture of possible adjustments that could be developed from the basic defense:

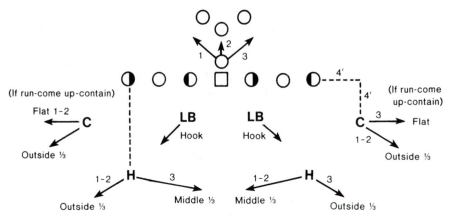

Basic Coverage Responsibilities (Right or Left)

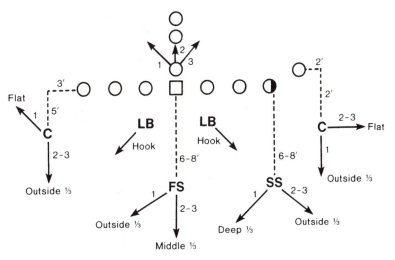

Wing Set (Right or Left)

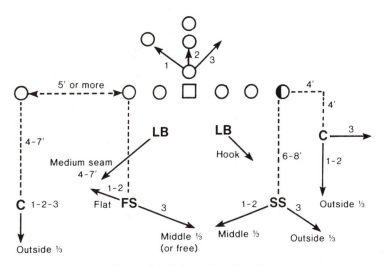

Split End (Right or Left)—Invert

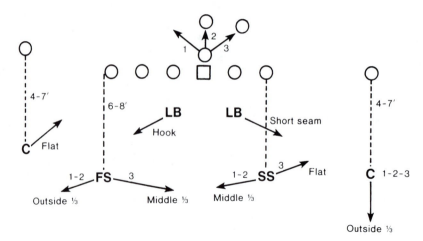

Pro Set (Split End and Flanker)

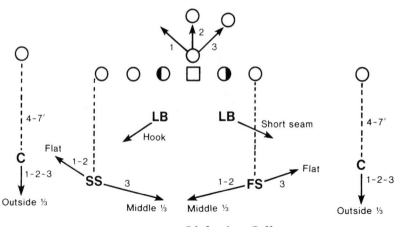

Lightning Call

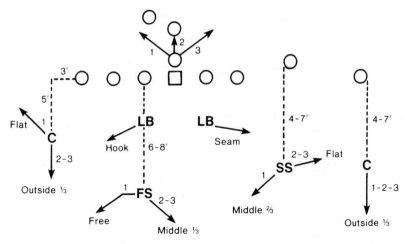

Slot (Pre-Rotate). Three Deep Invert to Slot Side

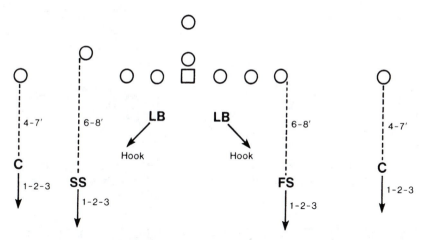

Special (No Rotation versus Four Quick Receivers—Prevent Defense)

STUNTING AND BLITZING

We will utilize stunts and blitzes from our basic defense when (1) we feel we can predict what the offense is doing and (2) when we want to surprise the offense.

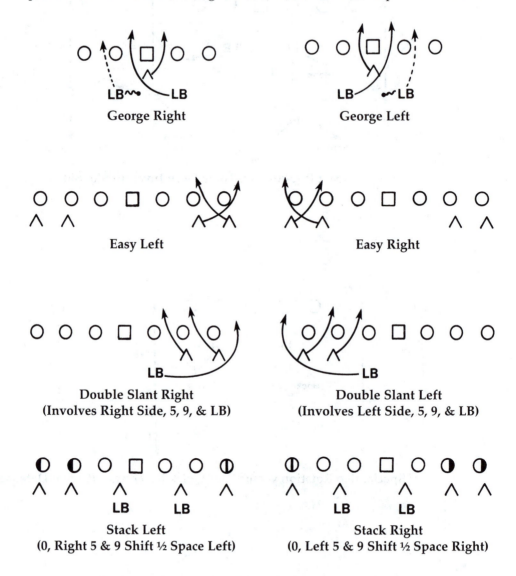

George Right

George Left

Easy Left

Easy Right

Double Slant Right
(Involves Right Side, 5, 9, & LB)

Double Slant Left
(Involves Left Side, 5, 9, & LB)

Stack Left
(0, Right 5 & 9 Shift ½ Space Left)

Stack Right
(0, Left 5 & 9 Shift ½ Space Right)

GOAL LINE AND SHORT YARDAGE (80 DEFENSE)

80 Defense can be used on short yardage situations (third and 1, second and 1) and anytime the opponent reaches or is within our ten-yard line.

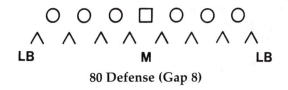

80 Defense (Gap 8)

One (1) Technique.   Align in the center–guard gap in a four-point low "frog" position. Bend elbows with legs coiled to extend six to eight inches off the LOS. All weight is on the hands. On the snap of the ball get penetration and keep shoulders parallel to the LOS. Bring inside arm up into the center's crotch, and scramble with the head up looking for the football. You are responsible for the center–guard gap, quarterback sneaks, and quick dive plays.

Three (3) Technique.   Line up in the guard–tackle gap approximately six to eight inches off the LOS. The inside leg is forward with shoulders parallel to LOS. Maintain a four-point stance with elbows bent. Get penetration by springing off the front foot. Stay low and come up hard after making penetration, looking for the football. You are responsible for the guard–tackle gap (B gap), quick dive plays, traps, and all other plays over this area.

Five (5) Technique.   Line up in the tackle–end gap (C gap) approximately six to eight inches off the LOS. The same stance and penetration moves apply as in the three technique. Stay low, and come up after penetration, looking for the football. You are responsible for the off-tackle hole and the power and trap plays. You must be aware of the trap plays. If no one blocks you, step down to the inside, stay low, and read the football.

Nine (9) Technique.   Line up approximately one yard outside the offensive end (D gap) in a two-point stance with the inside foot forward. The legs should be flexed at the knees to stay low and the arms should hang loosely. You are responsible for plays coming over the offensive end. Watch out for the trap and kick out blocks by the offensive backfield men. Meet all blocks with the inside shoulder and forearm. If the play goes away, trail as deep as the deepest man, and look for reverses, bootlegs, cutbacks, and the like. *Always* hit the offensive end as he comes off the LOS.

Defensive Halfbacks.   (LB) Align in a two-point stance about three yards outside the offensive end and two yards off the LOS. Your first responsibility is the run outside; you are the contain man. Read through the offensive end into the backfield. If the end blocks and the flow comes your way, quickly come up. You should not widen the gap between the defensive nine technique and yourself any more than you have to. Meet all blockers with the inside shoulder and forearm, with the inside foot forward. All plays must be met aggressively and turned in! You will be instructed from week to week on pass coverage responsibility.

Defensive Safety Man.   (M) Align in a two-point stance directly opposite the offensive center about two yards off the ball. Your feet and shoulders should be parallel to the LOS. Your key is the football and you should move down the LOS with shuffle steps, staying about one step behind the football. Move up into the LOS aggressively and tackle high. Your pass coverage responsibilities will vary from week to week.

All linemen on the 80 defense must explode across the LOS and try to break up the offensive play or tackle the football *behind* the LOS. Everyone must tackle high and drive through the ball carrier as he must not be allowed to fall forward.

GOAL LINE AND SHORT YARDAGE (6–5 DEFENSE)

6–5 Defense

The 1 and 5 technique linemen have their entire weight over the hands, nose close to ground, in "frog" stance. At snap of the ball explode as you uncoil, getting penetration and quickly getting your head up. *Stay off of your knees.* Scramble, grabbing anything you can and trying to penetrate into the backfield.

One (1) Technique.   Align in the A gap between the center and guard. On the snap of the ball, explode across the LOS while driving one arm through crotch of center. Reach and grab for QB's legs. You should tie up the center and guard on your side. Scramble to get head up. Get deep into the backfield.

Five (5) Technique.   Align on the outside shoulder of the offensive tackle, (C gap) angled in. Uncoil on the hip of the tackle. Get your head up; penetrate as deep as possible looking for the football. Do not get blocked out.

Nine (9) Technique.   Outside foot back—strong forearm or hand shiver to the end (or set back if end split). You *cannot* get blocked out. Stop all off tackle plays. Take QB on option; if there is a sprint out, contain and apply pressure. If the flow goes away trail as deep as the ball while watching for counters and reverses.

MLB.   Must tackle high and penetrate as you scrape. Play 2 yards back. Stop QB sneak, A gap and B gap runs.

LB.   Key offside HB (If there is none, key onside back or scouting key). If flow goes away, slide down LOS toward flow—look for counters. If flow comes, step up to meet blocker or ball. Tackle high. If flow is toward you but wide scrape into hole—do not get sealed off by TE. Fight through the pressure. As 9 technique jams end, scrape just off his hip, make tackle as corner turns play in, or penetrate, taking on as many blockers as you can.

Corners.   Outside foot back. You have contain responsibility on all runs to your side. Key through TE into backfield. Play pass first, run second. If flow goes away, check for counters and reverses. On option you have the pitch man.

General Note.   The front six should play the run first, the back six should play the pass first.

GAME-TO-GAME DEFENSIVE ALIGNMENTS

The following material is presented to give the reader greater depth in setting up a defense against a particular offensive set. This information is taken from a high school that uses a 6–3-2 defensive alignment and plays against the wish bone formation a great deal. The following diagram illustrates this basic defensive lineup against the standard wishbone attack and the following information describes the specific instructions to the players.

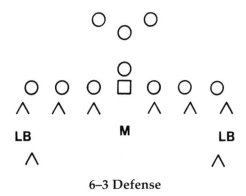

6–3 Defense

The defensive ends line up just outside the tight end or the position where he will be if he is split. Their responsibility is to slash hard on every play and tackle the quarterback no matter what he does (unless he has just released a pass). Tackles line up on the outside shoulder of the offensive tackles and are responsible for jamming up the off tackle hole. They do not try to get penetration but instead control their territory. The guards line up head-on to the offensive guards and try to get penetration on every play. They are not responsible for the quarterback sneak but simply try to break up plays before they develop.

The middle linebacker lines up with his toes even with the heels of the down guards and is responsible for tackling the first backfield man who dives into the line on either side. At the snap of the ball the middle linebacker follows the quarterback step for step laterally down the LOS. He cannot allow the center to block him and must tackle solidly the first back through the LOS.

Each outside linebacker lines up directly behind the defensive end and is responsible for the backfield man on his side. Each LB plays the offensive back man-for-man. If the play comes toward the linebacker, he scrapes off the end and comes up to meet the flow in a hitting position. The offside linebacker will move immediately to the middle of the field just behind the line-up position of the middle linebacker. He checks counters, reverses, or helps with the run or pass play. The diagram below illustrates these moves against a typical play.

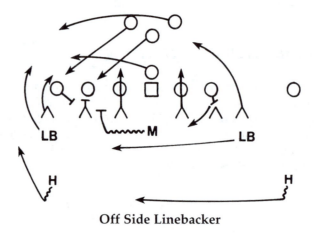

Off Side Linebacker

Both of the deep backs play over the offensive ends about six to eight yards deep. Their coverage is man-for-man and both backs play the pass every time until they are sure it is a run.

The diagrams that follow illustrate various situations that might be encountered during a game. The reader should examine these and then review this section in an attempt to understand the positional assignments that would be made prior to a game.

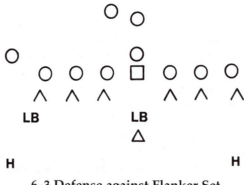

6–3 Defense against Flanker Set

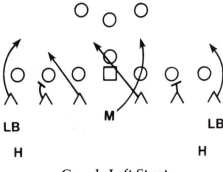

Guards Left Stunt

If, for example, the Wolverines played a team that ran the wishbone, the week prior to the game would be devoted, defensively, to making sure each player on defense knows what he is responsible for and where he is supposed to move in any given situation. The coaching staff will then hope that their team performs as they have practiced in the game. All coaches have to live with the fact that many players will not perform during a game as they have practiced during the week!

As with offense, specific defensive adjustments in alignment, keys, and reaction will vary from week to week. But a team should be well versed in a "basic" midfield defense as well as a short yardage/goal line defense. Defense is reacting to specific stimuli (movement) as quickly as possible while keeping the overall defensive scheme in mind and reacting to the football.

CLASS ACTIVITIES

1. Scout a high school game and concentrate on defense only.

2. Analyze the strengths and weaknesses of the 5–4 defense.

3. Develop additional stunts for the 5–4 defense and stunts for the 6–5 goal line defense.

4. Divide the class into LB and secondary units and have each react to movement of the ball or flow.

13

THE KICKING GAME

Chapter Objectives

After completing this chapter, the reader should be able to:

- Describe the basic mechanics of punting the football and be able to demonstrate these on the field.
- Draw on the chalkboard and explain on the field the basic spread punt alignment and responsibilities of all players.
- Analyze the mechanics of a deep snap, kicking, and punting.
- Draw, as well as explain on the field, the alignment and field coverage of a kickoff return and a kickoff.
- Draw, as well as explain on the field, the alignment of the field-goal and extra-point formation and responsibilities of all players, especially the holder.

KICKING IMPORTANCE

No other aspect of the game of football is more important, yet more frequently overlooked by coaches, than the skills involved in the kicking game. This aspect consists of kickoffs and returns, punts and returns, extra points, field goals, and special plays. The coaching staff must work constantly on the kicking game with as much, if not more, zeal and enthusiasm as they do when working on offense and defense. Because of the attitude of many coaching staffs toward the kicking game, errors due to sloppy play are evident in many games. These kicking errors are very often the difference between a win or a loss. Conservatively, over 25 percent of a football game is involved in some form of the kicking game. It would stand to reason that coaches would spend well over this percentage of practice time on these skills. Needless to say, most coaches do not spend this amount of time on kicking and most have their players practice these skills when they are tired, usually at the end of a practice session. Thus players often develop a negative attitude about the kicking game. Such an attitude can lead to one or more of the common mistakes and errors in kicking:

Moving offsides
Roughing the kicker
Slowing up on the coverage
Slowing up in the tackling zone
Clipping
Failing to contain

These and countless other mistakes can be largely eliminated if a coaching staff instills pride and a feeling of worth in the players about the kicking game. Adequate practice time and goal setting are two ways to develop a winning attitude. Common goals for the kicking team might include:

1. Perfect snap and hold 100 percent of time
2. No blocked punts or kicks
3. Hold opponent to an average of three yards or less on punt returns
4. Average forty yards per punt
5. Return all kickoffs beyond the twenty-yard line
6. Make 100 percent of extra points
7. Make 80 percent of field goals
8. Down every possible punt inside the ten-yard line
9. No penalties in kicking game
10. Allow an average of eighteen yards or less per kickoff return
11. Block a field-goal or extra-point attempt
12. Force a bad punt
13. Average ten yards or more per punt return
14. No punt fielded inside our ten-yard line
15. Kick a minimum of 75 percent of our kickoffs into the end zone.

Specific yardages and percentages can be adjusted for specific age players.

At the younger age levels, the inability of players to kick the ball often limits the scope and depth of enthusiasm and instruction in this area. Coaches need to recognize that instruction in kicking fundamentals and attitudes must be started early and developed over the years. If emphasis is placed on the kicking game, the

TABLE 13.1   The Kicking Time and Distance Table

	High School or College	Below High School Level
Distance of Snap	13–15 yards	10–12 yards
Time of Snap	0.6–0.9 sec.	1.0–1.3 sec.
Time of Kick	1.2–1.4 sec	1.4–1.8 sec.
Distance of Kick	35–45 yards	20–30 yards
Distance of Kickoff	5-Yard Line to End Zone	10–15-Yard Line
Extra Point Success When Kicking	90%	75% (7th & 8th usually run)
Field Goal Success	60–85%	Almost nonexistent

Adapted from: Paul ("Bear") Bryant, *Building a Championship Football Team* (Englewood Cliffs, NJ: Prentice-Hall, 1960).

younger player learns to respect this as an integral part of the total team effort. As an example of the limited abilities of younger age kickers, consider the statistics given in Table 13.1.

These few figures can give the reader some idea of the kicking limitations of players below the high school level. It should be noted that these statistics hold true no matter what the coaching emphasis has been. That is to say, although coaches can work on the kicker's technique and protection plans for them, the neuromuscular and strength development of younger individuals limits what they are capable of doing. With these statements in mind, this section attempts to give the reader a background of information to draw on as he prepares to coach the kicking game. Some of the overall areas of concern in coaching the kicking game are the snap, kick coverage, and performance of the kicker. These areas will be discussed separately and will include diagrams and information basic to punts, kickoffs, extra points, and field goals.

THE CENTER'S SNAP

We have already given a detailed discussion of the long snap for the center in Chapter 5. The reader may refer to that section as a review. It is important that team tryouts be held for the purpose of deciding who will snap for punts. The coach may be surprised as to which of his players can consistently snap the ball ten to twelve yards, quickly and on target!

Using data given earlier, you should strive to have a center get the ball back accurately twelve to thirteen yards in 0.07 to 0.09 seconds. Hitting the target, (usually the inside portion of the punter's kicking leg, or the hands of the holder) may be affected by a snap that is released too soon (low snap) or too late (high snap). Constant practice between the center and all punters and holders is needed.

Snapping for extra points and field goals is an abbreviated punt snap. The emphasis here is on accuracy. Each center must work on not being intimidated by sudden moves by the defense. Snapping for punts or goal kicks requires daily practice, and the coach should work with the player(s) in these areas to correct faults in basic stance, hand position, balance, or follow-through. Probably about 99 percent of all blocked kicks result from imperfect snaps from the center to the kicker.

PUNT COVERAGE

Opinion is divided concerning the best formation to use for protection of the punter and coverage of the kick. Some teams prefer to use a spread punt formation as shown below:

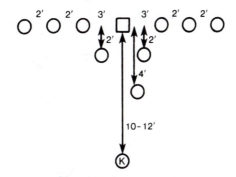

Spread Punt Formation

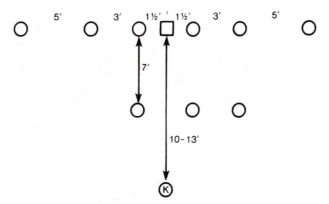

Spread Punt Formation

The main advantages of using a spread punt formation are that the defense has a difficult time holding up coverage, and the team is already spread over a larger area of the field for a broader coverage. The latter advantage is important because if a team can spread its men evenly across the field as they run downfield toward the receiver, they will have a much greater chance of limiting the runback. The main coaching problem in punt coverage is to get the players to stay in their "lane," keeping equidistant from each other as they go downfield. The long return is usually caused by an overbalance of coverage men on one side of the ball or the other. Various types of coverage patterns are shown in the following illustrations. Most coaches will teach that the first man to reach the receiver should tackle him high (with "reckless abandon") when he touches the football, or force him to call for a fair catch. Some teams use their center for this purpose, releasing him with no blocking rules. Others use the men playing at the end or wide positions.

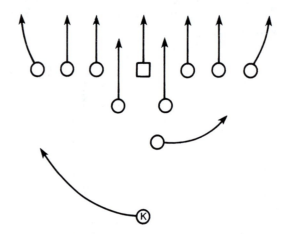

Coverage Pattern Variation

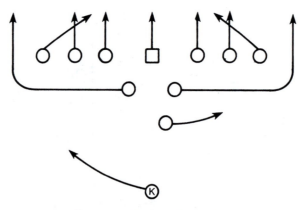

Coverage Pattern Variation

Still other teams feel that since the younger punter is generally close to the LOS a tight punt formation is best. A common type is shown in the following figure.

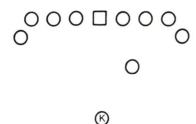

Tight Punt Formation

Any team having to punt from close to its own end zone (ten-yard line or less) may find it best to use a tight punt formation. Many teams have the kicker call in the huddle which side of the field he will kick the ball to so the linemen will have some predetermined area of the field to converge on. Even when they slant they will still keep an equal distance from each other as they move down the field.

As can readily be seen, this formation makes middle penetration very difficult but also narrows the initial coverage significantly. Many coaches favor the spread punt formation as an effective carryover skill to be taught to younger players. For clarification, the remainder of this chapter relates to the spread formation.

Punt Blocking Rules

Many types of blocking rules for the punt can be developed. Two player handout forms of rules are presented in the following sections. Basically, a coach wants his players to simply pick out a man to block, pointing to him if necessary, always being aware of inside rushers. Consider each of the following procedures and compare their applicability to practical situations.

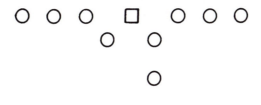

Wolverine Punt Formation

Procedure

  A. Huddle Call—"Spread Punt on Center's Snap" (punter calls play).
  B. Stance—Two-point stance. Linemen align with feet of center. Splits: Guard–Center, two feet; Guard–Tackle, three feet; Tackle–End, three feet; Backs, two yards behind LOS in space between center and guard.

C. Call and point out blocks.

D. Kicker will signal to center when he is ready. Center has last option. Kicker is twelve yards deep (depends on ability on center to snap the football).

Blocking Rules

A. Center—Snap (pop head up quickly), and release.

B. Guards—First man to outside—you must keep your inside foot stationary. Block for one count, and release.

C. Tackles—If two men line up between you and the guard, block inside. If not two men, block first man to outside. Block for one count, and release.

D. Ends—First man to outside unless there are two men between you and the tackle—then block inside. Block for one count, and release. You are the contain men.

E. Backs—Block anyone coming between the center and guard. If no one comes, release.

F. Personal Protector—Look up and down the LOS and block the most dangerous rusher as he approaches. In the event of an overload to one side or the other the personal protector will yell "overload" and indicate the side. You cover to the right side of the field.

G. Punter—get the kick off, cover the left side of the field.

General:

A. Success in covering a punt hinges on *desire*.

B. The kicking team can down the ball anywhere on the playing field and the receiving team will be in possession of the ball at the spot where the downing occurred. Do *not* leave the ball until the whistle blows.

C. Great effort should be made to prevent punts from going into the end zone without batting the ball from the end zone back onto the field. On all fair catch signals inside the ten-yard line, the first men down will run beyond the receiver and protect the goal line, to prevent the punted ball from going into the zone.

D. C, G's, T's don't be offsides and stay in your lanes approximately four to five yards from your teammate on either side.
Never cover directly behind a teammate!

E. Backs—maintain a position approximately five yards behind the front wall between the guard and tackle on your side.

F. Ends—you are the contain men. *No one gets outside of you.*

G. FB—cover to the right side as safety.

H. Kicker—cover to the left side as safety. *Call out direction of kick.* Take pride in the kicking game—it is a great offensive weapon, and field position is gained by it. Hold your opponents' kick return yardage to a minimum.

PUNT RETURN

Several punt return schemes will now be illustrated. The reader should be able to get the basic objectives of each man's position from these illustrations. Where possible, the return is shown from a defensive alignment that is similar to the basic 59 or 5–2 defensive formation. However, it is not necessary to align in this basic defense as most teams have a specific alignment and a specific unit for the punt return. The down linemen on the punt return scheme must be cognizant of the return plan. As can be seen from the figures, those individuals on the side of the return simply deliver a forearm lift or hand shiver and quickly peel off the LOS into the return wall. A deeper penetration is taken by each lineman the farther he is away from the return side. The last down lineman away from the return side will have the responsibility of (1) making sure the kicker kicks the ball or (2) covering any bad snap situations. The initial blow of these linemen should be to slow the offensive linemen down and delay their release from the LOS. Linebackers may have the responsibility of blocking or immediately dropping back into the return pattern. Since the players that the linebackers are assigned to block usually have a running start downfield, we recommend that the linebacker *not* leave his feet in an effort to knock the rusher down. A high shoulder block that delays the rusher is a more reliable type of block, and it allows the linebacker to stay on his feet and get into the return pattern more rapidly.

All other players who are fifteen to twenty yards downfield will have the problem of open field blocking. The crucial element is to get contact with your man. The cross-body block and roll technique is used where it is legal (local school and state regulations vary). The initial block across the rusher's body must be timed so that you don't find yourself blocking only air. Many times it is sufficient simply to "get up in the face" of the rusher or shield your ball carrier from the rusher till he has run past your position. Again, the major point is to pick a rusher and make contact with him.

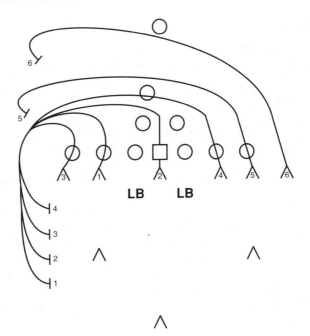

Punt Return Left (If End or Ends Split #3 & #6 Will Cover)

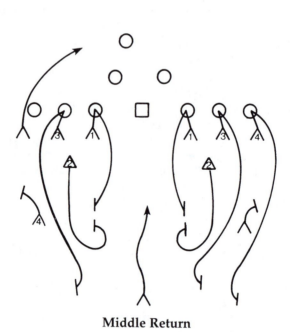

Middle Return

Receiving the Punt

At younger levels of football play, it is always advisable to have two players back to receive the punt. These men can line up either side-by-side or one in front of the other. The advantage of doing this is that one man can give the receiver information as to whether he should fair catch, let it go, or catch and run. The person receiving should keep his eyes on the ball at all times. He should always attempt to keep his elbows as close together as possible to form a cradle with which he can trap the ball against his chest as it hits his arms. He should avoid trying to catch the ball with his hands only, even when he hears those footsteps bearing down on him! Once he has the ball under control, *then* he looks upfield and begins his return.

The same instructions for receiving the punt apply to the kickoff receivers. The exception, of course, is that a kickoff receiver does not have to worry about the immediate pressure of the coverage. Whether instructing punt or kickoff receivers, the coach should stress to the youngsters that they should try to catch the ball before it bounces. If it has to bounce, try to catch it on the first bounce or you will increase the probability of a fumble.

Either a wall or alley is set up by blocking the kick coverage people away from the intended path of the ball carrier. Always have at least one man going to the

COACHING POINTS: Punt Reception

- Consider the wind, rain, and so forth when judging how far back to stand. (The coach should tell the kick receiver how far the opponent can kick the ball. Find out from scouting or watching during the pregame warm-up).
- Know where the goal line is.
- Never field a punt if the opponents are closer than five yards, (if you intend to run with the ball).
- Know when to fair catch (that is, good field position, pressure, etc.).
- Never field a punt inside your own ten-yard line. Always move to the ball as soon as it comes off the kicker's foot. Get to the ball and position yourself squarely under it.
- Relax the hands and arms as soon as the ball contacts them. Cradle the ball in the pocket formed by hands and arms.
- After catching the ball read your blocks, try to get outside the wall quickly; or, if returning up the middle, get started quickly, aim straight upfield, get close to your blockers, look for daylight, and move!

kicker. The people setting up the wall must be spaced evenly and have some conception of their relation to the receiver's position. This can be studied by the coach during practice as he stands downfield and watches the punt return develop. Repetition is necessary until this positioning is mastered.

Most teams will try to use some sort of wall return to one side of the field or the other as this seems to be the easiest to set up. Some teams like to hold up all linemen on the punting team to keep them from going downfield. This technique is used especially when the punting team is forced to punt from deep in their own territory. A typical formation for this return is shown below:

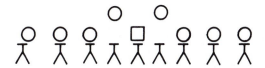

PERFORMANCE OF THE PUNTER

At the college level and beyond, many coaches feel that if a young man can kick the ball adequately, leave him alone. Don't worry about how many steps he takes, how he holds or drops the ball, or the way he ties his shoes! However, the junior and senior high school coach will have young men who need specific instructions in punting. The following information is typical, but additional descriptions of coaching the punter should always be investigated and discussed whenever possible.

Holding (If Left-footed, Reverse Technique)

1. Left hand underneath and to the side of the far point; hold tightly; this is the steady hand.
2. Right hand underneath and to the side of the rear point; hold tight; this is the guide hand.

The Drop

1. Keep the far point of the ball (nose) aimed in the direction you plan to kick.
2. Drop the ball with the nose lower than the near point (if drop is correct, the ball will bounce up and back toward the punter if dropped on the ground).
3. Keep arms extended and drop the ball while hands are slightly above the waistline.

Steps

1. Start with the left foot forward to meet the snap.
2. As the first short step is taken with the right foot, fix the ball as desired (do not overstride).
3. Take a full step with left foot.
4. Swing through for the kick with head down. (This description is for a step-and-a-half approach, with the punter taking the first step with the kicking foot, then a full step with the nonkicking foot, then the kick. The decision to have the youngster start with the kicking or nonkicking foot forward must be made based on the quickness of each punter in getting the ball away. If the center can snap the ball back thirteen yards, then use this approach. However, the closer the punter is to the center the quicker he will need to get the kick away. In such cases, the coach might want the punter to start with his kicking foot forward, which shortens his steps but does not allow for the buildup of much body momentum for the kick.)

The Punt

1. Extend the right hand slightly as the foot swings forward.
2. Lock the knee and point the toes as the foot contacts the ball, about one to two feet off the ground (knee high).
3. Extend the trunk slightly in order to open the waist angle and allow the leg to extend to its full swing.
4. Kick through the ball, making certain to swing the kicking leg above the waistline. The speed of the leg is increased by extension of the lower leg at the knee which is increased by a rapid and complete extension of the upper leg at the hip. The distance of the kick is determined by leg speed and contact of the ball with the foot.
5. Push off from the left leg to gain power. (Some players can push off and jump at least six inches off the ground for more power.)

6. Ways to strengthen the punter's leg:

    a. Lower leg extensions: (Universal Gym Apparatus or Cybex) three sets of ten repetitions with 20–30–40 lbs. (if adequate).

    b. Half-squats: three sets with 100 lbs.

    c. Bench jumps: 120

    d. Running: windsprints

    e. Hamstring stretch

KICKOFF TECHNIQUES

Most young players have a general idea of how to kick a ball using the standard kickoff procedure of teeing the ball up. A few specific suggestions (straight-on kick) may assist the coach.

- The ball should be placed on the tee leaning back slightly with the laces pointing away from the kicker.
- Have the player mark a spot on the ground approximately three inches to the side and six inches behind the ball. This mark will be for the placement of the nonkicking foot before the swing through. Depending on the strength of the kicker's leg, he should step back from five to ten yards and mark his starting point.
- Momentum is built up by increasing the speed of the approach to the ball, but the kicker should time it so that the nonkicking foot is planted on the mark and that the ball is met just below midpoint with a foot that is semiflexed (toe up) in a locked position. The head should be kept down when kicking and during the follow-through. A slight push-jump with the nonkicking leg is often helpful. Soccer style kicking is discussed in the extra point and field goal section.

Formation

One of the most dangerous plays in football is the kickoff. This is particularly true if the receiving team is using crisscross blocking when players will be hit from the blind side. Coach players to sprint as far as possible and keep their eyes on the football. This requires them to see the blockers indirectly with their peripheral vision, a technique which young players may not have developed to a great degree.

Although the manner of lining up players for the kickoff varies, a common formation is for the players to line up five yards from the ball in a two- or three-point stance, with all heads looking to the inside. A "starter" stands just to the side of the ball with hands raised. This formation is illustrated in the following diagram.

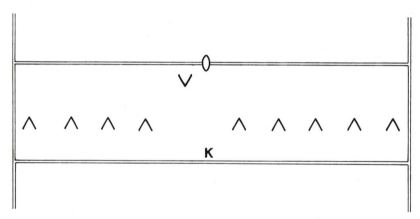

Kickoff Lineup

Coverage

Generally, the coverage of kickoffs, like that of punt returns, is best taught on the field rather than by chalk talks. As with the punt, the men covering the kickoff should keep an equal distance between themselves as they run downfield. Reckless abandon is required so that the team gets as far downfield as possible before the receiver fields the ball. Players should sprint at least thirty yards before beginning to come under control and moving to the ball. They must note where the ball is before they start angling over to one side or the other as they go downfield. One man must be assigned to go down each sideline and not let anyone get between him and the sideline.

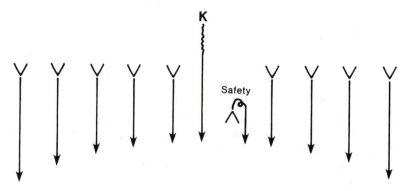

Straight Kickoff Coverage

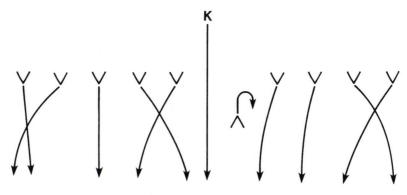

Crisscross Kickoff Coverage

Returns

Two kickoff returns are shown in the following diagrams. The numbering indicates that the blockers will count off the men on the kickoff team and be responsible for blocking those men.

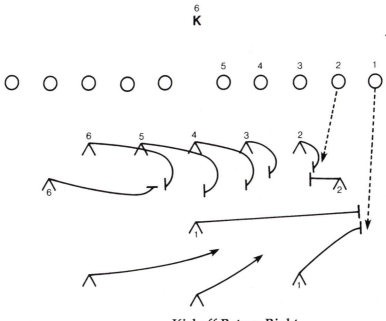

Kickoff Return Right

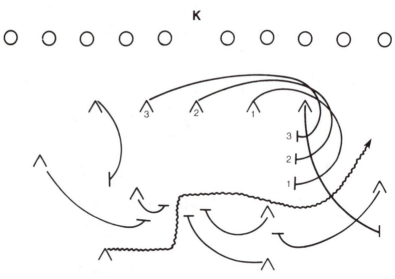

Kickoff Return Right with Middle Return Fake

The return illustrated above requires a call "right" or "left" to tell the front blockers which way to peel back. The back wall sets up ten yards in front of the ball. The far back not receiving the ball becomes a blocker looking for the most dangerous man. This type of return might be good for junior high school as it does not require players to number the opponent or block a specific man.

POINT AFTER TOUCHDOWN (PAT) AND FIELD GOALS

This area is not widely stressed in younger age levels due to the demands it places upon the strength of the kicker, accuracy and speed of the center, and skill of the holder. This does not, however, mean that we shouldn't coach kicking-related skills to younger players—they are the kickers of tomorrow.

The Holder:

1. The holder for PAT's and field goals should have good hands for catching and handling the football.
2. The holder positions himself on one knee (on the side of the kicker's kicking leg) with his back knee down just behind and about six inches away from the tee.
3. Arms are extended to make a target for the center. Hands are in a thumb-to-thumb position.
4. The primary responsibilities of the holder are (a) telling the kicker "keep your head down" (b) receiving the ball, letting the hands give toward the tee as the ball is caught, (c) placing the ball on the tee with the right hand or right index finger atop the ball, (d) rotating the ball as the left hand is removed so that the

laces face away from the kicker, and (e) quickly removing the left hand while holding the ball straight up and down with the right hand or index finger.

5. The holder's eyes should be on the ball throughout the kick and he should not take his finger or hand off the ball. The kicker kicks the ball out from under the holder's hand or finger.

Straight-On and Soccer Style Kickers

The straight-on kicker should make a lead step mark approximately three inches behind the ball. He should then walk off one-and-a-half steps away from the ball. Probably the best momentum advance on the ball is obtained by having the kicker step with his right foot pointed straight at the tee on the snap, followed by a step with the left foot landing on the lead step mark. The kick is made with a locked flexed (toe up) foot throughout. The head must be kept down during the kick, eyes on the ball.

Most of the following information relates to the soccer style kicker's technique. Note that since soccer style kicker's techniques have specific individual differences, the following suggestions should be regarded as generalizations. There are many exceptions when dealing with soccer style kicker's techniques.

Many soccer style kickers vary with respect to the exact part of the foot that makes contact with the football. Some kickers hit the football with the instep while others make contact with the top of their foot. This particular difference accounts for each type of kicker approaching the football at a slightly different angle. Kickers should experiment to find the best method for them. Remember, the individual kicker's steps in approaching the football must always be consistent. Also, the path or angle of the approach will be dependent on the field or hash mark position. *Practicing the placement and alignment of the kicking tee with the target from wide angles on the field is vitally important to success.* The tee will give the soccer style kicker a final check point for his non-kicking foot at the time of the kick. An accurate kick will be the result of the proper alignment of the foot with the tee. Note that kickers must sometimes compensate their aim according to wind conditions. Some kickers must allow for a hook or slice on their kick, if they cannot correct the problem.

Teaching the Soccer Style Kicker

1. *Starting position.* Most soccer style kickers stand just behind the ball; they take two steps back and one to three steps to the left, eyes on the ball. The kicker is now set. After the snap of the football to the holder, the placekicker steps with his kicking foot. The first step is a position step, (approximately a half step). Good body position must be maintained, and the head is down, concentrating on the target.

2. The second and final step is made with the non-kicking or aim foot. This final step is a full stride, with a little bounce or hop to it. The non-kicking foot is planted in the proper position in relationship to the kicking tee. *The aim foot is pointed directly down field at the target.* When planting the last step, the body should still be in good position, leaning slightly forward, head down, and eyes concentrating on point of contact.

3. With the kicker balancing on his non-kicking foot, his kicking leg is accelerated forward into the football. On impact the kicker's ankle and knee are locked, with the leg swinging in a sweeping type motion from the hip. The kicker's ankle is locked with the toes depressed (pointed position). The head is down, but the body position varies among styles.

4. *Follow through.* The football has left the tee. With the kicker's knee and ankle locked, the leg sweeps forward through the ball and tee. As the kicker's leg moves upward in the final phase of its swing, the kicker will go up onto the toes of his non-kicking foot. The kicker's body will continue forward out in front of the kicking tee. Some soccer style kickers, because of their individual technique, pivot on their non-kicking foot.

Coaches should stress the following stages with all kickers:

1. *Starting position and use of consistent steps into the football.* The kicker must always line up the same distance from the tee, so that the length of each step is consistent when approaching the football. Inconsistency in both the starting position and length of steps will lead to under or overstriding into the ball by the kicker. This will affect his final plant position. This point is your top teaching priority because starting position can affect everything else that happens.

2. *Placement and direction of the last step (non-kicking or aim foot).* The placement of this foot is important for two reasons:

   a. Accuracy—The foot should be planted so that it is pointing directly downfield at the target:

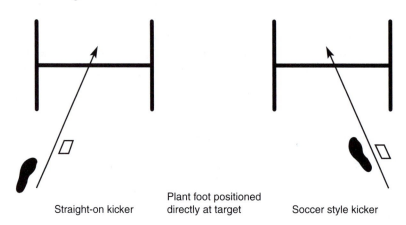

Straight-on kicker

Plant foot positioned
directly at target

Soccer style kicker

   b. Proper contact—The foot should be planted according to the kicker's preferred number of inches away from the tee. The foot should be placed consistently in the same spot, front to back and side to side, as shown in the following diagram. The proper positioning of this foot is important so that the kicking foot may swing in its natural arc and make proper contact with the football. If proper contact is made, then maximum transference of force from the foot to the ball is achieved.

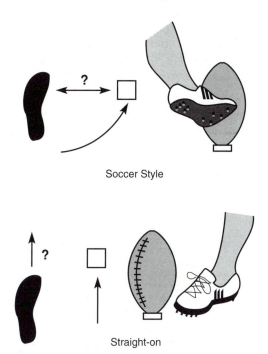

Soccer Style

Straight-on

Note that the height of the kicking tee 1 or 2 inches or kicking off grass will affect or change the amount of distance the plant foot is away from the football.

3. *Position and direction of the hips and shoulders on contact with the football.* Even though different kickers approach the football differently all kickers must have their hips and shoulders in the proper position on contact. The proper positioning of the body will result in a straight kick, provided that everything else is done correctly.

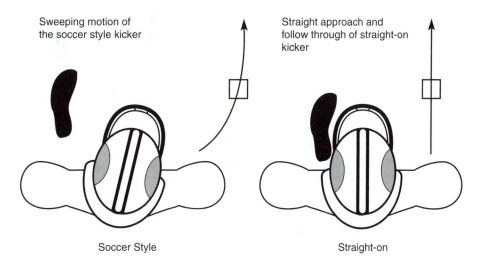

Sweeping motion of the soccer style kicker

Straight approach and follow through of straight-on kicker

Soccer Style   Straight-on

Note that the soccer style kicker must first get his non-kicking foot properly placed, if he is eventually going to get his body in the correct position for contact.

4. *Locking position of the leg and foot to make proper contact with the football.* As the kicking leg extends into the football the following must be done by each kicker.

    a. Soccer style kicker—As the leg swings into the football, the kicker's ankle must be locked in place, with his toes depressed in a pointed position. This position of the foot must be maintained into and during the follow-through of the placekick.

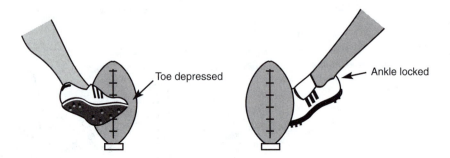

Toe depressed

Ankle locked

    b. Straight-on kicker—As the kicking leg swings into the football, the knee will lock out upon contact with the football. At the same time, the kicker's ankle must be locked in place, toes up. The foot is locked in at a 90 degree angle. The foot position into and through the kick is very important if proper contact is to be achieved. The knee and ankle remain locked throughout the entire kick. Coaches must stand back and off to the side to see if their kicker's ankle is remaining locked during the follow-through.

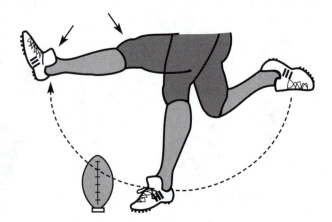

5. *Follow-through.* The kicker should always kick through the football. The follow-through should be the consequence of the energy imparted into the football by the kicker. It is important that the follow-through be natural, not a forced movement. As the kicker kicks through the football, his movement should carry him upward, onto the toes of his non-kicking foot. Many kickers then move forward beyond the tee.

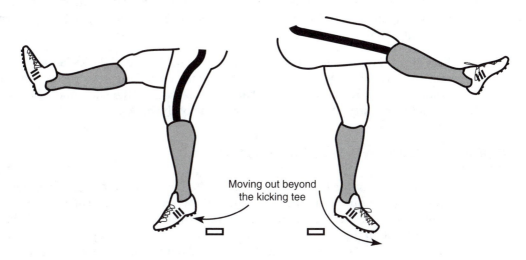

Moving out beyond the kicking tee

PAT AND FG BLOCKING RESPONSIBILITY

The following diagram and descriptions give a common formation and basic rules for a point-after-touchdown or field goal situation.

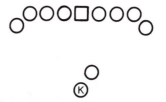

PAT and Field Goal Formation

Linemen. Two-point stance with elbows on knees. Area block. Keep outside foot anchored. Be passive—do not go out after defensive man. Guards line up with toes even with the heels of the center. All linemen in comfortable stance, shoe to shoe. On snap of the ball all linemen will place their helmets on the hip of the man next to them toward the center.

Center. Use a good solid stance and have a firm grip on the ball. You will snap the ball anytime that you are ready after the holder signals. Primary responsibility is to make a perfect snap and create a broad blocking surface.

Backs.   Two-point stance with hands on knees. Line up with your inside foot directly behind the outside foot of the end. Line up at a 45° angle. Keep inside foot anchored. Do not let anyone come between you and the end.

Holder.   Take position six-and-a-half yards from the ball. When the kicker is ready, tell him "Keep Your Head Down," then signal the center, "OK," by extending your hands.

Ball Play.   This will be used on a bad snap or muffed ball. The kicker and holder immediately call "BALL." The kicker blocks the most dangerous rusher while the holder goes for the ball. The two backs will fan out to the end zone. The holder will advance the ball and try to throw to one of the backs.

BLOCKING KICKS AND SPECIAL SITUATIONS

The opportunity for blocking kicks at the junior and senior high school level is great—mainly due to mechanical errors of the kicking team. The following diagrams give the reader some ideas for rushing the kicking team in an effort to break a man through the LOS for the block. This is usually accomplished by overloading one side of the line or taking rush paths that open holes in the offensive line.

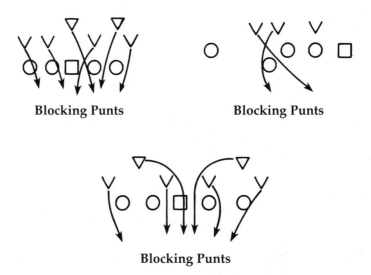

Blocking Punts   **Blocking Punts**

Blocking Punts

ONSIDE KICKS

The following diagram illustrates a typical onside kickoff. At the junior and senior high level many times simply placing the ball on its side and kicking a scribbler will enable the kicking team to recover. If a planned play is needed, the following figure illustrates a common attempt. The kicker simply kicks the football with his instep instead of his toe.

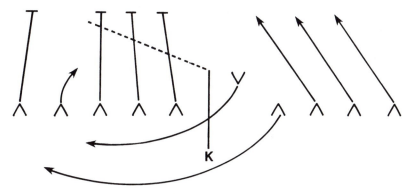

Onside Kick Coverage

Even at the Youth Football League level, the mechanics of the kicking game should be practiced regularly. The qualities of a well-coached team more often than not manifest themselves in the areas of scrimmage kicks and kick-offs; and what is more important, even if the players being coached do not possess the physical ability to execute, they can be drilled in the basic know-how: to line up, to protect the kicker, and to cover downfield. The reader is referred to an excellent text which breaks down errors of not only the kicking game, but all phases of the sport.[1]

CLASS ACTIVITIES

1. In groups of four have one person snap for a punt, one person serve as the punter, and one person identify errors in each performance. The fourth person becomes the receiver.

2. Have a full team cover a punt and a kickoff, demonstrating flow down the field in appropriate lanes.

3. Have a full team go over the movement of a receiving team when returning a punt and a kickoff to the right, left, and middle.

4. Time class members' snaps (from snap to punter's hands) as well as the time it takes the punter to kick the ball. Compare these to the norms in this chapter.

5. In groups of four (center, holder, kicker, receiver) practice field goals and extra point attempts. Have class members make coaching analyses.

NOTE

1. Donald Fuoss and Rowland Smith, *Effective Football Coaching* (Boston: Allyn and Bacon, 1981).

14

LEGAL RESPONSIBILITIES, EQUIPMENT, AND PRACTICE ORGANIZATION

Chapter Objectives

After completing this chapter, the reader should be able to:

- Define *negligence* in terms of the legal tort liability of a coach.
- Outline the main points to make in a preseason meeting with parents and athletes.
- Recite the major symptoms of brain and cervical spine injury and tell what to do when an injury is suspected.
- List the things a coach can do to eliminate avoidable injuries.
- Write out the general timetables for a typical preseason workout, in-season "hard-day" workout, and pregame organization.
- Give the specific breakdown of time for all activities in an in-season contact day workout.
- List the checkpoints for both shoulder pad and helmet fitting.

LEGAL LIABILITY

This chapter is written for all first-year coaches, as well as the twenty-year veteran who has had one year's "experience" repeated twenty times. The football field is filled with opportunities for legal liability as far as coaches are concerned. Every teacher is in a position to incur legal liability daily, and football coaches are particularly vulnerable. Every day coaches work with the potential of an injury situation: young, accident-prone students needing supervision for a wide variety of physical activities. *Negligence* can be defined as the failure to meet a standard of care that a reasonable and prudent football coach would exercise under the same or similar circumstances. The courts have said that teachers owe their pupils, and others with whom they deal, a duty of reasonable care and prudence. If teachers are negligent and someone is injured as a result, they may be found liable.

Teachers have traditionally been identified as surrogate parents (*in loco parentis*) during school hours and during other times while acting within the scope of their employment. A teacher can be liable if a pupil is injured as a result of negligence, whether the failure was by omission or commission. In this respect, a teacher's legal responsibility falls into the following broad areas:

1. Anticipating foreseeable risks
2. Taking reasonable steps to prevent those risks from causing an injury
3. Warning and care addressed toward those risks that for whatever reason cannot be reduced or averted
4. Aiding the injured
5. Taking care not to increase the severity of the injury

These five areas provide the basis for injury prevention and the avoidance of negligence. More specifically, a coach should attend to the following suggestions as frequently as he attends to the yearly coaching clinic:

1. Meet with parents and athletes as a group before practice begins or as early in the season as possible, and explain all the risks involved in the game of football.
    a. Stress that you have done and will continue to do everything possible to reduce those risks.
    b. Advise that equipment cannot totally eliminate injuries.
    c. Explain that despite all your efforts and the efforts of all coaches across the county, a few players will be seriously injured in football every year.

This is probably the most important point in this section. Communication was discussed in the first chapter, and this parents' meeting is a must in opening lines of communication and avoiding negligence suits. Stress your conditioning program which emphasizes strengthening the supportive muscles of the neck; explain your procedures for checking helmet and shoulder pad fit; explain your prepractice weighing to ascertain whether the athlete has rehydrated and is back within a safe range of body weight; and explain your system of getting an injured athlete proper medical help. Every school should have on its staff a qualified person whose sole concern is the health and safety of the athletes. Many times this is a certified athletic trainer. For schools where there is no certified trainer (and there are many), you must institute special measures (paramedic units, for example) for dealing with emergencies. The school must be certain that *immediately* upon the occurrence of an injury a telephone is available and that all members of the athletic staff know where to call for help. The ultimate goal of a school should be to have a good athletic trainer, good medical backup, a good communications network, good available transportation, and a good hospital facility singled out as the ultimate destination: in short, a good plan of action. These items as well as others will let parents know that you have performed all the reasonable cautions that can be taken to safeguard the athlete.

2. Stress the values of the game that justify the inherent risks and the far greater risks present in other common activities.

Be careful here. Too many football coaches oversell and overplay the values of football in respect to other areas of the educational scheme. Be realistic in talking to parents concerning what benefits their child will derive from playing football. Be positive without being overbearing. A good point to make when discussing football participation and injury concerns the accident rate for youth between the hours of 3:30 P.M. and 7:30 P.M. while participating in automobile- and motorcycle-related activities. Contact your local police department or state highway patrol for current figures. Even you might be surprised at the safety of football compared to these activities.

3. Make sure the parents understand your program, and keep your door open for questions and comments.

Think seriously about this open door policy. In your busy schedule you might not always have the time to discuss next week's opponent to a well-meaning parent. Nevertheless, your policy should certainly be one of openness concerning all aspects of your program that impact on the health of the athlete, and you should always be willing to discuss any comments and questions from parents related to the health and safety of their child.

4. Make sure your equipment is safe, sound, and in good condition. All helmets should meet the National Operating Committee for Standards in Athletic Equipment (NOCSAE) specifications.

Considering many schools' budget restraints, this recommendation may loom large. You, as the coach, may have firsthand information concerning the safety of certain pieces of equipment, while the person in charge of purchasing for the whole school system may be operating from a completely different perspective. Be fully aware of your school's policy and procedure in purchasing equipment and if you discover, for example, that your helmets are not (NOCSAE) certified, immediate but diplomatic negotiations with school board members, central administration personnel, and team physicians should be started. All coaches should, however, make it perfectly clear that (1) football helmets are not guaranteed to protect the neck from fracture, and (2) that National Athlete Injury surveys have revealed that there is no significant difference in the levels of severe head injury among the various NOCSAE approved helmets on the market today.

5. *Distribute to each player a written copy of the rules related to the use of the head in blocking or tackling. Stress these rules daily, especially in tackling situations.*
Probably the biggest challenge to coaches today is the need to change the philosophy of using the head as a "first contact" point. Coaches should bear in mind that involvement of the head in contact is the common denominator in all types of catastrophic injuries. By constantly reminding and teaching players not to use any part of the face or head as a primary point of contact, football coaches will take great strides toward eliminating injuries from the game, especially those of a catastrophic nature.

This is not to say that players should not keep their heads erect and move into a block or tackle with their eyes always on the target. However, it is imperative that the primary application of force not be to the face or neck. At the instant contact is made, the head must be slipped to the side so that force is applied to the shoulder.

6. *Be alert for, and if necessary, eliminate from the program, boys who are not adequately prepared physically, mentally, and emotionally for the violence of the game.*
It is a very wise and astute coach who can sincerely prevent a boy from playing or practicing with the health of the boy in mind, rather than the win–loss record of the team. It is the coach's responsibility to see that all players who report to the field have been physically prepared for contact and are cognizant of the challenges of the game. Unfortunately, in the case of many individuals, this is not discovered until the boy is in a contact situation. The coach who can handle the situation in a nonhumiliating, diplomatic manner is a credit to himself and to the profession. Individual conferences and parent conferences should take precedence if a coach suspects that a young man may be injured if he continues to play due to poor physical, mental, or emotional conditions.

7. *Give special attention to the development of neck strength and supporting musculature.*
Double your concentration on those developmental activities (both isometric and dynamic) which serve to develop the neck musculature.

8. *Make every effort to have present at every practice a person properly qualified to deal with severe injury. This would preferably be a medical doctor or a certified athletic trainer. In any event, know how to discern and properly deal with severe or potentially severe injury, especially to the head and neck, at all practice sessions.*
Every coach should know the first aid procedures relating to head and neck injuries. Usually the neck fracture/dislocation causes immediate paralysis, but this is not always true. The player may suffer an injury which causes pain or discomfort but

no apparent disability. If properly handled, the athlete will recover without serious problems. If, however, he is sent back into contact, the result could be tragic.

The player with a subdural hematoma would demonstrate minimal evidence of injury at first. The player may not be able to answer simple questions like name, date, opponent, score, and so on. He may have a different response of the pupils when light hits them. Of course, he may complain of a headache, or numbness, or tingling of a body part. However, these minimal signs act as a warning to be on the alert for more severe problems and to take every precaution for the player's well-being. Any player who has experienced a violent, sudden movement of the head followed by any concussion symptoms should be observed on the sideline, not sent back into the game, if any of the above symptoms are present and must be watched very carefully for 24–48 hours. This observation may include waking the athlete several times during the night to check his responses. Diagnostic tools are now available by which the presence of a developing subdural hematoma may be discovered before the problem becomes critical. Examination by a neurosurgeon is recommended if symptoms persist.

9. Have a physician qualified in sports medicine present at every game.
We will stress here that whenever humanly possible, a qualified sports physician should be immediately available at *all contact practices* as well as at all games. This does not mean the physician should physically be at all contact practices but he should be in a position to be contacted immediately if needed. A decision by the school and attending medical personnel should be made before contact begins concerning the qualifications of the team physician to diagnose adequately both orthopedic and neurological injuries.

10. If severe injury occurs, don't panic.
    a. Remind parents, press, and all concerned that no one is to blame.
    b. Make no speculative statements about how the injury occurred.
    c. Store any equipment involved and any films or photographs of the incident.
    d. Notify the manufacturer of the equipment involved immediately.
    e. Have the school seek the counsel and advice of a lawyer knowledgeable in the area of athletic injury liability.

Again, these statements apply to the overall game plan of a coaching staff relative to the handling of all severe injuries. Public exposure to the small percentage of catastrophic injuries in football, coupled with the fact that litigation arising out of athletic injuries is accelerating out of control, should push all individuals involved with the football program to do everything in their power to eliminate avoidable injuries to the players.

EQUIPMENT

The general guidelines here for helmet and shoulder pad fitting serve only as preliminary information. All coaches should obtain as much information as they can from manufacturing companies concerning guidelines. Most companies produce wall charts, pamphlets, and checksheets listing the major checkpoints for fitting. Examples of such material follow:

Helmet

To check helmet size, measure head circumference using measuring tape, approximately one inch above the eyebrows. Select the proper helmet size as shown on the chart.

	Size	Head Measurement
Small Shell	$6\frac{1}{8}$	$19\frac{7}{8}$
	$6\frac{1}{4}$	$19\frac{3}{4}$
	$6\frac{3}{8}$	$20\frac{1}{8}$
	$6\frac{1}{2}$	$20\frac{1}{2}$
	$6\frac{5}{8}$	$20\frac{7}{8}$
Medium Shell	$6\frac{3}{4}$	$21\frac{1}{4}$
	$6\frac{7}{8}$	$21\frac{5}{8}$
	7	22
	$7\frac{1}{8}$	$22\frac{3}{8}$
	$7\frac{1}{4}$	$22\frac{3}{4}$
Large Shell	$7\frac{3}{8}$	$23\frac{1}{8}$
	$7\frac{1}{2}$	$23\frac{1}{2}$
	$7\frac{5}{8}$	$23\frac{7}{8}$
	$7\frac{3}{4}$	$24\frac{1}{4}$
	$7\frac{7}{8}$	$24\frac{5}{8}$

Helmet Fitting (Padded Type Hat)

1. *Put on the Helmet.* Check helmet for proper size. Hold helmet with thumbs in the ear holes of the shell and fingers pointing toward the helmet top. Spread and bring helmet down toward head at a slight angle with jaw pads first touching at temples. Roll helmet back slightly and bring down straight into position.
2. *Check for Proper Fit.* Place both hands with fingers interlocked on top of helmet and press down. Put on chin strap. The helmet should fit comfortably and snugly. Check for rotation. The skin on the forehead should move with the sweatband. If the helmet slides easily, try the next smaller size helmet.
3. *Check Jaw Pads.* Jaw pads should feel firm against face. If loose, change to thicker pad. If too tight, change to thinner pad or change helmet sizes.
4. *Take off the Helmet.* Place thumbs in ear holes of helmet with hands on helmet. Bring helmet straight up until jaw pads reach temples; then begin to lift and roll helmet backwards using the nape of the neck as a fulcrum.

A properly fitted helmet is one of the important keys to maximum shock dispersion. Players should try on several helmets, selecting the one that provides the best fit. When wearing a helmet that fits properly, the player can feel the padding with firm, equal pressure against his head all the way around.

To check snugness of fit, a physician's plastic or wooden tongue depressor can be used. Insert it vertically between the player's head and interior helmet padding in front, back, and both sides of the head. With a proper fit, a noticeable drag should be felt on both insertion and withdrawal. Easy insertion or withdrawal at any of these locations would indicate a fit that is too loose. Be sure that the chin strap is tightly fastened while checking snugness. Also, while checking for fit be sure that the player wears the helmet down in front, as close as possible to a point just above his eyebrows. After the helmet is worn a few times, the helmet padding will adapt more exactly to the head shape, due to head pressure, perspiration, and regular use.

When properly fitted, a helmet should not drop forward over the eyes, twist or shift on the head, or "travel" or recoil against the head upon contact.

Several times during a season (and generally always following a haircut) the helmet should be inspected for proper fit. Also, players should not swap helmets unless proper fit has been checked.

Shoulder Pads

These points must be considered in fitting shoulder pads to provide maximum player protection:

1. The body arch of the shoulder pad must follow or hug the contour of the player's chest and back, and fit perfectly over the top of the shoulders.
2. Neither end of the body arch should protrude outward from the body. This would suggest an improper fit.
3. The shoulder padding should extend along the collarbone to a point beyond the edge of the shoulder.
4. The shoulder caps should extend down far enough to cover the upper parts of the arms and the outside point of the shoulder.
5. The epaulets should be centered directly in front of the shoulder joint.

Issuing Equipment

These two pieces of equipment, helmet and shoulder pads, are the prime protective pieces of a player's uniform. Careful attention and time should be taken when fitting all players with these. Issuing the players a complete uniform remains the biggest event in many coaches' yearly activity and one in which very little prior training has occurred if the coach is in his first year.

The four things that complicate issuing equipment are (1) the time it takes for one individual to draw a complete uniform; (2) the necessity of having everything fit properly; (3) the fact that some youngsters do not know the proper way to put on the various pieces of equipment; and (4) recording the number of each piece of equipment issued to each athlete for equipment control.

In order to solve all these problems and outfit a large number of athletes in an hour or less, the following method could be used. Lay out all the pieces of equipment in two lines down the gymnasium floor. The various items should be laid out separately, rather than in piles, and in the order in which an athlete would put on each article while dressing. As the youngsters walk down the line—varsity on one side, everyone else on the other—they put on each piece of equipment so that by the time they reach the end of the line they are completely dressed in full gear. At that point, a manager hands each athlete an equipment record card, and as the players undress in the locker room, they record the number painted on each piece of equipment and then turn the card in to another manager. All the while this is going on, the coaches walk up and down the line making sure the players select equipment that fits properly. This method is efficient, easy to control, and creates the atmosphere of careful organization, preplanning, and attention to detail that serves as an example to the team.

PRACTICE ORGANIZATION

Having done all that is possible to safeguard players from injury, and having all players adequately suited up, our attention should turn to practice organization. Preparation usually begins early in the summer when, as a first-year coach, you receive information from the head coach similar to the following:

Dear _____

It is time to start making our preparations for the upcoming football season. I am enclosing some information concerning coaching school and our schedule for the month of August.

I have assigned each of the high school coaches a lecture to attend at coaching school and to discuss when we have our staff clinic August 8. I feel we will all benefit from this. It will give you an opportunity to express yourself; also, it will afford all of us the opportunity to learn more about some phase of football. I am certain you will want to attend as many lectures as possible. However, it is difficult to attend them all. This method will assure us of getting a report over all the topics pertaining to football that are discussed at coaching school.

We will reserve one night in August for the coaches and wives to make ice cream, visit, and become better acquainted.

Sincerely,

Head Coach

The daily practice session becomes the lifeline for many players. Thus, these sessions must be well-organized with challenging activities that are geared toward specific goals. It is most helpful for team spirit and morale that several things be kept in mind:

1. Minimize and vary the practice time. Many football coaches feel that two hours is the maximum amount of time any practice session should last, while many others feel that an hour and a half should be the maximum time. Whatever time you decide on, it is probably a good idea to remember to give the players a day off once in a while.

2. Post a written schedule of the practice plan. Do this every day and if possible a day in advance. This schedule should reflect activities that your players hopefully will view as those which will strengthen their weaknesses. The plan should reflect a variety of activities, not only within this practice session, but also when compared to past practice sessions.

3. Attempt to allow your players to feel that they have a say in practice activities. Discuss with your players, individually or in a group, what they feel are the weaknesses that need to be worked on. Include fun activities in the practice session and stress positive reinforcement rather than negative reinforcement.

Naturally, all equipment that will be needed, as well as coaching personnel assignments for all activities, should be taken care of before practice starts. The coaching staff should be fully aware of the total practice breakdown as well as their individual assignments. All phases of practice should, above all else, start and end on time. Individual practice organization and breakdown are best illustrated by giving examples of actual planning schemes. The reader is referred to Appendix C for examples of master planning sheets for practice organization and typical practice assignment sheet. In the following schedule the reader should notice the attention to specific time breakdowns and personnel coordination. Although activities and time sequences may vary, these examples should serve as guidelines for the coach who is taking his first coaching job.

(A) Two-a-Day Practice (Preseason)

Chart 1   Overall Time Schedule

Morning

7:45–8:15	Staff meeting (coaches dressed), Taping
8:15–8:30	General squad meeting (Head Coach), Announcements, Offensive plays for the day. (Squad must be taped before 8:15.)
8:30–9:00	Group meetings
9:00–9:15	Squad suits up
9:15–9:20	Squad meeting, Head coach explains time schedule for morning workout

9:20	Report to field
9:20–11:00	Morning practice
11:00–11:45	Shower, check injuries
11:45–12:30	Staff meeting

Afternoon

2:00–3:00	Film and Rules Period (coaches)
2:30–3:00	Trainers report for taping
3:00–3:15	Squad meeting (Head line coach in charge), Defense for afternoon workout
3:15–3:45	Group meetings
3:45–4:00	Squad suits up
4:00–4:05	Squad meeting (schedule procedure)
4:05	Report to field
4:05–5:30	Afternoon practice
5:30–6:15	Shower, check injuries
6:15–7:00	Staff meeting

Chart 2   Specific Time Schedule

Morning Practice Schedule (Offensive)

9:20–9:25	Warm-up period (together)
9:25–9:30	Buddy drill (four groups)
9:30–9:35	QB: Warm-up passing drill with Backs; Pass protection drill Centers, Guards, Tackles, Ends: Gap blocking drill
9:35–9:40	Center: QB exchange drill Backs, Guard, Tackles, Ends: Fumble (2 min.) Backs: Inside-out blocking drill Guards, Tackles, Ends: Downfield blocking drill
9:40–9:50	Backs: Play drill Center and Guards: Quick trap drill, Double team drill Tackle and Ends: Double team drill, Hook and trap drill
9:50–10:00	Backs and Ends: Pass drill Centers, Guards, Tackles: Wedge blocking and Pass protection
10:00–10:05	Special Drill period (Hand-off challenge drill, Hamburger, Double Hamburger)
10:05–10:10	3 Team signal drill
10:10–10:40	Offensive team drill 3-Down Zone, 4-Down Zone, Special Zone

10:40–10:50	Specialty Period Punt Returns, Kickoff Returns
10:50	20-yard Sprints First Wk: 20 Second Wk: 30 Third Wk: 40 40-yard dash—Time
11:00	Shower

Afternoon Practice Schedule (Defense)

4:05–4:15	Kicking Drill for Punter, KO—receivers Individual lineman position instruction (Middle Guard, Linebackers, Tackles, Ends) Sled extension drills
4:15–4:20	Defensive buddy drill (four groups)
4:20–4:30	Backs, linebackers: Pass defense drills Middle Guard, Tackles, Ends: Pursuit drills
4:30–4:40	Backs, Ends: Pass defense drills MG, LB, T: Stunt techniques
4:40–4:50	Backs, Ends, LB: Defense coverages MG, T: Eagle techniques
4:50–5:20	Team Defense Goal Line defense (Inside ten-yard line—include extra point and field goal attempt) 4-Down 3-Down
5:20–5:30	Specialty Period Tight Punt Spread Punt Kickoff Safety
5:30	Shower

(B) In-Season Practice (Typical Week for Junior High School Squad That Plays on Thursday)

Monday and Tuesday

2:30–2:40	Squad warm-up—Calisthenics
2:40–2:50	Agility Drills
2:50–3:15	Defensive Drills—Divided into three groups

Group #1: Defensive Backs—Five basic drills
    (1) Initial move on key
    (2) Run defense filling and pursuit
    (3) Tackling
    (4) Pass Defense: Zone
    (5) Pass Defense: Man-for-Man

Group #2: Defensive Linemen—Four basic drills
    (1) Meeting a blocker and delivering a blow
    (2) Shivering a blocker and going into pursuit
    (3) Rushing the passer
    (4) Tackling

Group #3: Linebackers and Defensive Ends—Six basic drills
    (1) Meeting a blocker and delivering a blow
    (2) Shivering a blocker and going into pursuit
    (3) Plugging and Bouncing
    (4) Tackling
    (5) Pass Defense: Zone
    (6) Pass Defense: Man-for-Man

3:15–3:30   Defensive Scrimmage against the offensive formation we will be facing in Thursday's game.

3:30–3:35   Break

3:35–3:50   Offensive Drills—Divided into two groups:

Group #1: Offensive Linemen—Seven basic drills
    (1) Drive block
    (2) Cut-off block
    (3) Seal block
    (4) Scramble block
    (5) Half-line drill
    (6) Trap block
    (7) Pass protection

During this time the line will work against the defense they will face for the upcoming game.

Group #2: Backs and Designated Ends—Five basic drills
    (1) Ball exchange drill
    (2) Blast drill
    (3) Backfield skeleton drill
    (4) Blocking drill
    (5) Individual and team pass cut drill

3:30–4:05   Offensive Scrimmage against the defensive formation we will be facing in Thursday's game.

4:05–4:15   Offensive and Defensive coverage of kicking game

4:15–4:25   Conditioning

Wednesday*

2:30–2:40	Squad warm-up—Calisthenics
2:40–2:50	Agility Drills
2:50–3:05	Defensive Game Plan—(Half speed)
3:05–3:20	Offensive Game Plan—(Half speed)
3:20–3:30	Offensive and Defensive phase of kicking game
	*Squads suit up in shorts, helmets and shoulder pads only

Thursday

Game Day

Friday

2:30–2:50	Review of Thursday's Game
2:50–3:10	Scouting Report of next opponent
3:10–3:35*	Calisthenics and Agility Drills to stretch and exercise the muscles
	*Injury situation will be evaluated and necessary action will be taken during this time.

(C) Pregame Organization

Pregame Warm-up

6:30–6:45	Centers, backs, ends, kickers or field
6:45–6:55	Squad warm-up—Calisthenics
6:55–7:10	Agility
	(1) Linemen on north side of field; backs on south side
	(2) Punters and kickers warming up
	(3) Quarterbacks warming up by throwing to each other
7:10–7:20	Team Comes Together
	(1) 1st team offensive running plays against 1st team defense to review assignments for both sides
7:20	Return to dressing room for final review of game plan
	(1) Captains remain on field for coin toss
7:25	Return to Field
7:30	Kickoff

Thursday

Game Day

8:30–2:30	Classes
2:30–3:30	Team Meetings
	We will meet as a team for about fifteen minutes, then we will split up into offense and defense and go over the game plan.

4:00	Pregame meal—*Eat at Home!*
5:30	Players report to dressing room Any players needing to get taped should come in around 5:15.
6:30	Put on pads
6:45	Take field for pregame
7:30	Kickoff

These few examples should impress upon the reader how much thought should go into each and every phase of your workout. The ability of a coach to organize his time, both when coaching and when at home, will determine to a large extent his success in both his personal and professional life.

CLASS ACTIVITIES

1. Have the class choose a local school and develop an emergency plan for getting an injured player from that school to the nearest medical facility.

2. Have class members visit several coaches from local schools and find out different systems of checking out and fitting equipment.

3. Let students work in groups to develop a timetable for workouts at various times of the week during a football season.

4. Visit with a coaching staff prior to a workout; find out their practice schedule and then observe the timing to see if the schedule is followed.

5. Develop an agenda for a preseason parents' meeting, listing the specifics of what you will cover.

15

MOTIVATION, ETHICS, AND PUBLIC RELATIONS

Chapter Objectives

After completing this chapter, the reader should be able to:

- State his philosophy about the contribution of football to the individual as well as to the educational process.
- Analyze positive and negative teaching comments.
- List five ways to motivate a football team as a whole.
- List several ways to motivate individual players on a team.
- State several common problems encountered when working with members of the school community, the community at large, and players, and propose possible ways to eliminate these difficulties.

MOTIVATION

After all the drills, workouts, instructions, and practice, when game time finally comes, all attention centers on motivating the players to give their maximum effort. However, many coaches, as well as parents, overlook the fact that the feeling of closeness between a coach and player begins from the first time the player sees, hears, or interacts with the coach. Chapter 1 discussed the reasons and rationale that motivate people to become football coaches. Perhaps now would be a good time to reflect on the reasons a young man might want to play football:

1. Recognition
2. Ego reinforcement
3. Need for physical activity
4. Need for an emotional outlet; desire to be part of a team (group)
5. Material gain
6. Enjoyment and satisfaction

For whatever reasons they play, a coach must always keep in mind that all players on his team are individuals, each with his own feelings, opinions, experiences, and inner motivations. It is paramount that a coach remember that, for the most part, people play football because of self-motivation. Willingly and proudly, these boys submit to the drudgery, toil, and self-discipline of football practice. The very nature of football coaching creates an atmosphere for the development of perfection. The best eleven will start. The coach who is able to interact with his players, working with the regulars but at the same time remembering that the second and third team players need respect, acknowledgment, and positive reinforcement, is the successful coach, regardless of the win–loss record. Those players, at all levels, who spend most of their practice time laboring in anonymity on the "Kamikaze" squad (or scout team, blue team, or whatever the label might be) that prepares the regulars for the weekly games must never be treated as second-class citizens by any member of the coaching staff.

Most football coaches when asked if they treat all players equally will respond in the affirmative. This is a conscious response or, to put it another way, a "socially acceptable" response. Numerous studies have shown that a coach may exhibit an entirely different personality when he steps on the athletic field than he exhibits when not in that role. His actions become subconscious. Let's use a classical study from the classroom setting to illustrate the impact that a coach (teacher) can have on those who are under his direction.

A few years ago an experiment conducted by Rosenthal and Jacobson proved to be one of the most exciting (and controversial) reports to appear in the history of educational research.[1] These investigators presented data to suggest that teachers' experimentally induced expectations of student performance were related to the actual levels of student performance. Students who were expected to do better (even though there was no real basis for this expectation) did, in fact, do better.

After all students were given a test of general ability at the beginning of the year, randomly selected students were described to their teachers as "late bloomers" who would probably make very large gains. The information presented to teachers was not based on student test performance. Except for the expectation that had been created for the teacher by the experimenters, there was no reason to predict increased student performance. At the end of the year, the same test of general ability was readministered to all students, and the data indicated that the students identified as "late bloomers" did outgain their classmates on the test, although the difference was due mainly to large differences in grades one and two. The classes in grades three to six showed no differences. The labeled students in grades one and two also outperformed their classmates in reading achievement, and teachers described them as more likely to succeed in the future, more interesting, happier, and more intellectually curious than students who were not labeled as "late bloomers."

The study captured the imagination of the general public. Unfortunately, sources describing the study made exaggerated claims that went far beyond those made by Rosenthal and Jacobson. For example, one ad suggested that some "mysterious force can heighten your intelligence, your competitive ability, and your will to succeed. The secret: just make a prediction! Read how it works."

Some attempts to replicate Rosenthal and Jacobson's data were unsuccessful. However, more recent work by a large number of investigators using a variety of methods has established unequivocally that the expectations of teachers' as well as managers in the business world can and do function as self-fulfilling prophecies.[2]

ANALYZING COACHING BEHAVIOR AND VOCABULARY

Even though a coach may verbalize that he likes all players equally and that he treats everyone the same, Rosenthal and Jacobson's study shows that if we aren't sincere in these attitudes, students and players can tell how we feel about them by the many unconscious interactions that occur between the player and the coach. Many people feel that in the area of coaching and working with youth you are judged mainly by two things:

1. What and how you say things and treat the players.
2. How much you appear to know about the game.

Of these two, the first is of prime importance in the area of player motivation. Several years ago, fifty-one youth coaches in three Little League programs (ages 8–15 years) were studied. The accuracy with which coaches could perceive their own behaviors was very low. The only significant correlation between external observers and the coaches self-perception was in the area of punishment and it was a negative correlation.

This study also asked the players to rate the coaches behavior patterns at the end of the season. Correlations were low and nonsignificant, *except* in the area of punishment. Thus, current data reveal that the ability of coaches to give self-ratings of their behaviors that correspond with the perceptions of others is quite limited.

The potential importance of increasing coaches' awareness of how they behave has been determined to be the key to changing their behaviors. All coaches (first year and experienced) should have someone associated with the team, but not part of the coaching staff, review and observe their behavior when in the coaching role. A system of classifying coaches' behavior was devised and a brief description of the procedure follows.[3]

To begin with, the observer must become aware of a behavior classification system in order to have a common data base from which to operate. Such a system is illustrated in Table 15.1.

A simple analysis of what a coach says, how he says it, and under what conditions he says it will tell the coach much about his behavior and interaction with players. If nothing else, someone should tell the coach if he is making more negative

TABLE 15.1   Response Categories of the Coaching Behavior Analysis System

Class I. Reactive Behaviors

Responses to desirable performance

Reinforcement	a positive rewarding reaction (verbal or nonverbal) to a good play or good effort
Nonreinforcement	failure to respond to a good performance

Responses to mistakes

Mistake-contingent encouragement	encouragement given to a player following a mistake
Mistake-contingent technical instruction	instructing or demonstrating to a player how to correct a mistake made
Punishment	a negative reaction, verbal or nonverbal, following a mistake
Punitive technical instruction	technical instruction following a mistake which is given in a punitive or hostile manner
Ignoring mistakes	failure to respond to a player mistake

Response to misbehavior

Keeping control	reactions intended to restore or maintain order among team members

Class II. Spontaneous Behaviors

Game-related

General technical instruction	spontaneous instruction in the techniques and strategies of the sport (not following a mistake)
General encouragement	spontaneous encouragement which does not follow a mistake
Organization	administration behavior which sets the stage for plays by assigning duties, responsibilities, positions, etc.

Game-irrelevant

General communication	interactions with players unrelated to game

or neutral comments towards his players than positive ones. This is not to imply that a coach should not criticize, but the point is that the majority of statements should reinforce the positive aspects of what a player does, rather than emphasize the negative actions. It is difficult to pick out a good point in many player's actions, but each coach should strive to do so. It's a matter of attitude. It is also important that every coach understand the impact of what he says. The following list of comments can be heard on the practice fields and sidelines of any football game. For organization and emphasis they have been divided into negative and positive comments.

Negative Comments

Get your head in the game
Don't you know how to . . .
What are you thinking about?
Straighten up and play football
Shut up and listen
The referee cost us that game
They cheated; you really won
Knock somebody down
Run over that guy
Hit them; don't let them hit you

Are you afraid?
Are you scared?
Are you a sissy?
Are you a crybaby?
You'd better start playing or I'll . . .
Your little sister can kick, run, etc.,
   better than you
Why did you sign up to play?
I can't believe you're so lazy

The above statements (and many, many more) are generally said in a hateful tone accompanied by clenched fists, frowning facial expressions, and an overall attitude of disgust.

Positive Comments

Way to go
That's OK
Don't worry about it
Good hustle
Great kick
Good pass, block, run
That's better
It's not your fault
Way to stay with them
Super

Very good
That's the way to play
You played a good game
That's your best game
Good effort
I know you tried
I know you're hot
I know you're cold
I know you hurt

The above statements (and many, many more) are generally said in a peppy, enthusiastic tone, accompanied by smiling facial expressions and a relaxed but energetic attitude. The same statement can have either positive or negative effect depending entirely on the accompanying expression, tone, volume, mannerisms, or gestures.

In the same respect, coaches should actively strive for as much positive reinforcement, rather than negative reinforcement, as possible. Do more telling and showing your players the right way to do something rather than spending the majority of your time criticizing the wrong way or the imperfect attempt.

It is important that coaches communicate honestly with integrity and a genuineness that comes through. Do not try to communicate those things that you do not believe in, and that are not a part of your lifestyle, because there is no group of people smarter than young people. You are not going to fool them for one second. This statement is especially true for those players who don't start or even play regularly.

To be a good communicator you must be a good listener. Look people in the eye when they are talking to you. Listen to what they are saying, and think about what *they* are saying, not about what *you* are going to say (or do, later).

Before asking your players to set their goals, ask that they take inventory of themselves, honestly evaluating their good points, their handicaps, what their commitments really are, and how they envision themselves one, five or ten years down the road. Once they take stock, they are better prepared to set their personal goals, and then their ultimate goals.

PLAYER ASSESSMENT

The following are samples of a personal inventory attempting to assess the personal and ultimate goals of players.

Personal Inventory

  I. Assets (good points)

  II. Liabilities (handicaps)

  III. My true commitments

  IV. How I see myself ten years from now

Personal Goals

Ultimate Goals	*To be reached by*
Academic (mental)	
Athletic (physical)	
Social (spiritual)	

Intermediate Goals	*To be reached by*
Academic (mental)	
Athletic (physical)	
Social (spiritual)	

Name _____   Date _____

Ultimate Goal: **To be reached by:**

Ways to Reach My Ultimate Goal

1.

2.

3.

4.

5.

Rank the items on the above list according to their importance in reaching your ultimate goal.

1.

2.

3.

4.

5.

Use this same process to reach other goals. Goals should be set in all areas of your life: moral, social, physical, financial, and spiritual.

Goal Card

(FRONT)

Name _____   Class _____

Eligibl. Remaining _____   Ht. _____   Wt. _____   40 _____

Summer address _____
_____

Telephone # _____
Parent's Name _____
_____

Address _____
_____

Summer Employment _____
_____

Degree Plan (if applicable) _____
Major (if applicable) _____

Intermediate Goals

Academic Goals: 1. _____

2. _____

Athletic Goals: 1. _____

2. _____

(BACK)

Social Goals:	1.	_____
	2.	_____
Other:	1.	_____
	2.	_____

Ultimate Goals

Spiritual Goals:	1.	_____
	2.	_____
Financial Goals:	1.	_____
	2.	_____
Vocational Goals:	1.	_____
	2.	_____
Athletic Goals:	1.	_____
	2.	_____
Comments:		_____
		_____
		_____
		_____

TIME MANAGEMENT

Time management contributes to motivation. Players who see a well-organized practice session, as well as a well-organized program, are generally motivated to perform in a like manner. Set aside times for self-improvement, your family, your priorities in your life, and your profession. You have so much time between seasons; you have so much time between workouts; you have so much time during workouts; and you have so much time between games. All of that time must be properly managed if you are to be successful.

Persistence is that human capacity to stay with something, not give up, and not quit. If we teach this to the young people we are working with, we can give them something that will be everlasting, and see them through life's problems, as well as football games. Remember, what you tell yourself is very important, because of the positive action that can follow. Your success or failure depends on what you tell yourself. You literally become what you think about. Eliminate negativism in your thinking. The best way to eliminate a negative attitude is to replace it with a positive attitude. Adhere to a simple principle: input equals output. Whatever you put into your mind will come back out in behavior, performance level, and attitude. If you apply this simple principle, it means that you associate with positive people, you read positive things, you listen to positive things and, as a result, you become positive and your actions are positive.

When you are assessing your own goals, the following questions should be asked:

1. Are your goals and your motivation strictly based on direct benefits to you? You must be motivated by more than just material things. Remember, for instance, that people motivated only by money are never satisfied.

2. Does your motivation react to criticism? Are you the kind of individual who can defend your profession, or are you just in the coaching profession for what you can get out of it? Are you in it because you believe in coaching and believe in the young people you have the opportunity to work with? (If you do, honestly, your goals are large and your motivating factor is larger than any material things.) Are you a loyal individual? Are you loyal to the people that you work for, and work with?

3. What effect does motivation have on your talents and your abilities? One should believe that an individual can be as great as he or she wants to be. Likewise, one should believe that an individual can become whatever he or she wants to become. Take the talents that you have and use them. Look well into yourself.

4. Does your motivation activate you? Does it cause you to move forward? If it does not, then you are being motivated incorrectly. Find ways to motivate yourself, and then you will find ways to motivate others.

SPECIFIC MOTIVATION ACTIVITIES

The following story will introduce this section, which attempts to give practical examples of how some coaches have strived to generate self-motivation within their players.

As the players came in I told each group that I wanted to induct them into a secret society. They all looked at me strangely as if to say "What do you mean?" So I took out the gold dots, pulled off the backs and put one on each player's watch. I told them that the gold dot meant that as a football team and as individuals we had set goals. In order to attain those goals we had to diligently, day-by-day, work toward attaining them. "If you guys leave here after all we have done throughout the spring without the incentive to continue to believe and work, then we have wasted our time. This dot will remind you of that every time you look at your watch. That gold dot is going to slap you in the face and you're going to be reminded. You look at your watch approximately forty times a day, and that gold dot will remind you forty times a day of individual goals and team goals." I did that with each of the groups and explained that the reminder would be this: Gold, G-O-L-D. G stands for the goals you set individually, and team goals. O stands for the oneness it takes as a team. L stands for the loyalty it takes as a team, and individually to your teammates, coaching staff, and school. Loyalty is a vital part of success. D stands for determination to get the job done. The reason for the Secret Society of the Gold Dot was to stimulate within the players the tough line, the positiveness toward the goals that they have to accomplish.

It is not an easy job to work with each player in an effort to get the youngster to motivate himself. But coaches are in a position to do this, as they see individuals succeeding and failing in a variety of situations. The successful coach helps build individuals by his actions of acceptance and understanding regardless of the outcome of the game, or minutes played. There is within each of us this capacity to overcome adversity and defeat, and we must teach this to the young people we coach. It's not always championships and National Coach of the Year. It is tough at times but what is important is that we are able to psychologically accept this and overcome. The coach must remember this very important saying: *"I may give out, but I will never give up."*

To end this section we have listed "the best of the best" motivational sayings. We hope you can use these as well as your own favorite quotes, sayings, and anecdotes to motivate not only your players but yourself:

Motivational Locker Room Sayings

It is not a disgrace to be defeated, but it is a disgrace to stay defeated.

Today I will give my all to the Coronado Mustangs.

You are only as good as you think you are.

The first step in moving up is getting up.

Don't be irreplaceable. If you can't be replaced you can't be promoted.

I may give out, but I will never give up.

A winner never quits and a quitter never wins.

A winner in the classroom is a winner on the field.

Win as a team, lose as a team.

Be the hammer, not the anvil.

There can't be a US without "U".

If you fail to prepare, prepare to fail.

Though we walk through the valley of the shadow of death, we fear no evil because we're the meanest.

Play like your practice.

Bend but don't break.

It's not the size of the dog in the fight, it's the size of the fight in the dog.

48 minutes to play, a life time to remember.

Second efforts and playing 4 quarters can beat any amount of talent.

Success is 90% perspiration & 10% inspiration.

To give totally of yourself, to dream, to strive will never result in failure.

Winning isn't everything: Playing hard is everything.

Go hard or go home.

Tough times don't last, but tough people do.

A. O. E. P. = All Out Every Play.

Pain is temporary, pride is forever.

To produce winners, you must first be a winner yourself.

Success requires more backbone than wishbone.

Victory is sweet, but you can't have it without sweat.

Ice Men—"I" = Intensity; "C" = Concentration; "E" = Effort.

Football is 99% mental and 1% physical.

The meek may inherit the earth, but they don't win football games.

There is no "I" in Defense.

ETHICS AND PUBLIC RELATIONS

Much of what has been said concerning a coach's personality, manner, and motivational theory, impacts on the image of the coach in the public's eye. Three distinct segments of the population enter into this area of discussion: the school community, the community at large, and the players. At all times the coach must be aware of his professional image and he should work to broaden the scope of his character whenever possible. The reader is referred to chapter 1 to review some of the problems that arise when the X's and O's become the only interest of the coach.

The School Community

By displaying a genuine interest and level of participation in the activities of other faculty members and departments within the school, the coach will go a long way toward improving his relations with the faculty. First and foremost is the problem of members of a coaching staff who feel they deserve special treatment for all the extra time they put into coaching. This philosophy results in coaches who do not take their turn at hall duty, bus duty, cafeteria duty, or who feel their time is wasted at faculty meetings, PTA meetings, or presentations by various groups and organizations within the school. In the faculty lounge this type of coach does little or no talking with fellow faculty members about any subject other than the team or the next opponent. The coach does not seek out the political science teacher to discuss current topics, or the English teacher to discuss current novels on the market. Seldom does this type of coach enter into a political discussion, or a discussion of a current theatrical production or ballet that might be in town. In short, this coach fits the typical stereotype of the jock.

Everyone involved in the profession of football coaching should, very early in their careers, make a habit of reading the society, family news, and current events sections of the local newspaper, and of thoroughly reading the front-page stories *before* turning to the sports section. More importantly, the coach should remember that he is merely a member of the faculty with the same primary responsibility as all other members of the faculty: he is working for the welfare of all students in the school in a variety of activities.

Good relations with all other members of the staff, including those very important people who really make the school and your program run—the secretaries, custodians, janitors, and managers—is essential. Make it a practice to be genuinely interested in how people are doing. Remember their troubles or family illnesses. Remember to give the secretary a birthday card or flower arrangement. Be a positive person, a person who has a smile on his face and a friendly "hello" for others most of the time.

These are little things, and as a coach you may say "I don't have time for all that!" But, more than anyone else on the faculty, you should understand that people act on their priorities. If other people are not a priority with you, chances are when the going gets tough in the win–loss column, you won't be a priority with them, either.

Often the coach gives superficial lip service to his players' academic standing. By lip service we mean when a coach only contacts the teachers of his star players, or only contacts fellow teachers when one of his players is about to lose his eligibility due to low grades. Coaches should actively see that all players under their direction maintain an interest not only in high academic marks, but in all facets of the school's educational offerings (such as plays, concerts, and fund-raising programs for the band). The following "letter to the coach" illustrates how many faculty members view the coach's concern about their player's academic standing in the classroom:

Dear Coach Muscleman:

Remembering our discussions of your football men who were having troubles in English, I have decided to ask you, in turn, for help.

We feel that Paul Spindles, one of our most promising scholars, has a chance for a Rhodes Scholarship, which would be a great thing for him and for our college. Paul has the academic record for this award, but we find that the aspirant is also required to have other excellences, and ideally should have a good record in athletics. Paul is weak. He tries hard, but he has troubles in athletics. But he does try hard.

We propose that you give some special consideration to Paul as a varsity player, putting him if possible in the backfield of the football team. In this way, we can show a better college record to the committee deciding on the Rhodes Scholarships. We realize that Paul will be a problem on the field, but—as you have often said—cooperation between our department and yours is highly desirable, and we do expect Paul to try hard, of course. During intervals of study we shall coach him as much as we can. His work in the English Club and on the debate team will force him to miss many practices, but we intend to see that he carries an old football around to bounce (or whatever one does with a football) during intervals in his work. We expect Paul to show entire good will in his work for you, and though he will not be able to begin football practice until late in the season he will finish the season with good attendance.

Sincerely, yours,

Benjamin Plotinus
Chairman, English Department*

---

*Coach Muscleman letter © William Stafford. Originally published in *College English,* April, 1995 (National Council of Teachers of English). Reprinted by permission of The Estate of William Stafford.

Finally, above all, keep your administrators advised as to what you are doing. Let your principal or supervisor know about all aspects of your program, such as your policy with regard to practicing when it snows, rains, or is cold. Let them know if you are planning a series of long practices, or if you are going to start a new off-season program. Any and all of this information can serve to improve your public relations when that parent comes storming into the principal's office demanding to know "What's going on in that football program!"

A suitable ending for this section lies in this anonymous saying that can be applied to how coaches perceive themselves and their role in the school community: "The downfall of a magician is belief in his own magic."

The Community at Large

From the very first contact with parents, the media, and all "boosters" of the football program, the coaching staff must attempt to maintain honest, open lines of communication. This is especially important to the parents of your players. Early contact (possibly via a letter) with parents concerning the objectives of your program, practice schedules, your philosophy concerning injured players, playing time, and your win–lose philosophy will open many doors. This letter should be followed by a parent–coach meeting to discuss and clarify any points in the letter. Preseason get togethers, such as a watermelon party following a Saturday scrimmage, can be extremely helpful in avoiding future conflicts (and they are fun, too!).

Understanding the ego involvement and tunnel vision of most parents, a coach must do everything in his power to let parents know how the decisions on who plays, and how much they play, are made. These discussions during the preseason often will eliminate problems during the season if by some chance the team loses a few ball games. If parents understand the coach's willingness to discuss the objectives and goals of the program, and if the coach possesses the personality to sell the program to the parents, then many hurdles will be eliminated. A good thing for coaches to remember in this area of communication is "Never *assume* anything. It makes an *"ass* out of *u* and *me."* Never assume parents empathize with you or understand your approach and actions. Let them know what you are doing and why you are doing it.

All coaches should remember that they work as a staff, a unit. No coach should criticize a fellow coach, player, or operational method publicly. These matters should be resolved privately within the coaching staff or between the coach and the player. This rule should readily apply to the news media. The media can have as powerful an impact on the football program as any other factor. The media generally do a tremendous service to the football program by reporting on the accomplishments of players and the team as a whole. Trouble surfaces when for example, the coach uses the media to falsely publicize injury information or refuses to discuss the team or its activities with the media. Another example is when the media become authorities on football strategy and begin playing the role of critic, or publicizing comments concerning upcoming opponents, or criticisms of a coach or the program from a disgruntled player.

All members of the coaching staff should strive to have a cooperative working relationship with the media, stressing the type of information and publicity that is supportive of the goals and objectives of the football program and, more specifically, the players involved in that program. If the coaching staff makes a point of supplying information concerning team activities, and works to develop a good reciprocating relationship, many positive aspects can result.

Both the school community and the community at large will, at one time or another, become the coach's biggest critics, and most of the time the coach will find that he will be criticized no matter what he does. This comes with the territory, and a coach should attempt to do the best job he can for the good of *all* the players on his team. In so doing, he should strive to satisfy 100 percent of the people knowing that if he satisfies 75 percent he has done a great job! The following narrative suggests an excellent moral for the coach.

> There was an old man, a boy, and a donkey. They were going to town and it was decided that the boy should ride. As they went along they passed some people who exclaimed that it was a shame for the boy to ride and the old man to walk. The man and boy decided that maybe the critics were right so they changed positions. Later they passed some more people who then exclaimed that it was a real shame for that man to make such a small boy walk. The two decided that maybe they both should walk. Soon they passed some more people who exclaimed that it was stupidity to walk when they had a donkey to ride. The man and the boy decided maybe the critics were right so they decided that they both should ride. They soon passed other people who exclaimed that it was a shame to put such a load on a poor little animal. The old man and the boy decided that maybe the critics were right so they decided to carry the donkey. As they crossed the bridge they lost their grip on the animal and he fell into the river and drowned. The moral of the story is that if you try to please everyone you will finally lose your ass.

The coach who is able to keep his temper when being criticized, who does not lash out verbally in defense of his position, and who can maintain an attitude of listening even when he wants to speak, will do much for his public relations. Being competitive in nature may make such efforts very difficult indeed, and unfortunately not everyone can be the perfect diplomat. But all coaches should strive for such diplomacy—the rewards will be many.

The Players

Perhaps the group which most often is in the forefront of a coach's life are the players themselves. Since so much time is spent together it seems natural that the coach should get involved with the team and have the time and interest to participate in some of the activities mentioned earlier. This restricted involvement should be avoided if at all possible. Their can be many rewards from the relationship built up between the coach and his athletes, and many coaches will tell you that the kids are the reason they stay in coaching. If the coach can stay involved in outside activities while at the same time maintaining the bond between himself and his players, he has done an outstanding job.

Much of what was said concerning motivation applies directly to the player–coach relationship. How the coach handles all players, both on the field and off, determines the quality of this relationship. If these activities foster friendly, open lines of communication, the athlete will be more likely to put forth maximum effort on the field, in the classroom, and in society. A coach should not, however, let the student feel that he can confide in the coach (without anyone else knowing) concerning *any* subject. A coach might be approached by one of his athletes with this comment, "Coach, I'd like to discuss something with you but I don't want anyone else to know." The coach should respond to this opening with a comment such as "I'll be glad to talk with you, but let's discuss it before we make any other commitments." A coach should never be trapped by agreeing not to tell anyone else something an athlete tells him. But every coach should be the type of person that an athlete feels he can confide in. When such a situation occurs, it is generally best to let the athlete do the talking. You, as the coach, should help the athlete to see all sides of the problem, hoping that the solution will become evident to the athlete. Many times the athlete just wants a sounding board. With this in mind, every coach should take each opportunity to talk to students—especially the student who comes to you when you have a thousand things to do, and all of them are due immediately!

If a coach puts the welfare of each one of his athletes (we reiterate, not just the regular starters) before personal goals and ambitions, and if each athlete is made to feel that he is being taught and coached rather than used, good rapport will develop. (The reader should look back at Rosenthal's study and reaffirm that students have many ways of judging a teacher's true intentions, expectations, and feelings.)

THE COACH'S FAMILY

No amount of space is ample to discuss this crucial element in the life of a coach. Regardless of the individual makeup of the coach's family, it will be closely intertwined with the coach and his work. Early in the young coach's life he should take all opportunities to expose his family to the rigors and demands of being married to a football coach. The coach's wife will come in contact, directly and indirectly, with comments and criticisms about her husband's activities, via telephone calls (many anonymous), critics or grandstand coaches, comments and news stories in the local media, contact with community members, and finally, in the stands during the game itself.

The coach's children cannot escape involvement, as peer pressure is many times very cruel and very outward. The coach's children will be elevated in their status when the coach wins and the team is doing well. However, as with the fans in the stands, criticism will be very quickly given and blame laid upon the coach for the team's losing record or an individual game lost. As children can be verbally cruel to their peers, a coach should be ever aware of the pressures that will fall both on his wife and his children.

In that there is no way a coach's family can be completely insulated against criticism and exposure, the coach should do everything to keep his family involved in the operation and organization of the team. This, however, is a two-edged sword. The coach cannot allow his problems, worries, and anxieties to leave the locker room and follow him into the home environment. However, the family needs to be advised as to some of the upcoming pressures and some of the decision-making problems that occur on a week-to-week basis. How the coach approaches this problem depends upon the individual personality of everyone involved. Let us first speak to the concept of family time being prime time. Every coach should make an effort to advise his family exactly when he will be home on each day during the week, if at all possible. Hopefully, all coaches will be able to gather this information from their own coaching organization, and head coaches will be sensitive enough to allow such long-term planning so that within a close proximity the coach's family will know when to expect him home and for how long. If this is done, every effort should be made by the coaching staff to adhere to these hours. From the coach's standpoint, this time away from the office should be given to fortify his interest in both his wife's activities as well as his children's activities and upcoming events in their lives. Extreme attention should be paid to the problems and decision-making processes that the family has had to go through during the coach's absence. It should be recognized that the wife of a coach must do many things in the area of home repairs, doctor and veterinary appointments, auto repairs and a multitude of other activities. Thus, when the coach arrives home, he should be ever mindful of what his wife has been doing to continue the successful operation of the family, and should be most supportive and helpful in decisions that have not been made to that point.

Many coaches find it productive to designate one day a week, usually Sunday, where the family does non-sport-related activities as a group. This is a good tradition and allows the cohesiveness and interest of the entire family to be expressed in a very relaxed and productive atmosphere. It also allows the coach, as well as his family, to keep the game of football in perspective. That is to say, just because the team lost a game last Friday night does not mean the world has come to an end. It's always nice to go out in public after a win, but the coach should make a special effort to go out in public after a loss to exhibit to the world that the family and the coach's life still goes on and that the priorities of life—the relationships between people—are still the most important issue. Keeping this in perspective is a large problem for not only the coach, but also the family. Because coaching is such an overwhelming activity and because coaches expend a huge amount of personal, mental, and physical energy in the job of coaching, it's easy for them to fall into the trap of feeling that all things exist and revolve around the athletic event of the week. All coaches should guard against this and strive within their own interpersonal relationships to keep a view of what is going on in the world and an interest in what's going on in the family, especially during the season in which the coach is active. Readers are referred to several good articles written by the wives of football coaches and are strongly urged to consider these thoughts in their daily life.[4]

CLASS ACTIVITIES

1. Interview a coach or have a coach come to speak to your group on the aspect of player–coach relations or public relations.

2. Speak to several coaches about ethical problems that arise.

3. List several methods you feel are viable as far as motivating a football team.

4. Develop a list of motivational sayings for use in locker rooms and on handout materials.

NOTES

1. Robert Rosenthal and Lenore Jacobsen, *Pygmalion in the Classroom: Teacher Expectations and Pupil's Intellectual Development* (New York: Holt, Reinhardt and Winston, 1968).

2. For applications of this research, see Paul Loftus, "The Pygmalion Effect" *Industrial and Commercial Training* 27(4), (1995):17; and Matt Oechsli, "Pygmalion Revisited," *Managers Magazine* 69(3), (1994):16.

3. Frank Smoll and Ronald Smith, "Techniques for Improving Self-Awareness of Youth Sports Coaches," *Journal of Physical Education and Recreation* 51 (1980):46–49.

4. See, Barbara Norman, "Coaches Wives", *Texas Coach* 40(8), (April, 1996):58; Mary Ann Evans, "Job Descriptions for Coaches' Wives and Athletes' Mothers," *Texas Coach* 40(6), (1996):46; Evelyn Permenter, "Why Do I Go To So Many Games?" *Texas Coach* 37(5), (1993):22.

Appendix

A

CONDITIONING PROGRAMS

HIGH SCHOOL OFF-SEASON CONDITIONING PROGRAM

This program is divided into two phases (I and II) and is designed to improve aerobic power as well as emphasize anaerobic power improvements of your athletes.

Phase I

Divide your athletes into groups depending upon the strength of the individuals, tested by a maximum bench press strength test. This best minimizes the changing of weights during the progressive weight training program. The program consists of two 25-minute periods on Monday and Wednesday. One group (group A) undergoes a 25-minute progressive weight training program, using a combination of free weights and a Universal machine, which consists of the following exercises:

1. Bench Press—three sets of six repetitions on Universal
2. Military Press—three sets of six repetitions on Universal
3. Tricep Press—three sets of six repetitions with free weights
4. Clean—three sets of six repetitions with free weights
5. 1/2 Squats—three sets of twenty repetitions with free weights
6. Leg Press—three sets of twenty repetitions on Universal
7. Curl-ups—50 repetitions

At the same time the other group (group B) undergoes a 25-minute period devoted to reaction drills and anaerobic power exercises consisting of:

1. Ten-yard stance and starts—the players assume a three-point stance and run ten yards on voice command. The emphasis is placed on the quickness of the start.
2. Ten-yard wave drill—the players are placed in a two-point linebacker's stance and on sight command are given a signal to run parallel to their starting position, both left and right.
3. Ten-yard seat rolls—the players bear crawl on voice command, with seat rolls intermixed with the bear crawl on command.
4. Stands running—the players run up and walk down the football stands with the emphasis placed on the leg drive up the stands.

The groups switch after 25 minutes, with group A performing the reaction drills and group B undergoing the progressive weight training program. On Tuesdays and Thursdays, the entire fifty minutes of actual workout time is devoted to anaerobic work which consists of running four to six 220-yard dashes in groups of three with the rest period consisting of the time needed to walk back to the starting line. The players are encouraged to run the 220s at top speed. The times are recorded and reported to the participants.

Fridays are spent in competitive games such as basketball, rugby, wrestling, boxing, volleyball, or others.

Phase II

Phase II consists of a four-week period. The athletes are divided into football positions, using two coaches with each group, if possible. Group A are the linemen and tight ends. Group B are the backs and split ends. The purpose of Phase II is to develop muscular strength and promote the learning and performance of football related skills.

On Mondays, Wednesdays, and Fridays, group A works out for 25 minutes on progressive resistance weight training program which stresses upper body development, using free weights and a Universal machine. The progressive resistance weight training program consists of the following activities.

1. Bench Press—four sets of six repetitions on Universal
2. Military Press—four sets of six repetitions on Universal
3. Lateral Press—four sets of six repetitions on Universal
4. Tricep Press—four sets of six repetitions with free weights
5. Upright Press—four sets of six repetitions with free weights
6. Dumbbell Flies—four sets of six repetitions with dumbbells
7. Curl ups—50 repetitions

During this 25-minute period, group B (backs and split ends) participates in the practice of football skills which can consist of the following:

1. Stance and Starts
2. Ball-handling drills
3. Pass-catching drills
4. Running drills

After the first period, the groups are switched. Group A (linemen and tight ends) participates in the practice of football skills which consist of the following:

1. Stance and starts
2. Six-point drill
3. Stance-and-step drill
4. Pulls-down-the-line drill
5. Traps-into-the-line drill

During Phase II, on Tuesday and Thursdays, group A spends the first twenty-five minutes in a progressive resistance weight training program, which stresses lower body conditioning. The program consists of the following:

1. Half Squats—three sets of 25 repetitions with free weights
2. Toe Raises—three sets of 25 repetitions with free weights
3. Leg Extensions—three sets of 25 repetitions on Universal
4. Leg Curls—three sets of 25 repetitions on Universal
5. Leg Press—three sets of 25 repetitions on Universal
6. Curl-ups—50 repetitions

The groups are rotated between weight training and drills with Fridays being used for competitive team games.

AGILITY, TECHNIQUE, AND COMPETITIVE ACTIVITIES

An excellent form of work is running, agility, and endurance. Divide the athletes into six groups, and then rotate them. Run them eight minutes in each group. Here is what we do in each one of those groups.

Group One will start with a form-running drill.
Group Two will start with agility running.
Group Three with apparatus and so on down the line.

At the end of eight minutes they rotate stations until they go through all six stations in one day. The form-running is developmental running, the teaching of the correct form to run.

The first thing done is a "rip" drill: running in place. We train our coaches to look at an individual and see what is lacking in his basic running technique. It may be in the arm carriage, it may be in the knee lift, it may be in the way he turns his feet—a lot of young men turn their toes out in running which prevents them from running and driving to their fullest capability.

Relaxation is another thing that we stress; we never ask a football player to run at full speed. Instead, we ask them to run at three-quarter speed, because the first thing that results when you ask someone to run at full speed is a tight neck and tight arms and chest. Relaxed running increases speed.

The second group will be participating in agility running. Backward, parallel, three-sixty-degree run, wave drills, carrioca, side shuffles, all the things that we deem are important in the development of football playing skills. The apparatus run is where we use the various apparatuses for teaching the proper running form.

Quickness Drills.   These are involved drills where the players are looking and reacting. *Sight drill* is one we like very much in which players are watching the coach's hand, and they react off of his hand, either a roll forward or a roll backward, or down on all fours. Three-sixty is obviously doing a 360-degree turn, and players will either do two or three of these based on a five-yard spread in between. Lateral touch and running-jump runs are quickness type drills.

In the sixth period we use the inclines for starts and running. We think one of the great ways to teach proper running is to run up an incline. We have a ramp at our place that's perfect for that. Running down is also very good. We use the bleacher hop, which is another thing that we have that's available. Then we use the twelve-minute run a little later in the spring.

Competitive Drills

Bull Moose
1. Both players are in a four-point stance, with a line drawn in the middle of the area.
2. The two players hook up with each other by putting their heads under each other's shoulders.
3. On the whistle each man tries to force the other off of the mat without holding on to anything.
4. If any part of the body touches the area off the mat the man loses.

Indian Chief
1. Both participants sit on the ground with their legs crossed, hands on knees, and facing the same direction.
2. There are four referees. Referees 2 and 4 stand at the end of the midline facing in, holding two rags (one green and one white) behind them.
3. The referees take one of the rags from behind them and the contestants react to the color by getting up and going in the direction the rags indicate, (green indicates go left, white indicates go right) touch the wall if in a room or touch a line about ten yards from where they were sitting, and the first one back across the midline wins.

Lateral Jump

1. The two contestants will jump over a bench at the same time.
2. The first one to finish six repetitions and run ten yards wins. Over and back is one repetition.
3. The players must land on both feet and cannot use their hands on the bench.

Tube Tug

1. Two truck tubes are tied together with a rope about ten yards long.
2. There is one line and the two contestants start in the middle of the line, with each of them having one foot against his opponent's foot on the line.
3. The rest of the teammates stand in a neutral spot.
4. When the whistle blows the two players start in opposite directions trying to drag their opponents across the middle line.
5. If any part of a player's body crosses the line, he is disqualified.

Crab

1. The contestants start at one end with hands on a line in a backward crab position.
2. On the whistle the two crab to the end of the area, touch their seats, get up as quickly as possible, and run backwards to the opposite end.
3. The first to cross the starting line wins the point.

Shuttle Run

1. This event has two lines about ten yards apart.
2. On one line there are three objects (blocks, etc.).
3. Each begins lying on the starting line. On the whistle the contestants get up and race to the other line to get one of the objects and return it to the staring line.
4. The first contestant to get all three objects to the starting line and run across the line where the objects originated wins.
5. You do not throw the objects at the line. You place them on the line. The object must be completely on the line.

Take Down

1. Two contestants, each trying to throw the other to the ground.
2. The contestants kneel, facing each other with hands locked.
3. Only one knee may leave the ground at a time.
4. The contestant wins the point when they force the opponent to the ground.

Rooster Fights

1. Each player will hold one foot behind him with the opposite hand (right leg held by left hand) and use the other hand to hold his jersey. (They cannot hold on to the neck of the jersey.)
2. The object is to knock your opponent to the ground, make him let go of his ankle or jersey, or knock him out of the arena.
3. First man to fall or let go or be knocked out of the arena loses.
4. No intentional head shots.

Agility

Figure-8 Run

Purpose: To measure the ability to change direction of gross body movements accurately and quickly while moving rapidly.

Equipment: Stopwatch; five obstacles (chairs, cones) Procedure:

1. A gymnasium floor is the recommended testing surface.
2. From a standing start, run once around the obstacles placed as diagrammed in Figure A.1.
3. The starting signal is "on your mark," "get set," "go." Time to complete the circuit is determined with a stopwatch.
4. Two trials are allowed, with at least two minutes of rest between trials.

Scoring: Score is the number of seconds, to the nearest tenth, from the starting "go" until the finish line is crossed.

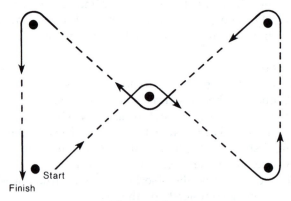

Figure 8 Run

Physiological Testing

Sargent Jump

Measuring the difference between a person's standing reach and the height to which he or she can jump and touch (similar to a basketball tipoff) has erroneously been used as a power test of the legs. If body weight and the speed in performing the jump are not a part of the measurement, one can't regard this test as a true measure of power. Certainly a 150-pound boy who jumps vertically two feet produces less power than the 160-pound boy who jumps two feet.

The Lewis Nomogram

In order to make the jump reach test more valid as a measure of leg power, the Lewis nomogram can be used as follows:

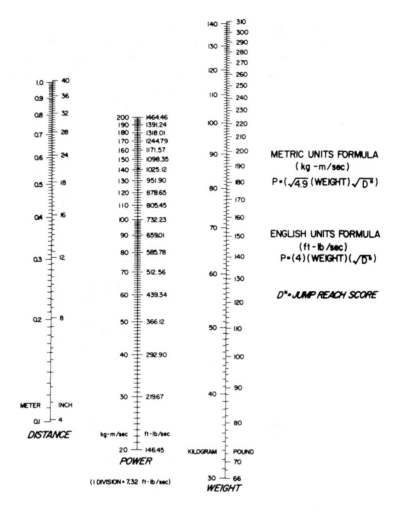

Body Weight = 180 pound
Distance jumped = 24 inches

Lay a straightedge across the nomogram connecting 180 lbs. (right column) and 24 inches (left column). Read, from the center column, foot-pounds per second (ft-lb/sec) as the power output. Note also that the measurements may be either in English or in metric system units. In the latter units the body weight in our example would be 82 kg. (1 lb = 0.454 kg.), the distance jumped would be equal to 0.61 meters (39.37 in = 1 m), and the power output would be 142 kilogram-meters/second (kg.-m/sec).

Margaria-Kalamen Power Test

R. Margaria suggested an excellent test of power, which has been modified by J. Kalamen. The modification results in greater power output than in Margaria's original test. The subjects stand six meters in front of a staircase. They then run up the stairs as rapidly as possible, taking two at a time. A switchmat is placed on the fourth and twelfth stair (an average stair is about 174 mm high). A clock starts as the person steps on the first switchmat (on the fourth step) and stops as he or she steps on the second one (on the twelfth step). You may time these steps visually using a stop watch if your physics teacher can't make switchmats or you can't purchase them. Time is recorded to a hundredth of a second. It is best to administer the test several times, recording the best score.

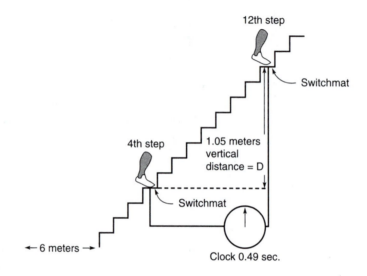

Power output is computed using the formula:

$$P = \frac{W \times D}{t}$$

In which

P = Power

W = Weight of person

D = Vertical height between first and last test stairs

t = Time from first to last test stairs (a stopwatch can be used to time the ascent)

The test is scored as follows:

W = 75 kg.

D = 1.05 meters

t = 0.49 second

$P = \dfrac{75 \times 1.05}{.49} = 161$ kg. – meters per sec.

161 kg.-meters per sec. is the anaerobic power score.

Appendix

B

DRILLS

DRILLS FOR WARM-UP AND CONDITIONING

The following drills can be used by a coach for whatever time period or specific emphasis is needed. This will vary from week to week or from season to season.

Drill: Stance and Start

Type: Reaction and Conditioning

Participants: All players

Purpose: Emphasize form and acceleration

Instructions:
1. From the team warm-up position (if lines are used) a line of players take their stance (three- or four-point) and on command, drive off the line and run ten yards.

Coaching points:
1. Check stance of all players before they fire off line.
2. Emphasize staying low for the first three steps.

Drill: High Knee

Type: Warm-up–Agility

Participants: All linemen

Purpose: To teach high knee action and balance

Instructions:

1. Set up equal lines on the sideline opposite a yard stripe.
2. The players line up facing the field.
3. On command from the coach, the groups proceed across the field keeping as close to each other as possible, moving in unison with their same foot hitting the line each time.
4. Players will lift knees high and hit the yard line with their right foot.
5. When the groups reach the opposite sideline they will turn left to the next yard line and come back across the field, this time hitting the yard line with their left foot.
6. Once they reach the original sideline, they will start again, this time using a crossover step while being careful not to touch the line.

Coaching points:

1. Players should use knee action with thighs parallel to the ground.
2. The coach should stress head up, eyes up, and have players feel the lines. For proper frame of mind the players should keep in step.
3. This drill should be done at ¾ speed or slower.

Drill: Carrioca

Type: Agility (and stretching if done slow)

Participants: All linemen

Purpose: To stretch and warm up, while developing good lateral movement

Instructions:

1. Set up players on a yard line facing the coach.
2. The drill should progress the width of the field or at least 10 yards.
3. Players should be in a football position, head up, back arched, lower legs flexed, and arms "hanging" in front of the body.
4. On the starting command, players move laterally across the field.
5. When moving left, the player steps laterally with his left foot, crosses his right foot in front of the left, steps laterally with the left foot, crosses the right foot behind and repeats this until he has covered the required distance.
6. Once the group reaches the endline, the process is reversed. The player faces in the same direction but now he moves right, back across the field. The steps are right laterally, left foot in front, and so on.

Coaching points:

1. The coach should "walk" through the carrioca until the players have mastered the steps. Having boys go in "slow motion" improves flexibility.
2. The players should try to develop a rhythmical rather than mechanical move. Always stress players staying low, butt down, head up.

Drill: Wave

Type: Agility

Participants: Linemen (from down position) and Backs (from up position)

Purpose: To teach and stress agility and reaction

Instructions:
1. Set up four lines with three players in each line.
2. The coach faces the players.
3. The first row steps up, five yards away from the other players, in appropriate three- or four-point stance for linemen, two-point "hitting" stance for backs.
4. The coach may give verbal signals or use a football to show movement.
5. The coach may use the following maneuvers:
   a. Forward, back, right, left
   b. Forward roll, backward roll
   c. 360-degree right—player places right hand on ground and runs all the way around the hand. (Process reversed for 360-degree left.)
   d. Lateral right or left—Players roll over and assume a four-point stance.
   e. Pass—players jump to block pass and come down to the ground with feet chopping.
   f. Fumble—players dive out on their stomachs.

Coaching points:
1. When the coach finishes his maneuvers the players sprint ten yards and get to the end of the line.
2. After the team knows the moves, the coach will be able to move just the football for the maneuver he desires.

Drill: Crab-Circles

Type: Agility

Participants: All linemen

Purpose: To develop quickness of body movement and to locate the ball

Instructions:
1. Set up four lines of players, three to a line, facing the coach.
2. On the command from the coach, the first man in each line sprints five yards, explodes out, and lands on his stomach.
3. The player then scrambles on all fours for five yards, places his right hand on the ground, and runs around his hand 360 degrees.
4. The player then scrambles on all fours for five yards, places his left hand on the ground, and runs around his hand 360 degrees.
5. After another five-yard scramble, the coach yells fumble and the players locate and scramble for the ball. (Fumble portion optional.)

Coaching point:
1. When the player is running around his hand, the coach should stress keeping his body as horizontal to the ground as possible with the head up.

Drill: Shoulder Roll

Type: Agility and Quickness

Participants: All players

Purpose: To get players used to getting up off ground quickly; loosen shoulder joint

Instructions:

1. Players form two lines one on each side of coach, facing up field (can be in a two-, three- or four-point stance):

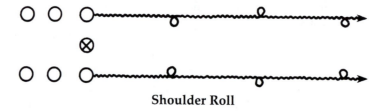

Shoulder Roll

2. On command, first players in line move out five yards and do a right shoulder roll, move five more and do a left shoulder roll, move five more, and finish with a forward roll and up.

Coaching points:

1. Players crab on all fours when moving each five yard distance.
2. Emphasize quickness and coming up in a hitting position after front roll.

DEFENSIVE DRILLS FOR LINEMEN AND LINEBACKERS

Drill: Eye Opener

Type: Tackling and Correct Pursuit

Participants: All defensive players

Purpose: To teach players to pursue from an inside-out position and to not overrun the football

Instructions:

1. The drill can be set up in a number of ways.
2. Emphasize shuffle steps, eyes open, shoulders square to LOS.

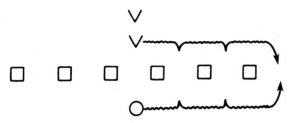

Tackling and Correct Flow Down the Line of Scrimmage

Coaching points:
1. This is an all-purpose drill that can be used by offense and defense alike (especially good with linebackers).
2. For defense, stress tackler staying a step behind ball carrier and coming up into the hole to tackle, facemask across the bow (in front).

Drill: Rapid Fire

Type: Reaction and Toughness

Participants: Defensive players

Purpose: To meet blockers correctly and deliver a blow

Instructions:
1. Players line up as shown:

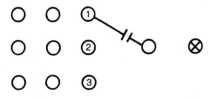

Reaction and Toughness

2. Player facing the three lines assumes a hitting position.
3. Coach signals one player from one of the lines to approach and shoulder block. Alternates lines in rapid succession.
4. Defender strikes a blow with near-foot-near-shoulder or hand shiver.

Coaching points:
1. Coach should stress the near-foot-near shoulder approach.
2. Defender should not get driven back.

Drill: Shed (Man in the Well)

Type: Toughness

Participants: Defensive players

Purpose: To stress good hitting position

Instructions:

1. Players position themselves as shown:

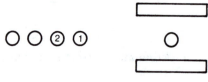

Man in the Well

2. Blockers alternately attempt to right and left shoulder block the defensive man.
3. The defender sheds the blockers as they come in successive order (that is #1 right shoulder, #2 left shoulder, etc.).

Coaching point:

1. Emphasize good hitting position and left shoulder block the defender.

Drill: Form Tackling

Type: Tackling

Participants: Defensive players

Purpose: To teach correct form and position in tackling

Instructions:

1. Players are lined up in two lines facing each other.
2. One line becomes ball carriers, just inside a five-yard marker.
3. The other line becomes ball carriers, just inside the next five-yard marker.
4. On command the ball carrier runs half-speed at the tackler who steps across the stripe when the ball carrier is one yard away.
5. Execute a face-form tackle with the ball carrier (who keeps his chin down, neck bulled) hopping or jumping up and stiffening out as the tackle is made—stress facemask on ball. The ball carrier should put his hands on the tackler's shoulder pads.
6. Tackler carries the ball carrier back across the five-yard marker.

Coaching points:

1. The coach checks to see that tacklers' eyes are open, head up, straight, good leverage.
2. Can perform drill in mass or individually down the line.

Drill: Wave Over Bags

Type: Lateral Pursuit–High Knee Lift

Participants: Linebackers

Purpose: To teach linebackers to move laterally by stepping with the near foot and not crossing the feet

Instructions:

1. Lay four bell dummies out about two yards apart.
2. Players go one-at-a-time, facing the coach and moving laterally over the bags with the right foot first.
3. Move over bags going right then come back stepping with left foot first.

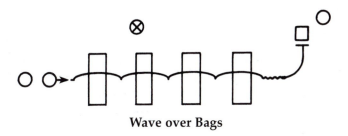

Wave over Bags

Coaching points:

1. Shoulders stay square to the line.
2. Raise knees, don't bob head.
3. Coach can wave players back and forth as development progresses.

DEFENSIVE SECONDARY DRILLS

Drill: Tip Drill

Type: Secondary Reaction to Loose Ball

Participants: Linebackers and defensive secondary

Purpose: To teach reaction to a ball that has been tipped into the air (that is, a pass deflection)

Instructions:

1. Players form single file line facing the coach fifteen yards away:

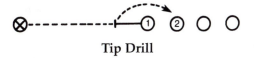

Tip Drill

2. First player in line runs toward coach who throws a pass over the head but not out of reach.
3. First player tips the ball into the air backward to the second man who catches it, yelling "Oskie!"

Drill: Lateral Recoil

Type: Position and Leverage

Participants: Defensive ends and cornerbacks

Purpose: To practice meeting blockers in good position, not giving ground or widening the hole too quickly, and turning the play in

Instructions:

1. Players are positioned as shown:

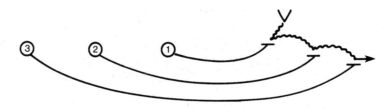

Lateral Recoil

2. On the command, the three blockers come toward the defender, who sprints to the towel and sets up in a low hitting position with his inside foot forward.
3. Blocker #1 tries to hook the defender in with a high shoulder block.
4. Blocker #2 attempts a low shoulder block and #3 rolls and tries to cut the defender's feet out from under him.
5. The defender meets each blocker and shuffles down the LOS not giving ground or getting hooked or knocked down.

Coaching point:

1. Always stress a hitting position with inside leg forward. Hit with inside arm and shoulder.

Drill: Hull

Type: Pass Defense Unit Working on Reaction

Participants: Secondary and/or linebackers

Purpose: To check flow, rotation, and reaction of defenders to various ball movements

Instructions:

1. The defensive secondary and linebackers take their positions as if in a game or scrimmage.
2. The coach serves as QB and either flows down the LOS, as if to run an option, or shows pass.
3. The defensive perimeter reacts and moves to the appropriate positions.

Coaching points:
1. Stress quick reaction and proper flow patterns.
2. Use two receivers and work with either dummy routes or actual pass plays.

Drill: Direction Change

Type: Quick Movement and Direction Changes while Moving Backward

Participants: Defensive backs and linebackers

Purpose: To practice moving backward while looking at QB and reacting to receiver moves and to the ball

Instructions:
1. Player(s) start facing the coach and on command start shuffling backward, yelling "pass."
2. On ball movement, left-for-right players turn and, with crossover step, move diagonally while watching coach.
3. On next movement player(s) throw shoulders and snap hips to other side, change direction without turning back on coach.
4. After two or three turns, drill can end with a pass thrown for interception and return blocking practice.

Coaching Point:
1. Stress chin over toes, arm pump when back pedalling.

Drill: Half Line

Type: Defensive (or Offensive) Unit Play

Participants: One-half of the defensive unit (can use secondary)

Purpose: To emphasize unit reaction to various run and pass situations working with specific personnel

Instructions:
1. Set up an offensive backfield unit and the line personnel on the side to be worked.
2. Have half the defensive unit set up in positions:

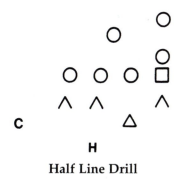

Half Line Drill

OFFENSIVE LINE DRILLS

Drill: 7-Man Sled Pop

Type: Blocking

Participants: Offensive linemen

Purpose: To teach the initial stage of blocking, which requires a blocker to bring his upper body into play

Instructions:
1. Line up seven men in front of the sled (or dummies).
2. Players assume a six-point stance (hands, knees, toes).
3. On the command from the coach, the players fire out into the sled.
4. Players should spring from their knees without using their feet.
5. After the first hit, they quickly resume the six-point stance.
6. The coach will call, "hit, hit, hit" each time the player assumes his original stance.
7. This should be done three or four times in a row, then the linemen can drive the sled or simply let the next group up.

Coaching points:
1. Coach should stress a stance that is coiled and ready for the hit.
2. Players should not "hitch" before they hit.
3. Players can drive the sled after the third hit. Check for good form: wide base, back arched, head up, feet moving in short, choppy steps.
4. Progression can be from knees, to four-, to three-point stances.

Drill: Offensive-Fire-Out-vs.-the Sled

Type: Blocking

Participants: Offensive linemen

Purpose: To stress good explosion and proper fire out

Instructions:
1. Line up seven linemen on the sled (or dummies).
2. A quarterback should be used for this drill. He will call the signals and take the ball from the center. Coach can serve as QB.
3. The coach and the linemen line up in the huddle five yards from the sled.
4. The linemen will explode into the sled and drive it two or three yards.
5. The coach will huddle the next line and the process is repeated.

Coaching points:
1. Backs may be added to this drill. They will line up at the end of the sled. On the starting count they will sprint five yards.
2. The coach should stress good huddle discipline, proper set at the line of scrimmage and proper fire out.

Drill: Boards

Type: Blocking

Participants: Offensive linemen

Purpose: To teach linemen to get off on the count and work on proper placement of the feet in blocking

Instructions:

1. Place stand-up dummies on the end of a board (2′ × 12′ × 10′). With one player holding a dummy, a blocker positions himself in front of the dummy:

Boards

2. On the starting count the blocker will try to drive the dummy off the end of the board.
3. Holder will give constant resistance.

Coaching points:

1. This is an excellent drill to teach young linemen to keep their feet wide and moving.
2. Can have dummy held firm, blocker explodes and sets up, explodes and sets up, explodes and drives the dummy back.

Drill: Double Team

Type: Blocking

Participants: Offensive linemen

Purpose: To teach the post and drive or the double team block

Instructions:

1. Set up groups of three players: two offensive linemen and one defensive lineman.
2. Place the defensive man head up (alternate right and left).
3. After the fundamentals have been mastered the defensive man may line up in any position he desires.
4. The post man has the main responsibility for stopping the charge of the defensive man, setting him up for the lead block. He may:
   a. Use strong arm shiver to arm pits of defender
   b. Drive head into midsection, going to a shoulder block.
   c. Drive head under crotch and lift.
   d. Drive to the inside leg, taking the leg away.
   e. Post man must step with his inside foot.
5. The drive man must assume that he has to take the defensive man by himself.
   a. Steps with his near foot and hits with his near shoulder.
   b. Aim at or above the hip of the defensive man.

   c. Uses head after contact to drive defensive man down the line.
   d. Keeps seam closed to the inside, shoulder to shoulder (hip to hip) with post man.

Coaching points:
   1. Blockers' hips must be close together in order to close seam, shoulder to shoulder.
   2. Post man must neutralize defensive charge.
   3. Drive man should drive defensive man to the side away from hole.

Drill: Man in the Well

Type: Run Blocking, Pass Blocking, Tackling

Participants: All linemen

Purpose: To teach the blocker to stay with his man and the defender to play off a blocker correctly

Instructions:
   1. Set up two dummies, lying on their sides, three yards apart.
   2. Set up one rusher and one blocker, in between the dummies.
   3. The third man becomes the ball carrier or QB if working on pass rush.
   4. The coach indicates the direction of the run and begins the drill with "Hit."
   5. The runner becomes the blocker after each drill is completed.
   6. The rusher and the blocker are two yards apart.
   7. The ball carrier is about three yards from the blocker.
   8. The rusher (if working on pass rush) can use an air dummy or arm shield. Later this drill will become live.
   9. On the signal from the coach, the rusher (or defender) tries to tackle the quarterback (or ball carrier).
   10. The drill is ended when the runner is tackled or gets by the defender or the rusher gets to the QB (or four seconds elapse).

Coaching points:
   1. This drill is the most widely used drill in this area. Highly competitive.
   2. The coach should be able to find his best rusher and his best blocker.
   3. Can be used to work on offensive ball carrier.

Drill: 1-2-3

Type: Pulling and Trapping

Participants: Guards and tackles

Purpose: To teach the pulling lineman the proper techniques for trapping a defensive lineman who (1) is on the line, (2) one step across the line, or (3) has penetrated into the offensive backfield

Instructions:
   1. Set up two linemen in their normal positions on the line of scrimmage.
   2. Set up three dummies, with holders, simulating defensive linemen.

3. The dummies are numbered 1, 2, and 3.
4. The coach stands in front of the linemen.
5. The coach will work one side at a time.
6. The coach will give the starting count. Once the lineman has started to pull, the coach will give the designated number of the dummy to hit.
7. The pulling lineman will always head for dummy number 1, and then proceed to the number called.
8. When pulling right the trapper will use his right shoulder on dummies 1 and 2 and his left shoulder on number 3, which will be a reverse shoulder block. The procedure is reversed when pulling left.

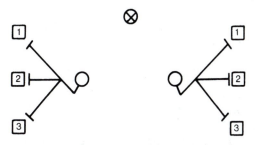

Pulling and Trapping

OFFENSIVE BACKFIELD DRILLS

Drill: Kick-Out

Type: Offensive Backfield Blocking

Participants: Offensive backs

Purpose: To teach backs to accelerate quickly, attack from an inside-out position, and explode through the defender

Instructions:

1. Arrange players as shown:

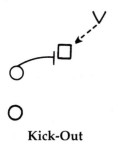

Kick-Out

2. Each blocker, on command, takes an inside-out route to the defender who has moved to a marked spot.

3. The blocker must blow the defender off the mark or in some way position himself between the defender and the dummy.

Coaching points:
1. Stress running through the defender.
2. Stress the inside-out route (more straight route if working on hooking the end to the inside).

Drill: Gauntlet

Type: Fumble Prevention

Participants: Offensive backs

Purpose: To aid runners in avoiding fumbles by teaching players to hold tightly to the ball while being hit, turned, and so on.

Instructions:
1. Several players line up facing each other about two yards apart. These form the chute or gauntlet.
2. Several ball carriers line up facing these lines. The first man in line is the ball carrier.
3. Each ball carrier runs through the gauntlet as each player in the gauntlet attempts to grab the ball.

Coaching points:
1. Ball carrier can only hold the ball with one hand and arm.
2. Gauntlet men cannot hold the ball carrier.
3. Stress explosive run by the ball carrier. Keep those legs churning, shoulders square.

Drill: Rapid Exchange

Type: Ball Handling

Participants: All ball carriers

Purpose: Practice many handoffs in a short period of time

Instructions:
1. Line up a row of ball carriers on one side of a yard line, with another row on the opposite side of the line, ten yards away.
2. The lead man in one row has a ball and begins by running forward and handing off the ball the lead man in the other row:

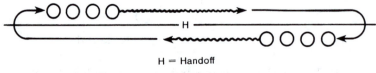

H = Handoff

Ball Handling

3. As soon as the second man gets the ball, the third starts running and accepts the ball from him.
4. This process continues (receive the ball, run, hand it off) until the coach stops the drill.

Coaching points:
1. Emphasize correct hand position for receiving the ball.
2. As skill progresses speed up the tempo of the drill.

Drill: Maneuvers

Type: Open-Field Running

Participants: Backs

Purpose: To teach the ball carriers open field tactics such as spinning, weaving, dodging, straight-arming, and ball changing

Instructions:
1. The dummies are lined up in a straight line about seven yards apart.
2. One player must hold each bag.
3. If air dummies are used the players can work on fundamentals because they can be moved around.
4. The players holding the bags can lift and maneuver them to create lifelike situations.
5. Ball carriers use straight-arm, weaving tactics, as well as ball changing, as they cut:

Maneuvers

Coaching points:
1. In cutting around dummies have players switch the football to the side opposite the dummy, crossover step with inside leg while stiff-arming the dummy.
2. Can use complete spin on last dummy.

Drill: Snap Perfection

Type: Center–QB Exchange

Participants: Center and QB

Purpose: To develop a smooth, rapid snap from center

Instructions:
1. Have the quarterback and center practice the snap and initial steps.
2. Work on smoothness and good exchange.

3. Have each quarterback work with each center; vary snap counts.
4. Perform this drill before and after practice if possible.

Drill: Mad Dog

Type: Fumble Recovery

Participants: All players

Purpose: To teach players to fight for fumbles and gain possession

Instructions:
1. Players line up two lines facing downfield on either side of the coach:

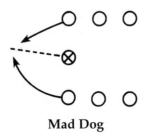

Mad Dog

2. Coach flips ball forward about five yards and players react by trying to cover the fumble.

Coaching points:
1. Stress quickness and aggression.
2. Emphasize getting control of the ball and curling body around it by bringing knees to chest.

PASS RECEIVING DRILLS

Drill: Frame-Up

Type: Concentration on the Ball

Participants: All receivers

Purpose: To get receivers to concentrate on the ball even though distracted

Instructions:
1. Form two lines with the receiver in back and the defender in front.
2. As the receiver and defender run in front of the passer the defender "frames" the ball allowing it to pass through his hands.
3. The receiver catches the ball using proper techniques with the added distraction of the defender's hands.

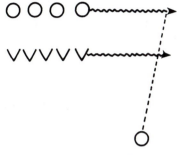

Frame-up Drill

Drill: Second Chance

Type: Concentration on the Ball

Participants: All receivers

Purpose: To draw attention to the ball even though defenders are in the path of the ball

Instructions:
1. Form two lines with the receivers on one side and the defenders on the other side.
2. As the receiver and defender run toward one another (with the defender in front of the receiver) the passer throws the ball to the receiver as the defender allows the ball to pass through his hands.

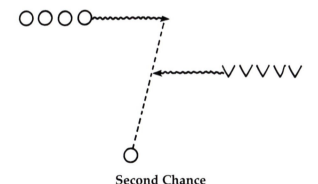

Second Chance

Drill: Problems

Type: Reception of Badly Thrown Ball

Participants: All receivers

Purpose: To strengthen skills in body position to catch badly thrown balls

Instructions:
1. As the receiver runs in front of the passer a bad pass is thrown, high, low, behind, and so on.
2. The receiver tries to adjust to the badly thrown ball and make the catch in any way possible.

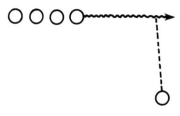

Problems Drill

Drill: First Down

Type: Staying In-Bounds

Participants: All receivers

Purpose: To practice keeping one foot in bounds

Instructions:
1. The passer throws the ball to the junction between the receiver and the sideline.
2. The receiver catches the ball and drags at least one foot before going out of bounds.

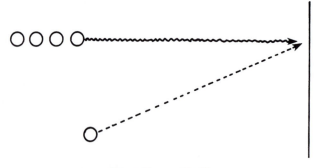

First Down Drill

Drill: Contest

Type: Pass Reception during Contact

Participants: All receivers

Purpose: To work on ball control and concentration while being contacted by a defender

Instructions:
1. The receiver comes back toward the passer to a spot directly in front of a defender.
2. The passer throws a high pass and as the receiver jumps for the ball the defender pushes or jumps with the defender to contest for the ball.

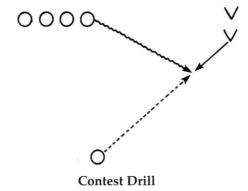

Contest Drill

There are countless ball catching drills. The above drills are just a few of the catching drills that can be used by the coach to improve the pass reception skills of his players. It is important for the coach to use drills that simulate every situation which a receiver might encounter in a game situation. It is important that the coach give the athlete drills which the receiver can work at away from the actual practice field situation, because catching skills are developed, for the most part, away from organized practice.

Appendix
C

SAMPLE SCOUTING FORM

SAN JACINTO OFFENSE

Running Plays:
- 47-28 Option (HB takes pitch)
- 17-18 Option (QB keeps)
- 47-28 Sweep
- 23-44 Pop
- 43-24 Counter
- 35 Slant
- 31 Trap
- QB Sneak (Wedge blocking)

Pass Plays:
- 18 Sprint out pass
- 44 Bootleg pass
- 35 Bootleg pass
- Screen pass (Left and right)
- Drop back passes (Favorite)

Helpful Hints:

1. Plays are run in Series: Ex. pop, slant, option (This is their favorite series.)

2. Threw dropback pass on 78% of pass plays (14 of 18); usually deep post patterns. Favorite receiver is #23, Jones.

3. They threw only one "sprint-out pass" (18 sprint out).

4. Harrell, #11 (QB and RHB), will throw deep when at QB and will run 44 pop when at RHB.

5. #61, #76, and #77 are tough aggressive blockers.

Favorite Play (Option Series Lt & Rt)

O'George pulls on this series

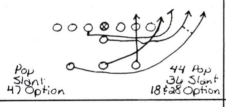

Pop
Slant
47 Option

44 Pop
36 Slant
18 & 28 Option

Screen Pass (Left & Right)

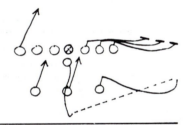

Sweep (28 & 47 Sweep)

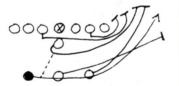

Offside G & Onside T pull and lead

Counter (24 & 43 counter)

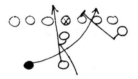

Play Passes

44 Bootleg Pass

35 Bootleg Pass

24 Counter Pass

SAN JACINTO DEFENSE

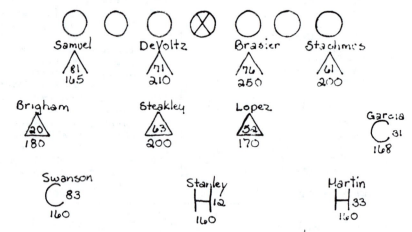

Samuel 81 165
DeVoltz 71 210
Brasier 76 250
Stachmes 61 200

Brigham 20 180
Steakley 63 200
Lopez 52 170
Garcia 31 168

Swanson 83 160
Stanley 12 160
Hartin 33 160

"Stack-3 Deep" (from '27') – This is San Jacinto's basic defensive alignment in Normal situations

---

OTHER DEFENSIVE ADJUSTMENTS & ALIGNMENTS

Split-Six 3 Deep	Umbrella – on Passing Downs
Split-Six (G's in 3 tech)	Split-Six (Umbrella)
	'27' Regular

SAN JACINTO KICKING

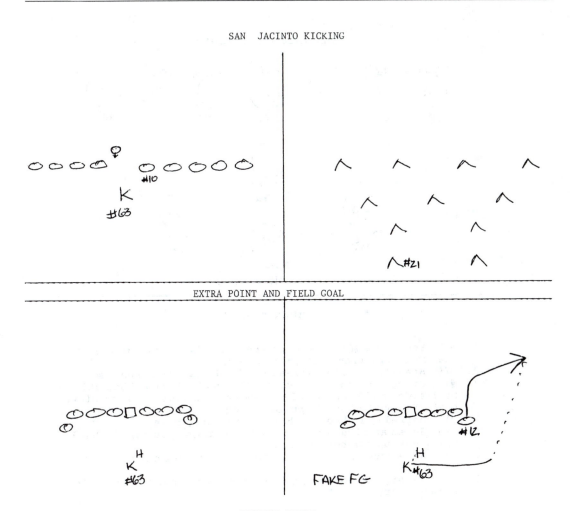

EXTRA POINT AND FIELD GOAL

KICKING NOTES

1. Kick off goes to the 10-15 yard line. We can run one back on this bunch!
2. #10 is a speedster- He will be the first one to the ball. BLOCK HIM!
3. They like to return the kickoff straight down the field. #21 is their best return man. We will kick away from him.
4. They line up shoe to shoe on Pat's & fg' s and turn in to the inside. We can split the right up back #12 and BLOCK THE KICK!
5. Watch out for the fake kick. #63 can throw the ball.

SAN JACINTO OFFENSE

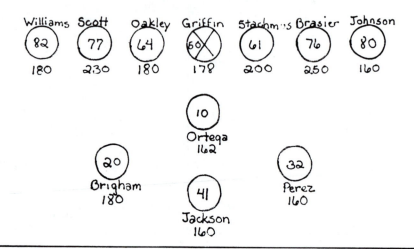

BEAR TRACKS

1. #77, Scott and #61, Stachmus are the only two offensive starters back from last year's team.
2. #76, Brasier is being pushed for "All District" Honors.
3. #10, Ortega is an explosive quarterback. He runs the option to both sides and keeps it often. He can and does throw the long bomb. You must stop him before he gets strung out.
4. #11, Harrell, is the toughest runner they have.
5. #23, Jones at right end, likes to out fight you for the ball thrown deep down the middle.
6. They have used the screen (both sides) to get out of a bad situation.
7. They're big but not bad, treat them rough from the start for a DEER victory.

SETS WE'VE SEEN

DEFENSIVE NOTES

1. The "Golden Bears" are basically a good defensive ball club.
2. They are good tacklers--"gang tackling" being their strong point.
3. The defensive secondary comes up quickly and tackles sharply on sweeps.
4. The LB'ers run thru quite frequently--the Right LBer fired thru on a "#1 call."
5. The secondary usually went into an "umbrella" on passing downs.

6. <u>Standout Defensive Personnel:</u>

   #52 - David Lopez, 5'9" 170 Lb., LB and Def. Signal caller

   #61 - Julius Stachmus, 6'1" 200 Lb., Rt. 7 Tech (Two-Way Performer)

   #76 - Derek Brasier, 6'3" 250 Lb., Rt 2 Tech

   #20 - Wardell Brigham, 6'0" 180 Lb., LLB (Two-Way Performer)

With "aggresive scrambling" and "good second effort", we can score on the Bears and post Victory No. 1 !!

"SKIN THE BEARS"

GLOSSARY

Adenosine Triphosphate   (ATP) The molecule which releases energy which can be used for muscular work.

Aerobic   Activity levels which can be met with adequate oxygen supply and energy delivery without the buildup of lactic acid.

Anaerobic   Activity which requires more energy than the aerobic system can supply, resulting in lactic acid production.

Area Blocking   When the offensive line blocks anyone in the attack area. This is freelance blocking, where the offensive blockers clear the hole anyway they can.

ATP-PC System   The anaerobic energy system which supplies the immediate source of ATP (PC = Phosphocreatine).

Audible   (Automatic; Check-off) A change of play by the quarterback while at the LOS.

Ballistic Stretching   Warming-up a muscle by bouncing it back and forth when stretching.

Blitz   The charge of a defensive linebacker or defensive back across the LOS at the snap of the ball in order to disrupt the offensive flow.

Buddy Drills   Prepractice competition between two players emphasizing speed and agility.

Conditioning   Activities which stress and seek to improve the energy supply systems of the body.

Corner (Cornerback)   Defensive secondary man aligned to the outside of the safety and corner linebacker or defensive end.

Counter Play   A misdirection offensive play that starts in one direction and comes back the other way, usually ran between the tackles.

Crackback Block   A block thrown usually by a player aligned in a wide position, on a defender aligned more toward the center of the field. The blocker must make contact above the waist. Illegal in many leagues.

Cup Blocking   Pass blocking by the offensive line sealing off the quarterback.

Cushion   The space between the defender and the pass receiver.

Defensive Numbering   A method of identifying where a defensive lineman will lineup.

Defensive Line   Any defender in a "down" position along the LOS. The first line who usually defend against the run and put pressure on the QB if passing.

Defensive Linebackers   Players that usually stand immediately behind defensive lineman. The second line of defense who have responsibility for both pass and run coverages.

Defensive Secondary   Those players who cover receivers coming downfield; they are the last line of defense and usually play pass first, run second.

Double Coverage   Two defensive secondary men are assigned to cover one offensive receiver.

Double Team Block   Two offensive men blocking one defender.

Downfield   Any area on the upfield side of the line of scrimmage (offensively).

Eagle   Where defensive men switch alignments. Usually a LBer and a defensive lineman.

Eligible Receiver   Usually any one of five offensive players eligible to receive a forward pass (i.e., two ends, three backfield men).

Even Defense   A defense with an even number of down linemen.

Face Guarding   When a defender deliberately obstructs an offensive receiver's vision (usually by waving his hands in front of the defender's face) without playing the ball.

Fill   When an offensive running back fills a space vacated by a pulling lineman.

Five (5) Technique   A defensive position which aligns on the outside shade of the offensive tackle.

Flag Pattern   An offensive receiver's pattern, which is run down the field and out at a forty-five degree angle (usually to the flag marker of the goal line).

Flat   A pass coverage area immediately outside of the TE, 2–3 yards down field.

Flip Flop   Generally when offensive line players are moved from one side of the line to the other to gain blocking strength. An offensive line will thus have a strong side (G, T, E) and a weak side (G, T, SE) that switch as a unit on all plays.

Flood   When two or more offensive receivers are sent into one area of the defensive secondary.

Flow   The direction of the ball or the running backs on an offensive play.

Fold Block (Load Block; Cross Block)   A type of cross block where offensive linemen switch blocking assignments in an effort to improve blocking angles.

Forearm Lift   Striking the chest plate of the player with the forearm.

Forehand (hand) Shiver   Driving the heels of both hands into the defender.

Four-Point Stance   Both feet and both hands are in contact with the ground.

Free Safety   A defensive secondary man who usually plays to the formation (i.e. strong safety to strong side of formation).

Gap Defense   (Gap 8) Where a defensive lineman is lined up in every gap or running lane.

Head-On Block (Base Block; 1, 2, 3 block)   An offensive charge at a defender lining up directly over the blocker.

Hitting Position   A "break down" position—feet chopping, bull neck, ready to strike a blow.

Hook (Curl) Zone   A fish hook pattern in a short zone 8–10 yards past LOS.

Influence (Brush) Block   An offensive block usually used to set up a defender for a trap block. The blocker just makes contact with less than full impact and then leaves for another block (usually on the linebacker).

Inside-Out Position   An approach to the target from a position inside the target rather than outside.

Interior (Down) Lineman   Usually denotes C, G & T on the LOS.

Invert   Where a corner and defensive back exchange responsibilities.

Isolation Block   When a defender is initially not blocked by anyone. Usually followed by a lead block from an offensive back.

Keys (also called Reading)   When a defensive player will watch the movement of a specific offensive player in an effort to predict what he will do or as a signal of how the defender should move on the snap of the ball.

Lactic Acid System   The anaerobic energy system which can produce ATP from the incomplete breakdown of glucose, resulting in lactic acid production.

Live Color   The color called by the quarterback that is predetermined to be the one which signals an audible or play change at the LOS.

Load Block   Cross blocking by offensive blocker or a kick out block by an offensive back.

Look-In   A quick pass route where the offensive receiver runs a slant-in pattern toward the center of the field. Usually thrown very quickly.

Man Coverage   When a defender is assigned to a specific receiver and he stays with that receiver wherever he goes.

Metabolism   Chemical reactions which occur in cells.

Mike   Another name for the middle linebacker.

Monster (Rover)   A defensive secondary man who lines up in a different T position each play according to strength of the formation, field position, or defensive call.

Near Back   The running back positioned on the side closest to where the play is designed to go.

Neutral Zone   The area between the offensive and defensive line as defined by the position of the ball.

Neutralize   Defeat the blockers attack and gain position.

Nine (9) Technique   A defensive position which aligns on the outside shade of the offensive tight end.

Nonrhythmic Cadence   The spacing or pause between digits and/or words is irregular and unevenly timed.

Nose   The defensive "0" Technique that lines head up the offensive center.

Odd Defense   A defensive front with an odd number of men aligned on the LOS.

Off-Side   The side of the offensive line opposite that to which the play is directed.

One (1) Technique   A defensive position which aligns in the gap between the offensive center and guard.

On-Side   The side of the offensive line to which the play is directed.

Oxygen System   The aerobic energy system which produces the greatest amount of ATP with no production of lactic acid.

Pick   When one offensive receiver runs a pattern which impedes or draws the defender away from the primary receiver.

Prevent Defense   A defense designed to prevent the long pass. This is a deep zone coverage where the secondary men play much farther from the line of scrimmage, usually allowing short pass completions but not the long pass.

Pursuit   The angle of approach that a defender takes in order to intercept or cut off the ball carrier.

Quick Release   The ability of the quarterback to get rid of the ball quickly once he has decided to pass.

Reach Block   An offensive block which attacks the outside leg of the defender in an effort to cut him off from the flow of the ball.

Read   The defender's key or man that he watches to determine what reaction to take.

Release   The quick movement of an offensive pass receiver off the line of scrimmage and into his pass route.

Rhythmic Cadence   The spacing or pause between digits and/or words is regular and evenly timed.

Safety Blitz   When a defensive secondary player (usually the free safety or strong safety) leaves his normal position just before or right at the snap of the ball and charges across the line of scrimmage into the offensive backfield.

Safety Valve   Usually a secondary receiver who runs a pattern into the flat so that the quarterback can have a receiver if the primary target is covered.

Scat Back   A speedy offensive back.

Scramble Block   An offensive block which attacks the middle of the defender (low) while the blocker scrambles on all fours in an effort to maintain contact.

Set Back   The position label given to all offensive backs lined up behind the quarterback from tackle to tackle.

Shooting the Gap   When a defensive player attempts to charge through the space between two offensive linemen.

Shotgun Formation   When the quarterback takes a deep snap (seven yards) from the center. Eliminates the dropback activity on passing downs.

Shoulder Block   Getting close enough to a defender that shoulder pads are in contact with him.

Slot   The gap between the offensive tackle and the offensive end or wide receiver.

Spearing   An illegal contact with the helmet when a defensive player dives head first into a player (who is usually down or going down).

Specificity   Training and conditioning the muscles at exactly the speed and range of motion that is required during performance (i.e., a passer must move his arm through the exact movement pattern of his throw when using weights or an isokinetic machine).

Static Stretching   A flexibility-stretching procedure in which the muscle is stretched and held for 10–30 seconds, rather than bounced.

Strong Safety   A defensive secondary man who aligns on the side of the field with the offensive tight end.

Stunt   A slanting or looping charge on the snap of the ball to cover an adjacent gap or lane.

Submarine   A low, penetrating charge by a defender.

Three-Deep Coverage   (Cover 3) where three defenders divide deep coverage into thirds.

Three-Point Stance   Both feet and only one hand are in contact with the ground.

Three (3) Technique   A defensive position in the gap between the offensive guard and tackle.

Training   Activities which stress and seek to improve skill as well as the energy supply systems of the body.

Trap Block   Usually an offensive lineman coming from the other side of the line to block a defender who has been set up or isolated.

Trap Reaction   If a defensive lineman senses that he is going to be trapped he should step down to the inside and brake for the blocker.

Two (2) Technique   A defensive position which aligns directly head-up on the offensive guard.

Unbalanced Line   An offensive alignment which has an unequal number of men on each side of the center.

Veer   An offensive formation similar to the wishbone but without a FB. The FB becomes a wide receiver.

Wishbone   An offensive formation with a full house backfield with the FB behind the center (very close), and running backs aligned behind the guards.

X   A term labeling one of the wide receivers.

Y   A term labeling the tight end.

Z   A term labeling the split end.

Zero (0) Technique (Nose)   A defensive position which aligns head-up over the offensive center.

Zone Coverage   Each defensive linebacker and secondary man has a certain area of the field to cover rather than a specific man.

INDEX